COLLECTOR'S
VALUE GUIDE

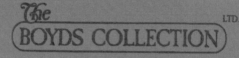

Boyds Plush Animals

Collector Handbook and Secondary Market Price Guide

FIFTH EDITION

BOYDS COLLECTION LTD.

The Boyds Collection Ltd. and associated trade marks, copyrights, and photography are owned by The Boyds Collection Ltd. and used under license. All Rights Reserved. The Boyds Collection Ltd. is not affiliated with CheckerBee Publishing or shares the opinions expressed in this publication.

Managing Editor:	Jeff Mahony	Creative Director:	Joe T. Nguyen
Associate Editors:	Melissa A. Bennett	Production Supervisor:	Scott Sierakowski
	Jan Cronan	Senior Graphic Designers:	Lance Doyle
	Gia C. Manalio		Susannah C. Judd
	Paula Stuckart		David S. Maloney
Contributing Editor:	Mike Micciulla		Carole Mattia-Slater
Editorial Assistants:	Jennifer Filipek	Graphic Designers:	Jennifer J. Bennett
	Nicole LeGard Lenderking		Sean-Ryan Dudley
	Joan C. Wheal		Kimberly Eastman
Research Assistants:	Timothy R. Affleck		Jason C. Jasch
	Priscilla Berthiaume		Angi Shearstone
	Heather N. Carreiro		David Ten Eyck
	Beth Hackett	Web Graphic Designer:	Ryan Falis
	Victoria Puorro		
	Steven Shinkaruk		
Web Reporters:	Samantha Bouffard		
	Ren Messina		

ISBN 1-888-914-75-0

CheckerBee PUBLISHING

306 Industrial Park Road • Middletown, CT 06457
www.CollectorBee.com

Table of Contents

Introducing
The Collector's Value Guide™

Welcome to the Collector's Value Guide™ to Boyds Plush Animals. This guide serves as your definitive source for information on the plush critters in The Boyds Collection Ltd. It introduces you to every plush animal in the Boyds forest and provides you with up-to-date information on secondary market values, new releases and retirements.

In addition, it gives you information and history on The Boyds Collection Ltd. family tree. It explores all of its branches, from the many plush series to the other collections in the line. And it looks at the man who serves as the roots of it all: the "Head Bean Hisself" artist Gary Lowenthal.

The Collector's Value Guide™ is filled with everything you need to make your way through the wilds of The Boyds Collection Ltd. It is sure to become a favorite companion through all of your collecting adventures!

Look Inside To Find:

· An inside look at "The Wacky World of Boyds"

· What's new for 2000

· A backstage look at the popular "Mary Beth and Gary Show"on QVC

· The latest Bearwear and accessories on the market

· The story of Burke P. Bear and his tour around the world

· And much, much more!

The Wacky World Of Boyds

The Boyds Collection Ltd., one of the most recognizable and successful companies in the world of collectibles, has been manufacturing jointed plush teddy bears and friends since 1987. But not many people realize that The Boyds Collection Ltd. began years before that first plush teddy bear hit stores. Eight years before, to be exact.

Boyds Goes On-Line!

The Boyds Collection Ltd. launched their official company web site on November 5, 1999. The site, which can be accessed at www.boydscollectibles.com features all of the latest Boyds news as well as club information, a store locator, gift and decorating ideas and a history of the company. Visitors to the site can also sign up for a free e-mail newsletter.

The Boyds Collection was founded by Gary M. Lowenthal and his wife, Justina, in 1979. The couple had recently moved to the small, rural town of Boyds, Maryland to escape the hassles of city life. Gary cultivated both his entrepreneurial skills and his artistry skills in Maryland, where he and his wife opened up their very own antique shop and made hand-carved wooden duck decoys.

Then Gary met artist Gae Sharp, and history was made. The two joined forces and released a line of jointed teddy bears that made The Boyds Collection "almost famous." Of course, the bears needed some animal friends to share their success with, so the line soon expanded to include hares, cats, dogs and nearly any other animal you can imagine, from frogs to elephants! As The Boyds Collection Ltd. grew, it moved to new headquarters in Pennsylvania. In recent years, The Boyds Collection Ltd. and its enterprising founder, lovingly known as "Uncle Bean," have ventured into the world of resin figurines, creating The Bearstone Collection® in 1993, The Folkstone Collection® in 1994, Yesterday's Child - The Dollstone Collection™ in 1995, The Shoe Box Bears™ and Yesterday's Child . . .™ The Doll Collection in 1996, DeskAnimals™ in 1998 and most recently, The Purrstone Collection™ in 1999 and Bearly-Built Villages™ in 2000.

ONE OF A KIND

While there are over 1,000 plush animals in the Boyds collection, each one is very different from the rest! Each animal has a distinct personality that is conveyed through its outfit (which can range from a simple collar around the neck to an intricate Halloween costume), its facial expression and especially its name. And boy, do these animals have some

unique names! When you buy an animal with a name like "Perriwinkle P. Snicklefritz" or "Taffy C. Hopplebuns," you can be sure that nobody else is going to have a name anything like it!

Even though every animal is different, Boyds does group animals with similar characteristics into categories called series. The series are helpful for collectors who prefer a certain style or type of animal. For instance, collectors who are searching for a fully dressed animal should look for those in the *T.J.'s Best Dressed* series, while those who are looking for a classic, antique-style bear might want to look at the *Archive Series* instead. And those looking for plush moose would do best by looking in the *Animal Menagerie* or *Northern Lights* series. A complete listing and description of each series is on pages 13-15.

FOR A LIMITED TIME ONLY

Another unique aspect of the Boyds collection is the release of limited editions. While Boyds releases several limited edition pieces a year, it also produces a small group of annual limited editions. "Bailey" the bear, named for Lowenthal's daughter, leads the pack that includes "Edmund" the bear and "Emily Babbit" the rabbit. Since 1992, these pieces have been released twice each year, once in the spring and once in the fall. Each season, the friends make their debut in a new themed outfit. "Matthew" the bear (named for Lowenthal's son and Bailey's brother) and his loyal dog, "Indy," are also included in this group, although they are traditionally released only in the fall. These pieces are some of the most popular in the collection,

and collectors look forward to each season to discover what "Bailey" and her friends will be up to next!

WHAT YOU'RE MISSING BY NOT WATCHING TV!

A few retailers and outlets are lucky enough to have the Head Bean Hisself design an exclusive piece for them. Usually limited in number, these pieces can only be bought through that store, catalog or outlet and are only available until the stock runs out. Therefore, many exclusives are gone before collectors realize they exist! QVC, the television home shopping network, is one of the largest and most popular dealers of Boyds exclusive pieces. Items, which are usually listed before the show on the web site, have been known to sell out before they were even featured on television!

LOOKING THEIR BEARY BEST

No animal is complete without accessories! Boyds makes specialty items for every animal and occasion. From stylish sweaters and glasses to stoves and furniture, your animal may soon have more possessions than you do! But don't worry, because under the threat of "Big Women With Sticks," The Head Bean designed a wide variety of items available for bear and hare owners too. From hats (with or without ears) to sweatshirts, quilts to cookie jars, Boyds addicts can quench their craving for "more Boyds!" as well. For more information on Boyds accessories, see pages 236-239.

FRIENDS (OF BOYDS) FOREVER

In June of 1996, The Loyal Order of Friends of Boyds (known as F.o.B. for short) celebrated its first year with an overwhelming number of charter "membears." In fact, demand to join the club was so high that The Boyds Collection Ltd. could not keep up, and several members did not receive their club kits until much later in the year. Since then, the club has continued to grow in leaps and bounds, and now boasts a membership of over 100,000!

Among other special benefits, club members receive a yearly subscription to Boyds' official newsletter, *The Boyds Inquirer*. The *Inquirer* is written by The Head Bean Hisself (in his own unique language) and gives collectors insight to upcoming events within the line, such as releases, retirements and signings. It also gives collectors a chance to learn about the recent antics of their favorite artist and his creations. While the *Inquirer* had traditionally been issued twice a year in the past, it was changed to four times a year in 1999.

AND THE WINNER IS...

Gary's success has been recognized within the collectibles industry as well. In 1997, he was named "Artist of the Year" by the National Association of Limited Edition Dealers (NALED), one of the most prestigious awards in the industry. This came on the heels of three Teddy Bear of the Year (TOBY) Public's Choice Awards from *Teddy Bears and Friends* magazine for "Corinna" and "Noah & Co.... Ark Builders" in 1996 and "Neville . . . Compubear" in 1997. His success continued when he won NALED's Collectors' Choice Award for "Best Manufactured Teddy Bears" in 1998, and in 1999 had five finalists for NALED's "Plush Collectible of the Year" and three nominations for the TOBY Awards.

Happy Anniversary!

The Boyds Collection celebrated its China Anniversary with a 20th Anniversary Fall Special Event on October 16, 1999. All Boyds retailers were invited to participate in this event, at which two commemorative plush pieces were made available. A replica of "Matthew," the first Boyds plush bear ever created, called the "Anniversary Edition Matthew Bear," made its debut at this event as well as the "Special Event T.F. Wuzzie Collector Pin."

CORPORATE ON-GOINGS

In 1998, The Boyds Collection Ltd. announced that the company was being sold to the investment firm of Kohlberg, Kravis and Roberts.

While many collectors worried about the fates of their favorite collectible line and artist, G.M. Lowenthal stepped up to assure his fans that he would still play a vital role in the company. The merger would give him some help with running the "business end" of the company, so he could have more time to focus on his creative talents. And as time progressed, collectors recognized that this merger was very much a success.

In 1999, The Boyds Collection Ltd. went international as it established its first overseas subsidiary in the United Kingdom, with hopes of bringing the "almost famous" bears and hares to England and Europe. The company also announced in March 1999 that it would allow the general public to buy stock in The Boyds Collection Ltd.

Boyds collectors around the world know that Gary and The Boyds Collection Ltd. will continue to manufacture the same top-quality plush animals that have been making lives brighter for nearly two decades. With the winning combination of a great personality, a dedicated group of fans and irresistible plush animals, Gary Lowenthal and The Boyds Collection Ltd. are sure to be celebrating success for many years to come.

The Man Behind The Menagerie

Anyone who has seen a Boyds collectible can tell you about the charm, humor and whimsy that shines through in every piece. That personality is a direct reflection of the comical nature of the line's personable creator, Gary M. Lowenthal. Gary is just as unique, and as much a part of the line, as any of his pieces. Those who know the bear artist know that the line would not be a success without his sense of humor, family values and the T.L.C. that he puts into each item.

Born on February 9, 1949, Gary was raised in Manhattan before leaving to attend Alfred College in upstate New York. He graduated in five years with both a bachelor's and master's degree in biology under his belt. Young Gary joined the Peace Corps, where he worked as a teacher in the Fiji Islands. When his assignment was finished, Gary returned to Manhattan and accepted a job with Bloomingdale's as a purchasing, design and merchandising representative.

After seven years in the heart of the Big Apple, Gary longed for a change of pace, and he moved to the rural town of Boyds, Maryland with his new wife, Justina. Gary and Tina, both young, creative and ambitious, opted for self-employment and opened their first "mom and pop" organization: an antique shop, which they named The Boyds Collection Ltd. The couple soon tired of their small shop, however, and tried their hands at several other enterprising ideas. They made decorative flowered wreaths and oak baskets, and Gary carved wooden duck decoys, so authentic that he actually shot them to give them a "used" look. The couple eventually decided to get into collectibles and manufactured a series of small ceramic cottages called "Gnomes Homes." But it wasn't until a few years later that the Lowenthals really found their niche in collectibles. In the early 1980s, Gary paired up with designer Gae Sharp and the two created a line of jointed plush teddy bears. The bears were an instant success, and Gary and Gae began to incorporate other animals into the line as well.

In 1991, Gary put his creative talents to another use, by creating resin figurines in the images of his popular plush teddies. The venture was enormously successful, and The Boyds Collection Ltd. now boasts several themed resin lines, each of which is as popular as the plush.

Much of Gary's success is due to his "slightly off-centered" personality and the sense of humor he brings out in his works and his fans. He is very social with collectors, and feels that it is important to listen to them and incorporate their ideas into his works. His interactive relationship with Boyds collectors has earned him a following unlike that of any other artist in the world of collectibles. Gary's appearances at trade shows and signings elicit a response much like that of a famous movie or rock star. Tickets to his "live studio audiences" at QVC are a hot item, and "The Head Bean Chat," as his seminars are called, are always packed with fans.

Despite his overwhelming popularity with collectors and success as a collectibles artist, Gary insists that the most important aspect of his life is his family. He and Tina have two children, Matthew and Bailey, and a dog, Indy, who have been featured in many of his pieces. Over the years, collectors have had the opportunity to watch the family grow, and with so many pieces based on the family, collectors feel as though they are a part of the Lowenthal clan. And that's exactly what the world of Boyds is all about – one big family.

Spotlight On Boyds Plush Series

With over 1,000 plush animals in the line, it can be hard to pinpoint the exact piece you are looking for. Boyds makes it easier to find your ideal animal by categorizing pieces with similar characteristics into groups called series. Here's a look at the many series within the line:

ANIMAL MENAGERIE – This series is home to the less common animals in the Boyds collection. With an assortment of pigs, monkeys, cows, gorillas and more to choose from, you're bound to find a piece here to bring out both your tame and wild side.

THE ARCHIVE SERIES – Created in the style of the traditional classic teddy bear, these hand-embroidered teddies inspire delight in both young and old with their jointed limbs and shiny neck ribbons.

THE ARTISAN SERIES – The pieces in this small series are all designed by talented "up and coming" artists.

BABY BOYDS – Double-lined and soft to the touch, these critters are designed especially for the youngest Boyds collectors, but are a big hit even with the oldest!

BEARS IN THE ATTIC – These animals are soft on the outside, with fur made of chenille and sherpa pile, but they're extra durable on the outside too, to protect them from the wear and tear that comes with lots of love! Each of these pieces is designed to give it the look of long-lost toys that have been hidden in the attic for years.

THE BUBBA BEARS – These adorable bears come with poseable faces that can be molded into a variety of expressions, a trait that makes them very popular, but hard to find, since the last bear of this collection retired in 1997!

THE CHOIR BEARS – No, these bears and hares can't sing (at least we've never heard them) but they can sit, stand and kneel in prayer!

CLINTONS CABINET – You will find some familiar names in this bunch! These bears all get their names from members of the president's family and his advisors.

DOODLE BEARS – Patriotic teddies make up the *Doodle Bears*, the smallest series in collection. Named after U.S. presidents, the last of these teddies retired in 1998.

THE FLATTIES – These floppy critters are at their happiest just "hanging around." The bears, hares and dogs in this collection are soft, floppy and great for cuddling!

GRIZZLY BEARS – These tough teddies all come with leather collars and hearts of gold!

HARES IN TOYLAND – One of the oldest series in the Boyds collection, these bunnies all retired by 1995. They are best known for their floppy ears.

HIMALAYAN DANCING BEARS – These primitive bears and hares are easy to recognize! Each has a sloped back, curved paws and a face that only a mother (or father or sister . . .) could love.

IMAGINEBEARY FRIENDS – Introduced in 1999, this collection of puppets consists of members of the Chatsworth family. These puppets serve as the "voice of Boyds plush," and they aren't afraid to speak their minds!

J.B. BEAN & ASSOCIATES – One of the largest and most popular series in the line, these bears, hares and friends are filled with bean pellets and are fully poseable.

THE MOHAIR BEARS – Each of these "upah clahss" sweeties has real mohair fur and suede paws. These members of the Bearington, Cattington and Harington families are limited editions. *Mini-mohairs*, which joined the collection in 1999, are sold in open editions.

NORTHERN LIGHTS – Here you'll find the Von Hindenmoose clan who represent the northernmost (or is it northern moose?) branch of the Boyds family tree!

ORNAMENTS – Ever try to hang a regular-sized Boyds up for decoration? It's not easy. So Boyds has designed a line of smaller bears, hares and angels that are perfect not only for hanging on the Christmas tree, but for hanging around all year as well.

PRIME MINISTER'S CABINET – These teddies are all exclusive to Canada, and are named for prime ministers of the country.

SNOW BEARS – Proven to warm the hearts of collectors all around the country, these pieces are known for their beautiful white fur and ice blue eyes.

SQUEEKIES – Give these love-starved animals a hug, and you may be surprised to hear them give cries of joy!

T.F. WUZZIES – Even though Boyds' collection of jointed miniatures, *The Fuzzie Wuzzies*, or *T.F. Wuzzies* for short, are all 5" tall or shorter, they still command a huge amount of love.

T.J.'S BEST DRESSED – These animals have a special way of showing off their personalities – proving that the clothes really do make the bear and hare and mouse ... Each comes with an outfit specially designed to best suit its personality.

UPTOWN BEARS – Only available through select Boyds retailers, these limited edition teddies and friends are all hand-numbered, come in decorated gift boxes and come with custom-designed accessories.

WEARABLE WUZZIES – If you thought those *Wuzzies* couldn't get any smaller, take a look at these! The 2" miniatures have been adapted into pins, so you can wear them proudly everywhere you go!

WOOL BOYDS SERIES – The Von Bruin family from Germany and their pet dog, Fritz, make up this collection. Each of the animals comes with a warm, wooly coat and a bright bow tie.

Sneak Peek At Boyds Resin Figurines

Always the entrepreneur, Gary Lowenthal took the success of his plush collectible critters and turned it into a whole new line of collectibles. The Boyds Collection Ltd.'s line of resin figurines made its debut in 1993 with The Bearstone Collection, and has grown to include these other lines.

THE BEARSTONE COLLECTION

Based on everyone's favorite characters from the plush line, these finely detailed bears, hares and friends have the same whimsical appeal as the plush pieces. Since the collection's debut in 1993, nearly 400 pieces have been introduced, including three themed series: *Classic Beary Tales Series, Holiday Pageant Series* and the *Noah's Pageant Series*.

THE FOLKSTONE COLLECTION

From seraphim to snowmen, you can find a piece to match every personality in this collection of mismatched characters, introduced in 1994. *Carvers Choice, Santa & Friends,* and *The Wee Folkstones* are all series within the collection, while *The Garden Gang, Ribbit & Co.,* and *The Tuxedo Gang* are sub-series of *The Wee Folkstones.* The *Not Quite Guardian Angels* (NQGA's), a crew of "wannabe" angels, are another favorite within the line.

YESTERDAY'S CHILD...THE DOLLSTONE COLLECTION

This magnificent group of smoothly finished doll figurines made its debut on QVC in 1995. An immediate success, the collection soon made its way to retail stores, and has been charming doll-lovers everywhere since. The nostalgic line focuses on "Yesterday's Child," who brings us back to the days of teddy bears and make-believe. Nearly 100 pieces have been introduced in this line to date, including figurines, musicals, ornaments, porcelain dolls, votive holders and waterglobes.

THE SHOE BOX BEARS

The Grizberg family of bears are the stars of this small collection of jointed resin figurines that was introduced in 1996 and named for the childhood toys and treasures that Gary Lowenthal kept under his bed. They are truly unique, as each body part has been delicately crafted and connected to one another with rubber bands, so that each of the animals is fully poseable!

YESTERDAY'S CHILD...THE DOLL COLLECTION

A new group of stars made its debut on QVC in 1995, as "Yesterday's Child" expanded into a group of porcelain dolls. The 16" limited edition dolls, who have delicate resin hands and feet, quickly won the hearts of collectors,   are now available in retail stores in 12" open editions as well as the original 16" limited editions.

DESKANIMALS

Introduced in 1998, these water-loving wild animals are made to look as though they are partly submerged in water. These unusual collectibles make great conversation pieces and are perfect for displaying on your desktop, tabletop or anywhere else where you could use some extra inspiration (or a chuckle).

THE PURRSTONE COLLECTION

The newest branch in the Boyds family tree, the Purrstone Collection made its debut in 1999. Eleven kitties have joined the litter so far. The fashionable felines each come in different outfits, and are all intricately detailed, right down to the tips of their whiskers.

BEARLY-BUILT VILLAGES

Boyds Town was erected in the Spring of 2000, as the first set of buildings made its mark on the map. Each building also features a hidden character inside, which can be found by removing the detachable roof of the building.

Boyds In The Spotlight

What is the favorite show of Boyds fans across the country? It's not the Super Bowl, the Miss America Pageant or even "Who Wants To Be A Millionaire?" It's the "Mary Beth and Gary Show" on QVC!

Since 1995, those lovable Boyds bears, hares and friends have enjoyed their "15 minutes of fame" on the cable home shopping network QVC. The animals and their creator, Gary Lowenthal, make several appearances a year on the network and have become one of QVC's most popular features. Launches and exclusives are not unusual to find on these shows, so Boyds collectors all across the United States eagerly tune it to see their ol' Uncle Bean and the new products he will introduce. And practically every piece offered during these shows, whether it be an exclusive, launch or even a regular-line piece, sells out in minutes, sometimes before it can even be described on camera.

QVC Senior Program Host Mary Beth Roe runs the show with Gary and the rapport that has developed between the co-hosts has become as much of a draw to viewers as the pieces themselves. ". . . [W]e just hit it off from the beginning. I love humor and he just was so humorous," remembers Mary Beth. And indeed, Gary's humor is one of the main highlights of the show. Collectors love his zany, "slightly off-centered" personality.

Each show kicks off when Gary first appears on stage, always in a different costume. Over the years, The Head Bean has arrived in outfits of all sorts, from a top hat and tails to a full fuzzy cat costume, and collectors love to try to guess what he will appear as next.

Mary Beth and Gary also have a wonderful chemistry that allows them to play off each other well. Mary Beth says, "The more Gary and I started to get to know each other, the more the teasing started to escalate. When that began to happen, the e-mail and the mail that I got was from Boyds Bears collectors siding with me .... Now, we have such

a good rapport that I feel like I can tease him back a few times."

The network occasionally opens tapings of the "Mary Beth and Gary Show" to a live studio audience. Collectors travel from around the country to attend these shows, and the studio fills up quickly. These shows always have a lively atmosphere, as collectors, decked out in Boyds t-shirts and sweatshirts, bring signs and cheer loudly for Gary, Mary Beth and the Boyds collection. Members of the audience often get to meet Gary, as he answers their questions during shows, holds signings afterwards and sometimes even wanders into the audience to sit and chat during commercial breaks! Since Boyds collectors are such a close-knit group, the fans watching the live-audience shows from home have just as good a time as those in the studio, as they recognize their friends on television and watch the antics of The Head Bean Hisself.

The "Mary Beth and Gary Show" is typically broadcast six times a year, including a five week mini-series in November that kicks off the holiday gift-giving season. Other appearances are held in January, March, May or June and August. For more information on upcoming episodes of the "Mary Beth and Gary Show," check your local TV listings or the *F.o.B. Inquirer* or visit QVC's web site at www.iqvc.com.

What's New For Boyds Plush Animals

The Boyds Collection Ltd. welcomes in the millennium with a giant release of Y2K-compliant animals. This section spotlights these critters alphabetically within their species. Look for them on the shelves of your favorite retailer and for several others on the shelves of exclusive outlets as well.

AGATHA SNOOPSTEIN . . . This "hare" is really Agatha Snoopstein – bear master of disguise!

AISSA WITEBRED . . . Her unusual name is only one reason you'll remember this teddy!

AUBREY TIPPEETOES . . . Looking charming in her tutu, this star ballerina has all the right moves to win your heart!

AUNT MAMIE BEARINGTON . . . Aunt Mamie serves as the kind-at-heart matriarch to the mohair Bearington family.

AUNTIE LAVONNE HIGGENTHORPE . . . Everyone's favorite aunt, Lavonne always has a smile and a good word for all!

B.A. BLACKBELT . . . Don't mess with this tough teddy! B.A. is a master in the martial arts to the highest degree!

BAILEY (SPRING 2000) . . . It's off to camp for Bailey this spring, and she just can't wait for the fun to start!

BAMBOO BEARINGTON . . . Newly arrived from China, this Asian panda needs a loving home. Will she find one with you?

BILLY BOB BRUIN WITH FROGGIE . . . Billy Bob never goes anywhere without his "toad-ally" cool best friend.

BRIANNA TIPPEETOES . . . Brianna practices hard so she can dance as well as her older sister Aubrey.

BRISTOL B. WINDSOR . . . This dapper darling always impresses the ladies with his English accent!

BROOKE B. BEARSLEY . . . All ready for a day of play, Brooke's the picture of comfort in a plaid jumper and headband!

BUMBLE B. BUZZOFF . . . This "bumblebear" is on the lookout for fresh spring flowers to pollinate.

CAMBRIDGE Q. BEARRISTER . . . The pinnacle of class, this "black-tied" bear only attends the most formal of affairs.

CLARK S. BEARHUGS . . . The "Superman" of bears, Clark has stolen Lois Bearlove's heart with his superpowers!

CORI BEARIBURG . . . With the luck of a ladybug, this soft brown teddy will envelop you in one of her famous "bear hugs!"

DARBY BEARIBURG . . . Darby is a close-knit companion to his sister Cori in their matching sweaters.

DOVER D. WINDSOR . . . Bring this teddy to your next social gathering. He's always the life of the party!

DWIGHT D. BEARINGTON . . . This unique-looking teddy was made in the style of bears from decades past.

EDMUND (SPRING 2000) . . . Edmund has a new friend, and can't wait to introduce his slimy sidekick to Bailey and Emily!

ELEANORE BEARSEVELT . . . Eleanore looks downright presidential in her red sweater and blue dress with white stars!

ELMER O. BEARROAD . . . Elmer proves that uniforms don't have to be unfashionable in his striped overalls and flashy scarf.

GINNIE HIGGENTHORPE . . . Ginnie wears her best hat while having tea with her Auntie Lavonne!

HAMPTON T. BEARINGTON . . . Hampton chooses to celebrate the warm weather by spending a day on his new sailboat!

HASTINGS P. BEARSFORD . . . Whether you need a shoulder to cry on or a friend to laugh with, Hastings will be there.

HAYDEN T. BEARSFORD . . . Hayden is studying hard in school, with hopes of being accepted to "Bearkeley" College.

HAZELNUT B. BEAN . . . Like a hot cup of coffee, this bear is perfect for snuggling up to on a cold winter morning.

HUNEY B. KEEPER . . . Huney wears a screen to protect her from the bees that surround her as she searches for sweets!

HUNTER BEARSDALE WITH GREENSPAN . . . Hunter insists that even a pet frog should get a good night kiss at bedtime.

JULIET S. BEARLOVE . . . Juliet wears her best red sweater in hopes that you will ask her to be your Valentine.

KEVIN G. BEARSLEY . . . In anticipation of days spent at the beach, Kevin puts on his favorite blue lighthouse sweater.

KOOKIE SNICKLEFRITZ . . . Better than a cookie, this huggable plush honey promises to brighten your day right up!

 KYLE L. BERRIMAN . . . He may look like an angel, but Kyle likes to stir up trouble when no one is looking!

LADY B. BUG . . . The cutest critter around, this "ladybug" is sure to crawl into your heart as soon as you see her!

 LOIS B. BEARLOVE . . . Looking lovely in a red plaid dress and bow, it's no surprise that Lois won Clark's heart!

MEGAN BERRIMAN . . . This classic teddy also enjoys a classic look, as you can see from her jumper and bow!

 MELINDA S. WILLOUGHBY . . . A natural beauty, Melinda prefers this basic khaki dress to flashier outfits.

MIKAYLA SPRINGBEARY . . . Mikayla has put away her winter blues and is dressed in her best springtime pink!

 MR. BOJINGLES . . . This comical and colorful bear promises to turn even the biggest frown upside down!

NANETTE DUBEARY . . . Nanette welcomes in the spring with a flowery hat in the colors of clear skies and sunshine!

NANTUCKET P. BEARINGTON . . . A little spring shower won't stop this determined bear from his travels!

NAOMI BEARLOVE . . . Naomi Bearlove can fix any injury, from a bruised ego to a broken heart, with some T.L.C.

PAIGE WILLOUGHBY . . . Paige looks like quite a "little lady" in a purple dress and matching hair bow.

PATCHES B. BEARILUVED . . . Who says wear and tear is a bad thing? It makes Patches even more lovable!

POOF PUFFLEBEARY & BLANKIE . . . Poof won't leave home without her blanket, and you won't want to leave without Poof!

RADCLIFFE FITZBRUIN . . . On leave from the "U.S.S. Bearmerican," Radcliffe can't wait to tell you about his travels!

ROCKWELL B. BRUIN . . . You'll never have to worry about losing this tall teddy, who wears a bell around his neck!

ROSS G. JODIBEAR . . . Ross plans to show off his American pride by playing his trumpet in the 4th of July parade!

SALLY QUIGNAPPLE & ANNIE . . . Sally's inquisitive eyes ask you to play with her and her favorite doll, Annie.

SAMUEL ADAMS . . . Who can resist this Casanova of teddy bears who's looking for your love?

SINCLAIR BEARSFORD . . . We think it's clear that you'll find that this bear is as sweet as his cinnamon-colored fur!

SNOOKIE SNICKLEFRITZ . . . Snookie is the perfect companion for babies (or adults) who like to snuggle up to softness.

TUMBLE F. WUZZIE . . . What would a circus be without a clown? Tumble steals the show with a red nose and pointy hat.

UNCLE BEN BEARINGTON . . . Uncle Ben always looks his best, even while working on the farm in his denim overalls!

WEBBER VANGUARD . . . Webber proves that classics are always in the front of the line!

WOOKIE SNICKLEFRITZ . . . Feeling a little blue? Wookie is the perfect bear for you!

BLAKE B. WORDSWORTH . . . This gray and white tabby makes every move poetic!

BUNDLES B. JOY WITH BLANKIE . . . Like her name implies, this kitty will bring you hours of comfort and joy!

CALLIE FUZZBUCKET . . . This gray and white tabby is considered by some to be the "pick of the litter" of Boyds cats.

DICKENS Q. WORDSWORTH . . . We have "great expectations" for this cuddly new gray and white kitten!

DORCHESTER CATSWORTH WITH ARTIE . . . This angler licks his chops in anticipation of the fish he'll catch.

EMERSON T. PENWORTHY . . . This friendly feline is best known for spinning "yarns," like the writer he was named for.

JAVA B. BEAN . . . The "purr-fect" companion, Java will keep you intensely "a-mew-sed" for hours with her games and tricks.

MILTON R. PENWORTHY . . . This black and white ball of fuzz is sure to write his way into your heart in no time.

MISS PRISSY FUSSYBUNS . . . Persian cat lovers will fall in love with this enchanting longhaired diva.

MOMMA McFUZZ & MISSY . . . Momma McFuzz gives Missy a hug and a nuzzle to show how much she loves her!

PHOEBE PURRSMORE . . . Freshly groomed, Phoebe puts on her best hat and heads out to visit good friends.

ROBYN PURRSMORE . . . Wide-eyed Robyn insists that she hasn't eaten her dinner yet, but her bib tells another story.

TESSA FLUFFYPAWS . . . With her soft white fur and pleading eyes, this kitty is the "cat's meow" of plush!

ELFORD BULLSWORTH . . . Elford may look gruff on the exterior, but this "ladies' man" is hardly a bully.

T. FODDER WUZZIE . . . He may be the smallest cow around, but he has a big job as the only *Wuzzie* cow!

BINKY McFARKLE . . . You'll do a double take when you first see Binky! This pup looks almost exactly like brother, Barkley!

CARSON B. BARKER . . . Carson is fiercely loyal, a trait that makes him a "bone-a fide" pro at guarding your home!

INDY (SPRING 2000) . . . Who said camps are for kids? Indy put on a Camp Bearibriar shirt and snuck into camp himself!

SNUFFY B. BARKER . . . Playful Snuffy the puppy will win your heart with his antics and games.

T. FOLEY WUZZIE . . . Foley promises to show you why he's "man's best friend" if you will take him home with you!

BEDFORD BONEAH II . . . Exchanging his scarf for a plaid vest, Bedford looks ready for a night out on the town.

BRIGHAM BONEAH II . . . Following Bedford's lead, Brigham has traded in his stripes for a flashy star-patterned vest.

BUFFIE BUNNYHOP . . . Buffie, a cream-colored cutie, and her sister Fluffie hope to hop into your heart and home.

BUNKIE HOPPLEBY . . . Don't let this busy bunny just hop on by – this hare is worth snatching up.

CARA Z. BUNNYHUGS . . . Just as her name suggests, Cara is full of care and hugs for the lucky person who adopts her!

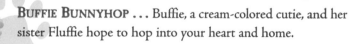

CATHY J. HIPHOP . . . Cathy feels grown up and groovy in her pink silk bow, even though she hasn't quite grown into it yet.

EMILY (SPRING 2000) . . . Emily puts on her Camp Bearibriar sweatshirt before heading down to the lake to test her new net!

FLUFFIE BUNNYHOP . . . Buffie's snow-colored sibling looks adorable in a pastel pink bow that matches her nose!

JENNA D. LAPINNE . . . Jenna's snowy fur and blue eyes are well-accented by her royal blue jumper and flowered hat.

JULIANA HOPKINS II . . . It's like a brand new Juliana as she makes her debut in a mauve corduroy sweater and jumper set!

LILA HOPKINS . . . This friendly little bunny is sure to hop right into your heart to make a big impression!

LOTTIE DE LOPEAR . . . A proud member of the distinguished de Lopear family, Lottie is only seen in the newest fashions!

MIPSIE BLUMENSHINE . . . A touch of lace brings out the feminine side of tomhare Mipsie!

NATALIE NIBBLENOSE . . . The only biting this hare will do is giving nibbles of affection.

NICKIE NIBBLENOSE . . . Nickie puts on a brightly colored ribbon to express his excitement over the new spring season!

PAULA HOPPLEBY . . . Now that the winter is over, Paula hops from hutch to hutch visiting friends and socializing.

POOKIE C. HOPPLEBY . . . Pookie looks forward to a springtime filled with munching on lettuce leaves and carrots!

REGENA HARESFORD . . . When not working the runway, this bunny supermodel likes to dress in denims and khakis.

ROSALYNN P. HARINGTON II . . . Rosalynn has traded in her bow for a more feminine look – and it suits her fabulously!

ROSLYN HIPHOP . . . Roslyn's long shaggy coat kept her warm through winter, and now it makes her very cool and cuddly!

SAVANNAH BUTTERCUP ... This Southern belle looks "just mahvalous" in her soft yellow springtime ensemble.

STELLINA HOPSWELL ... Stellina wears a green ribbon in excitement of the tasty grass and lettuce leaves to come.

STERLING HOPSWELL ... This "Easter bunny in training" has a lot of work ahead of him before springtime arrives!

T. FARRELL WUZZIE ... This hare better have a big appetite if he's planning on eating this carrot – it's as big as he is!

T. HOPPLEWHITE ... This rabbit's fur is as soft and as white as freshly spun cotton. And she's got a soft heart to match!

DIPSEY BAADOODLE ... The phrase "as gentle as a lamb" could have been made for this tender-hearted white creature.

EMBRACEABLE EWE ... This huggable lamb's heart is much bigger than the one she wears on her dusty blue sweater.

MATILDA BAAHEAD ... We promise that "ewe" will fall in love with this lamb as soon as you set eyes on her!

I.M. UPROARIUS ... I.M. may claim to have a rough exterior, but on the inside, he's as sweet and gentle as a kitten!

THEO F. WUZZIE ... He may be small, but Theo has a roar (and a heart) that's 20 times his tiny size!

ROMANO B. GRATED ... This Italian mouse would "mange" cheese all day if he was given the opportunity!

TOODLES F. WUZZIE . . . Toodles grinds the organ to welcome guests to the first-ever *T.F. Wuzzie* Circus!

MUDPUDDLE P. PIGLET . . . Mudpuddle is a great cook – her specialty is mud pies and will make a pig out of you!

PRIMROSE IV . . . While her friends like to frolic in mud all day, this well-dressed pig prefers to mingle with high society.

TRUFFLES O'PIGG & BLANKIE . . . This adorable oinker brings new meaning to the phrase "pig in a blanket!"

BANDIT BUSHYTAIL . . . Who is that masked critter? He's Bandit, The Boyds Collection Ltd.'s first plush raccoon!

DINKLE B. BUMBLES . . . This honey-loving teddy tries to camouflage himself as a bee in order to infiltrate the hive!

GONNA LUVYA . . . This lovable angel teddy extends his arms to give you a very special gift – his heart!

JOSANNA JAVA . . . Josanna is guaranteed to put an extra spring in your step when you first see her!

KATALINA KAFINATA . . . Katalina is the perfect-sized dose of "cat-feine" to help you get through your day!

LADY B. LOVEBUG . . . Lady flitters through the air, bringing love and warmth to all whom she passes!

LILITH ANGEL EWE . . . This lamb was sent from "a-baa-ve" to serve as your guardian angel and bring you joy!

LILLY R. RIBBIT . . . We've all heard of "raining cats and dogs," but frogs? Lilly, the first flying frog, debuts this season.

PINKLE B. BUMBLES . . . Pinkle looks as sweet as cotton candy in her pastel bee outfit!

T.F. BUZZIE WUZZIE . . . This "bumblebee" promises not to sting you if you give him some sweet honey!

TWEEDLE F. WUZZIE . . . What's black and white and red all over (but looks like a bear)? It's Tweedle!

TWIDDLE F. WUZZIE . . . You won't want to use the fly swatter on this bug, who's the latest fuzzy buzz of the town!

WINKLE B. BUMBLES . . . This periwinkle "bee" serves as a lookout while his two friends try to steal honey from the hive!

TEEDLE F. WUZZIE . . . Wear your love of Boyds on your sleeve with Teedle, one of three Boyds pins available this season.

THISTLE F. WUZZIE . . . This black and white critter will coordinate with all of your favorite outfits, no matter their color!

TINGER F. WUZZIE . . . Your friends won't "bee-lieve" their eyes when they see you wearing your latest Boyds find!

HOWLIN P. CHATSWORTH . . . The first canine Boyds puppet, Howlin is sure to live up to his name!

KATAWALIN P. CHATSWORTH . . . Katawalin has nine lives worth of talking to do and thoughts to share!

Collector's Club News

As The Loyal Order of Friends of Boyds roars into its fourth year of providing a "Slightly Off-Center Collector's Club for people who still believe in . . . Bears And Hares You Can Trust™," the wily Head Bean has enough surprises up his sleeve to guarantee excitement for both new and long-time members. This year's offerings give members the chance to sit down (or stand up) and enjoy some scrumptious "Tea for Three."

Settle down for a spot o' tea with "Caitlin Berriweather," a beautiful 6" plush bear who will make you wish that tea time could be all the time.

Membership also includes the exclusive Bearstone figurine "Catherine and Caitlin Berriweather . . . Fine Cup of Tea." One look at this heart-warming resin piece makes those tea parties from childhood long ago seem like they happened only yesterday.

Members can also show off their favorite bear in style with the spiffy Official "Brewin' F.o.B. Bearwear Pin," featuring Caitlin Berriweather as well as her favorite refreshment.

In addition, club members will receive the poem "Tea for Three." It's suitable for framing and sure to warm the hearts of all who read it.

Club members will be able to stay "in-the-know" with the handy, pocket-sized Boyds Bears & Friends Product List, the Boyds Dealer Directory for 2000 and a year's subscription of four big issues to the *F.o.B. Inquirer*.

For those of you who are computer inclined, the F.o.B. membership number will grant you access to the "V.I.P." area of the brand-new Boyds website. Here, club members have the privilege of even more insider news, ranging from hot stories to scoops on new products!

Of course, you cannot have a proper tea party without the proper china. For just a mere $7.50, you can be the perfect host with the "Brewin' F.o.B. Official Mini Tea Set." This table for three is a special member exclusive.

Members are also invited to purchase two member exclusive redemption pieces that can be ordered through your friendly Boyds retailer. "Catherine Berriweather" is an 11" plush bear that comes with a special surprise tagalong – "Little Scruff," a 3" *Wuzzie*. The Bearstone resin masterpiece "Catherine And Caitlin Berriweather With Little Scruff . . . Family Traditions" is a resin depiction of mother, daughter and *Wuzzie* sharing tea and conversation.

But this year isn't all play and no work for the characters in The Loyal Order of Friends of Boyds. To complement "Noah's Genius At Work Table," "Noah's Tool Box" will be available exclusively to members as Noah will not be able to get much accomplished without his tools.

Club membership is still only $32.50 and applications must be received by December 31, 2000. An application is at the back of this book or you can pick one up from your local Boyds retailer. Send your application to:

**THE BOYDS COLLECTION LTD.
P.O. BOX 4386, F.O.B. DEPT.
GETTYSBURG, PA 17325-4386**

Future Retirements

*E*ach year, The Head Bean goes through the Boyds warehouse and orders pieces "outta da pool" through retirement. Retirement usually means that a piece will retire at a specified date. A "sudden death" retirement means that the piece retires immediately, and when the Boyds warehouse runs out of its stock, that's it. Here is a list of pieces that will be retiring by December 31, 2000, with issue year, item number and series abbreviation in parentheses (*see chart on page 38*).

RETIRING IN 2000!

BEARS

❏ Ace Q. Dooright . . . .(1999, #900203, UB)
❏ Alex Berriman With Nikita . . . .(1999, #900202, UB)
❏ Alvis Q. Bearnap With Snoozy T. Puddlemaker .(1999, #900208, UB)
❏ Anya Frostfire . . . .(1999, #912023, TJ)
❏ Bailey . . . .(Spring 2000, #9199-14, TJ)
❏ Arthur C. Bearington . . . .(2000, #590060-03, MB)
❏ Bamboo Bearington . . . .(2000, #590030, MB)
❏ Betsey . . . .(1997, #913952, TJ)
❏ Bevin B. Bearski With Willie Waddlewalk . . . .(1999, #900206, UB)
❏ Billy Ray Beanster With Petey Poker . . . .(1999, #900207, UB)
❏ Bonnie . . . .(1997, #913951, TJ)
❏ Courtney . . . .(1997, #912021, TJ)
❏ Dwight D. Bearington . . . .(2000, #590081-03, MB)
❏ Hampton T. Bearington . . . .(2000, #590052-08, MB)
❏ Hartley B. Mine . . . .(1999, #91521, TJ)
❏ Kelsey M. Jodibear With Arby B. Tugalong . . .(1999, #900209, UB)
❏ Margarita . . . .(1998, #911062, TJ)
❏ Matthew . . . .(Fall 1999, #91756-12, TJ)
❏ McKenzie . . . .(1997, #5840-03, GB)
❏ Meredith K. Pattington . . . .(1999, #900204, UB)
❏ Momma McBear And Delmar . . . .(1997, #91007, TJ)
❏ Monroe J. Bearington . . . .(2000, #590023-11, MB)
❏ Rutherford . . . .(1998, #912610, TJ)
❏ Tabitha J. Spellbinder With Midnight Sneakypuss . . .(1999, #900201, UB)
❏ Tasha B. Frostbeary . . . .(1999, #900205, UB)
❏ Townsend Q. Bearrister . . . .(1999, #57001-03, AS)
❏ Winstead P. Bear . . . .(1998, #515210-03, JB)
❏ Worthington Fitzbruin . . . .(1997, #912032, TJ)

CATS

- ❏ Kattelina Purrsley .... (1999, #91978, TJ)
- ❏ Lindsey P. Pussytoes .... (1998, #912091, TJ)
- ❏ Mrs. Partridge .... (1998, #919750, TJ)

COWS

- ❏ Angus MacMoo .... (1999, #91341, TJ)
- ❏ Elmo Beefcake .... (1993, #5532-03, AM)

DOGS

- ❏ Clancy G. Hydrant, Jr. .... (1998, #5404, JB)
- ❏ Indy .... (Spring 2000, #91757-14, TJ)

FROGS

- ❏ Racheal Q. Ribbit .... (1997, #566340, BA)

HARES

- ❏ Cousin Rose Anjanette .... (1998, #91112-01, TJ)
- ❏ Dudley Hopson .... (1999, #91663, TJ)
- ❏ Edith Q. Harington II. .... (2000, #55901600-03, MB)
- ❏ Emily Babbit .... (Spring 2000, #9150-14, TJ)
- ❏ Iris Rosenbunny .... (1999, #91651, TJ)
- ❏ Millie Hopkins .... (1999, #91123, TJ)
- ❏ Rosalynn P. Harington II .... (2000, #5901400-01, MB)
- ❏ Wedgewood J. Hopgood .... (1999, #52401-10, JB)

LAMBS

- ❏ Tallulah Baahead .... (1995, #5520-01, AM)

PIGS

- ❏ Lofton Q. McSwine .... (1997, #55391-09, AM)
- ❏ Sheffield O'Swine .... (1997, #55391-07, AM)

Boyds Plush Top Ten

This section showcases the 10 most valuable Boyds plush animals as determined by their values on the secondary market. In order to qualify for this section, the piece must have top dollar value and show an increase in value from its original price. Secondary market values for some older Boyds plush animals have not been established. As a result, several rare and valuable pieces do not appear on this list but are extremely coveted by collectors! (Please note, this list does not include Boyds plush exclusives.)

BAILEY (Fall 1992)
Issued 1992 – Retired 1993
Original Price: N/A
Secondary Market Value: **$750**

ELEANOR BEAR (set/3)
Issued 1990 – Retired 1990
Original Price: N/A
Secondary Market Value: **$575**

RUDOLF
Issued 1992 – Retired 1992
Original Price: N/A
Secondary Market Value: **$540**

NANA
Issued 1991 – Retired 1992
Original Price: $27
Secondary Market Value: **$510**

BEATRICE

Issued 1991 – Retired 1991
Original Price: $63
Secondary Market Value: **$460**

MEMSY

Issued N/A – Retired N/A
Original Price: N/A
Secondary Market Value: **$440**

BAILEY (FALL 1993)

Issued 1993 – Retired 1994
Original Price: N/A
Secondary Market Value: **$380**

BEAR-AMONG-BEARS (#5050)

Issued pre-1990 – Retired N/A
Original Price: N/A
Secondary Market Value: **$360**

PHILLIP BEAR HOP

Issued 1991 – Retired 1992
Original Price: $27
Secondary Market Value: **$355**

BAILEY (SPRING 1993)

Issued 1993 – Retired 1994
Original Price: N/A
Secondary Market Value: **$350**

How To Use Your Value Guide

Addington
12" • #5701-05 • AS
Issued: 1993 • Retired: 1996
Orig. Price: $20 • Value: $50

1. Locate your piece in the Value Guide. Each piece appears alphabetically within its animal type, with the categories listed in the following order: bears, cats, cows, crows, dogs, donkeys, elephants, foxes, frogs, gorillas, hares, lambs, lions, mice, monkeys, moose, penguins, pigs, raccoons, ornaments, pins, puppets, tree toppers and collector's club pieces. Exclusive pieces follow and are also in alphabetical order within each animal type. Use the handy Alphabetical Index, that is on page 240 to help you quickly find your piece. A guide to the abbreviations of the plush series appears below.

Bears	
Price Paid	Value
$20.00	$50.00
$20.00	$50.00
Totals	

2. Record both the original price that you paid and the current value of the piece in the corresponding boxes at the bottom of the page. Pieces for which a secondary market price has not been established are listed as "N/E." For those, write the price you paid in the "Value Of My Collection" column. The market value for current pieces is the 2000 suggested retail price (although retail prices may vary).

3. Calculate the value for each page by adding together all of the boxes in each column and recording it in the "Pencil Totals" section at the bottom of the box. Be sure to use a pencil so you can change the totals as your Boyds plush collection grows!

4. Transfer the totals from each page to the "Total Value Of My Collection" worksheets located at the end of the Value Guide section.

5. Add the totals together to determine the overall value of your collection.

PLUSH SERIES KEY

AM Animal Menagerie	**CC** Clintons Cabinet	**IF** ImagineBeary Friends	**SQ** Squeekies
AR The Artisan Series	**CH** The Choir Hares	**JB** J.B. Bean & Associates	**TF** T.F. Wuzzies
AS The Archive Series	**DB** Doodle Bears	**MB** The Mohair Bears	**TJ** T.J.'s Best Dressed
BA Bears In The Attic	**FL** The Flatties	**NL** Northern Lights	**UB** Uptown Bears
BB The Bubba Bears	**GB** Grizzly Bears	**OR** Ornaments	**WB** Wool Boyds Series
BY BabyBoyds	**HD** Himalayan Dancing Bears	**PM** Prime Minister's Cabinet	**WW** Wearable Wuzzies
CB The Choir Bears	**HT** Hares in Toyland	**SB** Snow Bears	

COLLECTOR'S
VALUE GUIDE™

BOYDS PLUSH ANIMALS

Over the years, the Boyds family tree has expanded to include nearly 1,500 animals of all types, shapes and sizes. Its branches consist of critters from every neck of the woods, from lovable hares and teddy bears to ferocious lions and tigers. There is something for everyone in this truly captivating line!

BEARS

Boyds bears continue to win the hearts of collectors around the world as they remain the most popular characters in the plush line. A new line up of over 50 teddies march into the line this season, bringing the total number available too well over 600.

Abercrombie B. Beanster
16" • #510400-05 • JB
Issued: 1999 • Current
Orig. Price: $26 • **Value: $26**

Ace Bruin
10" • #5122 • JB
Issued: Pre-1990 • Retired: 1996
Orig. Price: $14 • **Value: $43**

Ace Q. Dooright
12" • #900203 • UB
Issued: 1999 • To Be Retired: 2000
Orig. Price: $95 • **Value: $95**

Adams F. Bearington
6" • #590080-03 • MB
Issued: 1998 • Retired: 1998
Orig. Price: $18 • **Value: $42**

Addington
12" • #5701-05 • AS
Issued: 1993 • Retired: 1996
Orig. Price: $20 • **Value: $50**

Bears	
Price Paid	Value
1.	
2.	
3.	
4.	
5.	
Totals	

Agatha Snoopstein
8" • #91870 • TJ
Issued: 2000 • Current
Orig. Price: $17 • **Value: $17**

Aissa Witebred
12" • #912070 • TJ
Issued: 2000 • Current
Orig. Price: $27 • **Value: $27**

Alastair
5.5" • #5725-08 • AS
Issued: 1996 • Retired: 1997
Orig. Price: $7 • **Value: $25**

Alastair & Camilla
(set/2, bear and hare)
N/A • #98042 • TJ
Issued: 1996 • Retired: 1996
Orig. Price: N/A • **Value: $44**

Albert B. Bean
14" • #5123-03 • JB
Issued: 1993 • Retired: 1997
Orig. Price: $20 • **Value: $37**

Alec
(also known as "Alex")
5.5" • #5711 • AS
Issued: 1990 • Retired: 1991
Orig. Price: $7 • **Value: $82**

Bears

	Price Paid	Value
1.		
2.		
3.		
4.		
5.		
6.		
7.		
8.		
9.		
10.		

Totals

Aletha...
The Bearmaker (LE-500)
N/A • #9217 • N/A
Issued: 1994 • Retired: 1994
Orig. Price: $74 • **Value: $260**

Alex Berriman
With Nikita
16" & 6" • #900202 • UB
Issued: 1999 • To Be Retired: 2000
Orig. Price: $73 • **Value: $73**

Alexis Berriman
16" • #912022 • TJ
Issued: 1998 • Current
Orig. Price: $61 • **Value: $61**

Alice
11" • #1101-08 • CC
Issued: 1995 • Retired: 1995
Orig. Price: $12 • **Value: $25**

Value Guide — Boyds Plush Animals

1

Alice II
11" • #1101-08 • CC
Issued: 1996 • Retired: 1998
Orig. Price: $12 • **Value: $23**

2

Alouetta de Grizetta
6" • #91842 • TJ
Issued: 1996 • Retired: 1999
Orig. Price: $9 • **Value: $19**

3

Alvis Q. Bearnap With Snoozy T. Puddlemaker
14" • #900208 • UB
Issued: 1999 • To Be Retired: 2000
Orig. Price: $39 • **Value: $39**

4

Amanda K. Huntington
16" • #912025 • TJ
Issued: 1999 • Current
Orig. Price: $59 • **Value: $59**

5

Amos
12" • #5700-03 • AS
Issued: 1995 • Retired: 1995
Orig. Price: $20 • **Value: $182**

6

Andrei Berriman
5.5" • #917300-06 • TJ
Issued: 1998 • Current
Orig. Price: $13 • **Value: $13**

7

Andrew Huntington
6" • #918053 • TJ
Issued: 1999 • Current
Orig. Price: $12 • **Value: $12**

8

Anissa Whittlebear
12" • #912650 • TJ
Issued: 1999 • Current
Orig. Price: $26 • **Value: $26**

9

Ansel
6" • #91271 • TJ
Issued: 1996 • Retired: 1999
Orig. Price: $13 • **Value: $18**

10

Anya Frostfire
16" • #912023 • TJ
Issued: 1999 • To Be Retired: 2000
Orig. Price: $59 • **Value: $59**

Bears	Price Paid	Value
1.		
2.		
3.		
4.		
5.		
6.		
7.		
8.		
9.		
10.		
Totals		

Archibald McBearlie
6" • #91393 • TJ
Issued: 1998 • Current
Orig. Price: $13 • **Value: $13**

Arctic Bear
info unavailable
Orig. Price: N/A • **Value: N/E**

Arlo
8" • #9141 • TJ
Issued: 1994 • Retired: 1996
Orig. Price: $12 • **Value: $45**

Arlo
8 • #98040 • TJ
Issued: 1996 • Retired: 1997
Orig. Price: $12 • **Value: $46**

Artemus
8" • #1003-08 • CC
Issued: 1997 • Retired: 1999
Orig. Price: $7 • **Value: $16**

Arthur
16" • #5712 • AS
Issued: 1991 • Retired: 1992
Orig. Price: $32 • **Value: $170**

Bears	
Price Paid	Value
1.	
2.	
3.	
4.	
5.	
6.	
7.	
8.	
9.	
10.	
Totals	

Arthur C. Bearington
9" • #590060-03 • MB
Issued: 1999 • To Be Retired: 2000
Orig. Price: $29 • **Value: $29**

Ashley
14" • #5109 • JB
Issued: 1991 • Retired: 1992
Orig. Price: $20 • **Value: $200**

Ashley Huntington
6" • #918054 • TJ
Issued: 1999 • Current
Orig. Price: $12 • **Value: $12**

Asquith
8" • #5705-05 • AS
Issued: 1993 • Retired: 1995
Orig. Price: $13 • **Value: $40**

Value Guide — Boyds Plush Animals

1

Astrid
9" • #9137 • TJ
Issued: 1994 • Retired: 1996
Orig. Price: $20 • **Value: $46**

2

Attlee
8" • #5705B • AS
Issued: 1992 • Retired: 1993
Orig. Price: N/A • **Value: $95**

3
New!

Aubrey Tippeetoes
12" • #912054 • TJ
Issued: 2000 • Current
Orig. Price: $28 • **Value: $28**

4

Auggie Bruin
16" • #5125 • JB
Issued: 1992 • Retired: 1996
Orig. Price: $27 • **Value: $63**

5

Augusta
14" • #91010 • TJ
Issued: 1998 • Retired: 1998
Orig. Price: $36 • **Value: $17**

6

Aunt Becky Bearchild
12" • #912052 • TJ
Issued: 1998 • Current
Orig. Price: $29 • **Value: $29**

7

Aunt Bessie Skidoo
9" • #91931 • TJ
Issued: 1998 • Current
Orig. Price: $30 • **Value: $30**

8

Aunt Fanny Fremont
8" • #918350 • TJ
Issued: 1999 • Current
Orig. Price: $23 • **Value: $23**

9
New!

Aunt Mamie Bearington
4.5" • #590104 • MB
Issued: 2000 • Current
Orig. Price: $11 • **Value: $11**

10

Aunt Yvonne Dubeary
11" • #918450 • TJ
Issued: 1998 • Current
Orig. Price: $25 • **Value: $25**

Bears

	Price Paid	Value
1.		
2.		
3.		
4.		
5.		
6.		
7.		
8.		
9.		
10.		

Totals

1

Auntie Aleena de Bearvoire
10" • #918451 • TJ
Issued: 1999 • Current
Orig. Price: $23 • **Value: $23**

2

Auntie Alice
10" • #9183 • TJ
Issued: 1993 • Retired: 1996
Orig. Price: $21 • **Value: $46**

3

Auntie Bearburg
info unavailable
Orig. Price: N/A • **Value: N/E**

4

Auntie Erma
10" • #91832 • TJ
Issued: 1996 • Retired: 1997
Orig. Price: $21 • **Value: $39**

5

Auntie Iola
10" • #91612 • TJ
Issued: 1995 • Retired: 1997
Orig. Price: $30 • **Value: $50**

6

New!

Auntie Lavonne Higgenthorpe
12" • #918452 • TJ
Issued: 2000 • Current
Orig. Price: $25 • **Value: $25**

Bears

	Price Paid	Value
1.		
2.		
3.		
4.		
5.		
6.		
7.		
8.		
9.		
10.		

Totals

7

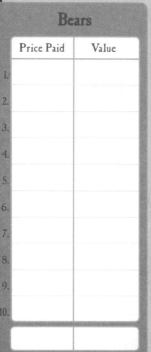

Avery B. Bean
14" • #5101 • JB
Issued: pre-1990 • Retired: 1990
Orig. Price: N/A • **Value: $190**

8

New!

B.A. Blackbelt
10" • #917361 • TJ
Issued: 2000 • Current
Orig. Price: $21 • **Value: $21**

9

Baaah'b
8" • #9131 • TJ
Issued: 1995 • Retired: 1997
Orig. Price: $17 • **Value: $40**

10

Baby
10" • #6105B • TJ
Issued: 1990 • Retired: 1991
Orig. Price: N/A • **Value: $300**

Value Guide — Boyds Plush Animals

Bailey *(Fall 1992)*
8" • #9199 • TJ
Issued: 1992 • Retired: 1993
Orig. Price: N/A • **Value: $750**

Bailey *(Spring 1993)*
8" • N/A • TJ
Issued: 1993 • Retired: 1994
Orig. Price: N/A • **Value: $350**

Bailey *(Fall 1993)*
8" • #9170 • TJ
Issued: 1993 • Retired: 1994
Orig. Price: N/A • **Value: $380**

Bailey *(Spring 1994)*
8" • #9199-01 • TJ
Issued: 1994 • Retired: 1995
Orig. Price: $26 • **Value: $155**

Bailey *(Fall 1994)*
8" • #9199-02 • TJ
Issued: 1994 • Retired: 1995
Orig. Price: $26 • **Value: $68**

Bailey *(Spring 1995)*
8" • #9199-03 • TJ
Issued: 1995 • Retired: 1996
Orig. Price: $26 • **Value: $57**

Bailey *(Fall 1995)*
8" • #9199-04 • TJ
Issued: 1995 • Retired: 1996
Orig. Price: $24 • **Value: $52**

Bailey *(Spring 1996)*
8" • #9199-05 • TJ
Issued: 1996 • Retired: 1997
Orig. Price: $26 • **Value: $52**

Bailey *(Fall 1996)*
8" • #9199-06 • TJ
Issued: 1996 • Retired: 1997
Orig. Price: $26 • **Value: $44**

Bailey *(Spring 1997)*
8" • #9199-07 • TJ
Issued: 1997 • Retired: 1998
Orig. Price: $27 • **Value: $42**

	Price Paid	Value
1.		
2.		
3.		
4.		
5.		
6.		
7.		
8.		
9.		
10.		

Bears

Totals

Bailey (Fall 1997)
8" • #9199-08 • TJ
Issued: 1997 • Retired: 1998
Orig. Price: $27 • **Value: $38**

Bailey (Spring 1998)
8" • #9199-09 • TJ
Issued: 1998 • Retired: 1999
Orig. Price: $27 • **Value: $33**

Bailey (Fall 1998)
8" • #9199-10 • TJ
Issued: 1998 • Retired: 1999
Orig. Price: $27 • **Value: $32**

Bailey (Spring 1999)
8" • #9199-11 • TJ
Issued: 1999 • Retired: 1999
Orig. Price: $27 • **Value: N/E**

New!

Bailey (Spring 2000)
8" • #9199-14 • TJ
Issued: 2000 • To Be Retired: 2000
Orig. Price: $27 • **Value: $27**

Bailey & Matthew
(w/resin ornaments, Fall 1996)
8" & 8" • #9224 • TJ
Issued: 1996 • Retired: 1996
Orig. Price: $70 • **Value: $90**

Bailey & Matthew
(w/resin ornaments, Fall 1997)
8" & 8" • #9225 • TJ
Issued: 1997 • Retired: 1997
Orig. Price: $70 • **Value: $92**

Bailey & Matthew
(w/resin ornaments, Fall 1998)
8" & 8" • #9227 • TJ
Issued: 1998 • Retired: 1998
Orig. Price: $71 • **Value: $83**

Bailey & Matthew
(w/resin ornaments, Fall 1999)
8" & 8" • #9228 • TJ
Issued: 1999 • Retired: 1999
Orig. Price: $70 • **Value: N/E**

Bears

	Price Paid	Value
1.		
2.		
3.		
4.		
5.		
6.		
7.		
8.		
9.		
Totals		

Value Guide — Boyds Plush Animals

1

Bailey With Dottie
(Fall 1999)
8" • #9199-12 • TJ
Issued: 1999 • Retired: 1999
Orig. Price: $30 • **Value: N/E**

2

Baldwin
5.5" • #5718 • AS
Issued: 1992 • Retired: 1999
Orig. Price: $7 • **Value: $12**

3

New!

Bamboo Bearington
14" • #590030 • MB
Issued: 2000 • To Be Retired: 2000
Orig. Price: $52 • **Value: $52**

4

Barnaby B. Bean
10" • #5150-03 • JB
Issued: 1994 • Retired: 1999
Orig. Price: $16 • **Value: $22**

5

Bartholemew B. Bean
10" • #5103 • JB
Issued: 1992 • Retired: 1998
Orig. Price: $14 • **Value: $30**

6

Baxter B. Bean
8" • #5151-05 • JB
Issued: 1994 • Retired: 1999
Orig. Price: $12 • **Value: $22**

7

Bea Bear
info unavailable
Orig. Price: N/A • **Value: N/E**

8

Bear-Among-Bears
16" • #5050 • N/A
Issued: pre-1990 • Retired: N/A
Orig. Price: N/A • **Value: $360**

9

Bear-Among-Bears
16" • #5051 • N/A
Issued: pre-1990 • Retired: N/A
Orig. Price: N/A • **Value: N/E**

10

Bear-Among-Bears
info unavailable
Orig. Price: N/A • **Value: N/E**

Bears	Price Paid	Value
1.		
2.		
3.		
4.		
5.		
6.		
7.		
8.		
9.		
10.		
Totals		

Value Guide — Boyds Plush Animals

1

Bear-Let
8" • #5020 • WB
Issued: pre-1990 • Retired: 1992
Orig. Price: $9 • **Value: $140**

2

Bear-Let
8" • #5021 • N/A
Issued: pre-1990 • Retired: N/A
Orig. Price: N/A • **Value: N/E**

3

Bearly-A-Bear
10" • #5030 • WB
Issued: pre-1990 • Retired: 1992
Orig. Price: $13 • **Value: $155**

4

Bearly-A-Bear
10" • #5031 • WB
Issued: pre-1990 • Retired: 1991
Orig. Price: $13 • **Value: $140**

5

Bears' Bear
12" • #5040 • WB
Issued: pre-1990 • Retired: 1992
Orig. Price: $18 • **Value: $270**

6

Bears' Bear
12" • #5041 • WB
Issued: pre-1990 • Retired: 1992
Orig. Price: $18 • **Value: $270**

Bears

	Price Paid	Value
1.		
2.		
3.		
4.		
5.		
6.		
7.		
8.		
9.		
10.		

Totals

7

Beatrice
14" • #6168 • TJ
Issued: 1991 • Retired: 1991
Orig. Price: $63 • **Value: $460**

8

Becky
6" • #91395 • TJ
Issued: 1995 • Retired: 1999
Orig. Price: $11 • **Value: $22**

9

Becky
6" • #91395-01 • TJ
Issued: 1996 • Retired: 1999
Orig. Price: $11 • **Value: $22**

10

Bedford B. Bean
10" • #5121-08 • JB
Issued: 1996 • Retired: 1996
Orig. Price: $14 • **Value: $65**

1

Benjamin
10" • #9159 • TJ
Issued: 1993 • Retired: 1994
Orig. Price: $20 • **Value: $50**

2

Berrybear
14" • #5762 • HD
Issued: 1992 • Retired: 1994
Orig. Price: $27 • **Value: $250**

3

Bess W. Pattington
14" • #92001-02 • AR
Issued: 1999 • Retired: 1999
Orig. Price: $40 • **Value: N/E**

4

Bethany Thistlebeary
6" • #913955 • TJ
Issued: 1999 • Current
Orig. Price: $13 • **Value: $10**

5

Betsey
6" • #913952 • TJ
Issued: 1997 • To Be Retired: 2000
Orig. Price: $13 • **Value: $13**

6

New!

Betsie B. Jodibear
9" • #92000-07 • AR
Issued: 2000 • Current
Orig. Price: $21 • **Value: $21**

7

Bianca T. Witebred
8" • #912076 • TJ
Issued: 1998 • Retired: 1999
Orig. Price: $19 • **Value: $25**

8

Big Boy
5.5" • #9108 • TJ
Issued: 1995 • Retired: 1997
Orig. Price: $12 • **Value: $43**

9

New!

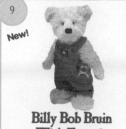

Billy Bob Bruin With Froggie
14" • #912622 • TJ
Issued: 2000 • Current
Orig. Price: $31 • **Value: $31**

10

Billy Ray
9" • #5850 • BB
Issued: 1992 • Retired: 1997
Orig. Price: $14 • **Value: $40**

Bears

	Price Paid	Value
1.		
2.		
3.		
4.		
5.		
6.		
7.		
8.		
9.		
10.		

Totals

Value Guide — Boyds Plush Animals

1

Billy Ray Beanster With Petey Poker
16" • #900207 • UB
Issued: 1999 • To Be Retired: 2000
Orig. Price: $51 • **Value: $51**

2

Binkie B. Bear
16" • #5115 • JB
Issued: pre-1990 • Retired: 1993
Orig. Price: $27 • **Value: $110**

3

Binkie B. Bear II
16" • #5115 • JB
Issued: 1994 • Retired: 1996
Orig. Price: $27 • **Value: $73**

4

Bixby Trufflebeary
12" • #56390-10 • BA
Issued: 1999 • Current
Orig. Price: $16 • **Value: $16**

5

Blackstone
6" • #5840-07 • GB
Issued: 1997 • Retired: 1999
Orig. Price: $9 • **Value: $16**

6

Blanche de Bearvoire
6" • #91841 • TJ
Issued: 1996 • Retired: 1999
Orig. Price: $9 • **Value: $22**

7

Blinkin
18" • #5807 • SB
Issued: 1991 • Retired: 1992
Orig. Price: $32 • **Value: $210**

8

Bluebeary
8" • #56421-06 • BA
Issued: 1998 • Current
Orig. Price: $11 • **Value: $11**

9

Bobbie Jo
12" • #5853 • BB
Issued: 1992 • Retired: 1997
Orig. Price: $20 • **Value: $50**

10

Bonnie
6" • #913951 • TJ
Issued: 1997 • To Be Retired: 2000
Orig. Price: $13 • **Value: $13**

Bears

	Price Paid	Value
1.		
2.		
3.		
4.		
5.		
6.		
7.		
8.		
9.		
10.		

Totals

Value Guide — Boyds Plush Animals

1

Boris Berriman
6" • #918021 • TJ
Issued: 1998 • Current
Orig. Price: $12 • **Value: $12**

2

Bosley
8.5" • #91561 • TJ
Issued: 1997 • Retired: 1999
Orig. Price: $12 • **Value: $23**

3

Bradley Boobear
8" • #919610 • TJ
Issued: 1998 • Retired: 1999
Orig. Price: $13 • **Value: N/E**

4

Bradshaw P. Beansford
14" • #51091-08 • JB
Issued: 1999 • Retired: 1999
Orig. Price: $20 • **Value: N/E**

5

Braxton B. Bear
14" • #51081-08 • JB
Issued: 1998 • Current
Orig. Price: $20 • **Value: $20**

6

Breezy T. Frostman
8" • #91522 • TJ
Issued: 1999 • Current
Orig. Price: $13 • **Value: $13**

7

**Breven B. Bearski With
Willie Waddlewalk**
14" • #900206 • UB
Issued: 1999 • To Be Retired: 2000
Orig. Price: $49 • **Value: $49**

8

Brewin
10" • #5802 • SB
Issued: 1992 • Retired: 1995
Orig. Price: $20 • **Value: $75**

9

Brewin
10" • #5806 • SB
Issued: 1991 • Retired: 1991
Orig. Price: N/A • **Value: $75**

10

New!

Brianna Tippeetoes
6" • #913959 • TJ
Issued: 2000 • Current
Orig. Price: $13 • **Value: $13**

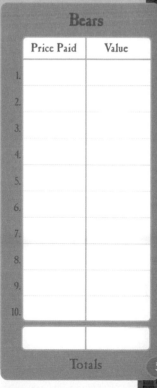

Bears

	Price Paid	Value
1.		
2.		
3.		
4.		
5.		
6.		
7.		
8.		
9.		
10.		
Totals		

1

New!

Bristol B. Windsor
8" • #57052-03 • AS
Issued: 2000 • Current
Orig. Price: $13 • **Value: $13**

2

Bromley Q. Bear
8" • #5151-03 • JB
Issued: 1998 • Retired: 1999
Orig. Price: $13 • **Value: $24**

3

New!

Brooke B. Bearsley
10" • #917400 • TJ
Issued: 2000 • Current
Orig. Price: $20 • **Value: $20**

4

Bruce
8" • #1000-08 • CC
Issued: 1993 • Retired: 1999
Orig. Price: $6 • **Value: $22**

5

Bruce
8" • #9157-08 • TJ
Issued: 1993 • Retired: 1994
Orig. Price: $14 • **Value: $65**

6

Bruce
8" • #98038 • TJ
Issued: 1996 • Retired: 1997
Orig. Price: $13 • **Value: $35**

Bears

	Price Paid	Value
1.		
2.		
3.		
4.		
5.		
6.		
7.		
8.		
9.		
10.		

Totals

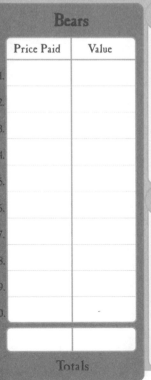

7

Bruinhilda Von Bruin
6" • #5010-03 • WB
Issued: 1994 • Retired: 1995
Orig. Price: $12 • **Value: $52**

8

Bubba
16" • #5856 • BB
Issued: 1992 • Retired: 1997
Orig. Price: $27 • **Value: $60**

9

Buckingham
21" • #57221 • AS
Issued: 1997 • Retired: 1999
Orig. Price: $55 • **Value: N/E**

10

Buckley
8" • #9104 • TJ
Issued: 1995 • Retired: 1996
Orig. Price: $16 • **Value: $56**

Value Guide — Boyds Plush Animals

1

Buffington Fitzbruin
10" • #912031 • TJ
Issued: 1997 • Retired: 1998
Orig. Price: $20 • **Value: $32**

2

Buffy
12" • #5639-10 • BA
Issued: 1995 • Retired: 1996
Orig. Price: $16 • **Value: $48**

3

Bumbershoot B. Jodibear
8" • #92000-03 • AR
Issued. 1999 • Current
Orig. Price: $20 • **Value: $20**

4 New!

Bumble B. Buzzoff
8" • #91773 • TJ
Issued: 2000 • Current
Orig. Price: $17 • **Value: $17**

5 New!

Bundles B. Joy & Blankie
12" • #56391-04 • BA
Issued: 2000 • Current
Orig. Price: $23 • **Value: $23**

6

Burke P. Bear
14" • #5109-05 • JB
Issued: 1997 • Current
Orig. Price: $20 • **Value: $20**

7

Burl
10" • #91761 • TJ
Issued: 1996 • Retired: 1998
Orig. Price: $20 • **Value: $32**

8

Burlington P. Beanster
16" • #510400-07 • JB
Issued: 1999 • Current
Orig. Price: $26 • **Value: $26**

9

Buttercup C. Snicklefritz
9" • #51760-12 • BY
Issued: 1999 • Retired: 1999
Orig. Price: $12 • **Value: $16**

10

Buzz B. Bean
10" • #5120 • JB
Issued: pre-1990 • Retired: 1990
Orig. Price: N/A • **Value: $200**

	Bears	
	Price Paid	Value
1.		
2.		
3.		
4.		
5.		
6.		
7.		
8.		
9.		
10.		
Totals		

Buzzby
8" • #9143 • TJ
Issued: 1994 • Retired: 1995
Orig. Price: $18 • **Value: $58**

Cabin Bear
info unavailable
Orig. Price: N/A • **Value: N/E**

Cagney
8" • #9189-01 • TJ
Issued: 1994 • Retired: 1996
Orig. Price: $20 • **Value: $52**

Caledonia
6" • #5840-01 • GB
Issued: 1997 • Current
Orig. Price: $9 • **Value: $9**

Callaghan
8" • #5704 • AS
Issued: 1990 • Retired: 1996
Orig. Price: $12 • **Value: $55**

Calvin Ellis
8" • #91223 • TJ
Issued: 1996 • Retired: 1997
Orig. Price: $18 • **Value: $35**

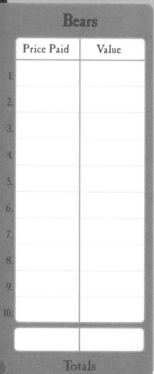

Bears

	Price Paid	Value
1.		
2.		
3.		
4.		
5.		
6.		
7.		
8.		
9.		
10.		

Totals

New!

Cambridge Q. Bearrister
12" • #57003-08 • AS
Issued: 2000 • Current
Orig. Price: $20 • **Value: $20**

Camille du Bear
6" • #91804 • TJ
Issued: 1996 • Retired: 1999
Orig. Price: $9 • **Value: $28**

Canute
6" • #9136 • TJ
Issued: 1994 • Retired: 1996
Orig. Price: $12 • **Value: $42**

Carmella de Bearvoire
6" • #918401 • TJ
Issued: 1999 • Current
Orig. Price: $9 • **Value: $9**

Value Guide — Boyds Plush Animals

1

New!

Caroline Mayflower
6" • #913958 • TJ
Issued: 2000 • Current
Orig. Price: $14 • **Value: $14**

2

Carter M. Bearington
10" • #590050-08 • MB
Issued: 1998 • Retired: 1999
Orig. Price: $31 • **Value: $55**

3

Cavendish
12" • #5701-02 • AS
Issued: 1994 • Retired: 1996
Orig. Price: $20 • **Value: $48**

4

Cecil
5.5" • #5726 • AS
Issued: 1993 • Retired: 1996
Orig. Price: $7 • **Value: $27**

5

Chamberlain
16" • #5709 • AS
Issued: 1990 • Retired: 1992
Orig. Price: $32 • **Value: $155**

6

Chamomille Q. Quignapple
10" • #91004 • TJ
Issued: 1997 • Current
Orig. Price: $24 • **Value: $24**

7

Chan
6" • #9153 • TJ
Issued: 1994 • Retired: 1998
Orig. Price: $12 • **Value: $27**

8

Chanel de la Plumtete
6" • #9184 • TJ
Issued: 1995 • Retired: 1999
Orig. Price: $9 • **Value: $15**

9

Chauncey Fitzbruin
6" • #912033 • TJ
Issued: 1997 • Retired: 1999
Orig. Price: $12 • **Value: $25**

10

Chipper
8" • #5642-05 • BA
Issued: 1996 • Retired: 1997
Orig. Price: $11 • **Value: $26**

	Bears	
	Price Paid	Value
1.		
2.		
3.		
4.		
5.		
6.		
7.		
8.		
9.		
10.		
	Totals	

Value Guide — Boyds Plush Animals

1

Christian
8" • #9190 • TJ
Issued: 1992 • Current
Orig. Price: $18 • **Value: $18**

2

Christmas Bear
info unavailable
Orig. Price: N/A • **Value: N/E**

3

Christopher
10" • #9161 • TJ
Issued: 1993 • Retired: 1998
Orig. Price: $20 • **Value: $33**

4

Churchill
12" • #5700 • AS
Issued: 1990 • Retired: 1999
Orig. Price: $20 • **Value: $60**

5

Claire
10" • #9179 • TJ
Issued: 1994 • Retired: 1998
Orig. Price: $20 • **Value: $34**

6

Clara
14" • #911061 • TJ
Issued: 1996 • Retired: 1998
Orig. Price: $20 • **Value: $35**

Bears

Price Paid	Value
1.	
2.	
3.	
4.	
5.	
6.	
7.	
8.	
9.	
10.	

Totals

7

Clarissa
16" • #91202 • TJ
Issued: 1996 • Retired: 1999
Orig. Price: $58 • **Value: $72**

8

New!

Clark S. Bearhugs
6" • #918055 • TJ
Issued: 2000 • Current
Orig. Price: $10 • **Value: $10**

9

Cleason
10" • #5121N • JB
Issued: 1992 • Retired: 1996
Orig. Price: $14 • **Value: $40**

10

Clement
16" • #5710 • AS
Issued: 1990 • Retired: 1992
Orig. Price: $32 • **Value: $130**

Value Guide — Boyds Plush Animals

1
Clementine
6" • #913953 • TJ
Issued: 1998 • Current
Orig. Price: $12 • **Value: $12**

2
Clinton B. Bean
14" • #5109 • JB
Issued: 1993 • Retired: 1998
Orig. Price: $20 • **Value: $33**

3
Clover L. Buzzoff
10" • #91772 • TJ
Issued: 1999 • Current
Orig. Price: $18 • **Value: $18**

4
Coco
10" • #5121 • JB
Issued: 1991 • Retired: 1995
Orig. Price: $14 • **Value: $50**

5
Colleen O'Bruin
6" • #91805 • TJ
Issued: 1995 • Retired: 1997
Orig. Price: $12 • **Value: $30**

6
Constance
16" • #91202-01 • TJ
Issued: 1998 • Current
Orig. Price: $48 • **Value: $48**

7
New!
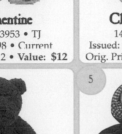
Cori Beariburg
8.5" • #915211 • TJ
Issued: 2000 • Current
Orig. Price: $14 • **Value: $14**

8
Corinna
16" • #91201 • TJ
Issued: 1996 • Retired: 1999
Orig. Price: $45 • **Value: $52**

9

Corinna II
16" • #912011 • TJ
Issued: 1997 • Retired: 1998
Orig. Price: $45 • **Value: $70**

10

Cornwallis
16" • #9126 • TJ
Issued: 1994 • Retired: 1996
Orig. Price: $45 • **Value: $82**

	Bears	
	Price Paid	Value
1.		
2.		
3.		
4.		
5.		
6.		
7.		
8.		
9.		
10.		

Totals

Cornwallis
16" • #9126-01 • TJ
Issued: 1996 • Retired: 1997
Orig. Price: $53 • **Value: $78**

Courtney
16" • #912021 • TJ
Issued: 1997 • To Be Retired: 2000
Orig. Price: $45 • **Value: $45**

Craxton B. Bean
10" • #510300-11 • JB
Issued: 1998 • Current
Orig. Price: $14 • **Value: $14**

D.L. Merrill
16" • #51100-05 • JB
Issued: 1999 • Current
Orig. Price: $29 • **Value: $29**

New!

Darby Beariburg
6" • #913960 • TJ
Issued: 2000 • Current
Orig. Price: $12 • **Value: $12**

Daryl Bear
16" • #5114 • JB
Issued: pre-1990 • Retired: 1993
Orig. Price: $27 • **Value: $150**

Bears

	Price Paid	Value
1.		
2.		
3.		
4.		
5.		
6.		
7.		
8.		
9.		
10.		

Totals

Delaney And The Duffer (LE-500)
N/A • N/A • N/A
Issued: 1993 • Retired: 1994
Orig. Price: $74 • **Value: $235**

Delanie B. Beansford
16" • #51101-10 • JB
Issued: 1999 • Current
Orig. Price: $29 • **Value: $29**

Delbert Quignapple
10" • #91003 • TJ
Issued: 1996 • Current
Orig. Price: $24 • **Value: $24**

Delmarva V. Crackenpot
10" • #91002 • TJ
Issued: 1997 • Retired: 1999
Orig. Price: $29 • **Value: $38**

Value Guide — Boyds Plush Animals

1

Denton P. Jodibear
9" • #92000-06 • AR
Issued: 1999 • Current
Orig. Price: $20 • **Value: $20**

2

Desdemona T. Witebred
10" • #912075 • TJ
Issued: 1997 • Retired: 1998
Orig. Price: $21 • **Value: $33**

3

Devin Fallsbeary
14" • #912621 • TJ
Issued: 1999 • Current
Orig. Price: $40 • **Value: $40**

4

Dewey P. Wongbruin
16" • #5154 • JB
Issued: 1997 • Retired: 1999
Orig. Price: $29 • **Value: $33**

5

Dexter
8" • #91331 • TJ
Issued: 1996 • Retired: 1998
Orig. Price: $25 • **Value: $40**

6

Diana (w/boy cub)
info unavailable
Orig. Price: N/A • **Value: N/E**

7

Diana (w/girl cub)
info unavailable
Orig. Price: N/A • **Value: N/E**

8

Dilly McDoodle
9" • #51710-12 • BY
Issued: 1999 • Retired: 1999
Orig. Price: $8 • **Value: $15**

9

Dink
16" • #5641 • BA
Issued: 1992 • Retired: 1994
Orig. Price: $21 • **Value: $48**

10

Dink
16" • #5641-08 • BA
Issued: 1995 • Retired: 1997
Orig. Price: $24 • **Value: $32**

Bears

	Price Paid	Value
1.		
2.		
3.		
4.		
5.		
6.		
7.		
8.		
9.		
10.		
Totals		

1

Disreali
5.5" • #5716 • AS
Issued: 1991 • Retired: 1993
Orig. Price: $7 • **Value: $70**

2

Doolittle Buckshot
12" • #51200-08 • JB
Issued: 1999 • Current
Orig. Price: $20 • **Value: $20**

3
New!

Dover D. Windsor
8" • #57051-03 • AS
Issued: 2000 • Current
Orig. Price: $13 • **Value: $13**

4

Dufus Bear
16" • #5112 • JB
Issued: pre-1990 • Retired: 1997
Orig. Price: $27 • **Value: $50**

5

Dunston J. Bearsford
6" • #57251-07 • AS
Issued: 1999 • Current
Orig. Price: $8 • **Value: $8**

6
New!
PHOTO UNAVAILABLE

Dwight D. Bearington
6" • #590081-03 • MB
Issued: 2000 • To Be Retired: 2000
Orig. Price: $14 • **Value: $14**

Bears

	Price Paid	Value
1.		
2.		
3.		
4.		
5.		
6.		
7.		
8.		
9.		
10.		

7

Eastwick Bearington
4.5" • #590101 • MB
Issued: 1999 • Current
Orig. Price: $11 • **Value: $11**

8

Eddie Beanberger
(formerly "Eddie Beanbauer")
10" • #9119 • TJ
Issued: 1995 • Retired: 1999
Orig. Price: $27 • **Value: $43**

9

Eddie Beanberger
10" • #9119-01 • TJ
Issued: 1996 • Retired: 1997
Orig. Price: $30 • **Value: $48**

10

Eden
5.5" • #5708 • AS
Issued: 1990 • Retired: 1996
Orig. Price: $7 • **Value: $28**

Eden
6" • #9139 • TJ
Issued: 1994 • Retired: 1996
Orig. Price: $13 • **Value: $42**

Eden II
6" • #91391 • TJ
Issued: 1996 • Retired: 1997
Orig. Price: $13 • **Value: $29**

Edmund *(Fall 1993)*
8" • #9175 • TJ
Issued: 1993 • Retired: 1994
Orig. Price: N/A • **Value: $260**

Edmund *(Spring 1994)*
8" • #9175-01 • TJ
Issued: 1994 • Retired: 1995
Orig. Price: $26 • **Value: $130**
Variation: black & white shirt
Value: $188

Edmund *(Fall 1994)*
8" • #9175-02 • TJ
Issued: 1994 • Retired: 1995
Orig. Price: $24 • **Value: $110**

Edmund *(Spring 1995)*
8" • #9175-03 • TJ
Issued: 1995 • Retired: 1996
Orig. Price: $24 • **Value: $55**

Edmund *(Fall 1995)*
8" • #9175-04 • TJ
Issued: 1995 • Retired: 1996
Orig. Price: $24 • **Value: $47**

Edmund *(Spring 1996)*
8" • #9175-05 • TJ
Issued: 1996 • Retired: 1997
Orig. Price: $26 • **Value: $44**

Edmund *(Fall 1996)*
8" • #9175-06 • TJ
Issued: 1996 • Retired: 1997
Orig. Price: $24 • **Value: $40**

Edmund *(Spring 1997)*
8" • #9175-07 • TJ
Issued: 1997 • Retired: 1998
Orig. Price: $24 • **Value: $40**

Bears

Price Paid	Value
1.	
2.	
3.	
4.	
5.	
6.	
7.	
8.	
9.	
10.	

Totals

1

Edmund *(Fall 1997)*
8" • #9175-08 • TJ
Issued: 1997 • Retired: 1998
Orig. Price: $24 • **Value: $35**

2

Edmund *(Spring 1998)*
8" • #9175-09 • TJ
Issued: 1998 • Retired: 1999
Orig. Price: $26 • **Value: $35**

3

Edmund *(Fall 1998)*
8" • #9175-10 • TJ
Issued: 1998 • Retired: 1999
Orig. Price: $27 • **Value: $33**

4

Edmund *(Spring 1999)*
8" • #9175-11 • TJ
Issued: 1999 • Retired: 1999
Orig. Price: $26 • **Value: $42**

5

Edmund *(Fall 1999)*
8" • #9175-12 • TJ
Issued: 1999 • Retired: 1999
Orig. Price: $27 • **Value: N/E**

6

New!

Edmund *(Spring 2000)*
8" • #9175-14 • TJ
Issued: 2000 • To Be Retired: 2000
Orig. Price: $26 • **Value: $26**

Bears

	Price Paid	Value
1.		
2.		
3.		
4.		
5.		
6.		
7.		
8.		
9.		
10.		

Totals

7

Eldora
14" • #91615 • TJ
Issued: 1996 • Retired: 1998
Orig. Price: $31 • **Value: $42**

8

Eleanor Bear (set/3, Eleanor, baby and chair)
N/A • #6102 • TJ
Issued: 1990 • Retired: 1990
Orig. Price: N/A • **Value: $575**

9

New!

Eleanore Bearsevelt
16" • #912010 • TJ
Issued: 2000 • Current
Orig. Price: $58 • **Value: $58**

10

Elfwood Bearington
4.5" • #590100 • MB
Issued: 1999 • Current
Orig. Price: $11 • **Value: $11**

Value Guide — Boyds Plush Animals

Elgin
6.5" • #9129 • TJ
Issued: 1994 • Retired: 1997
Orig. Price: $12 • **Value: $27**

Elliot B. Bean
14" • #5108 • JB
Issued: pre-1990 • Retired: 1998
Orig. Price: $20 • **Value: $36**

Elly Mae
9" • #5850-10 • BB
Issued: 1995 • Retired: 1997
Orig. Price: $14 • **Value: $40**

New!

Elmer O. Bearroad
12" • #911931 • TJ
Issued: 2000 • Current
Orig. Price: $27 • **Value: $27**

Elmore Flatski
8" • #5680-08 • FL
Issued: 1995 • Retired: 1997
Orig. Price: $13 • **Value: $30**

Eloise Willoughby
6" • #918402 • TJ
Issued: 1999 • Current
Orig. Price: $14 • **Value: $14**

Elsworth
12" • #1107-05 • CC
Issued: 1997 • Retired: 1999
Orig. Price: $12 • **Value: $22**

Elton Elfberg
10" • #917306 • TJ
Issued: 1997 • Retired: 1998
Orig. Price: $21 • **Value: $35**

Elvin Q. Elfberg
10" • #917301 • TJ
Issued: 1997 • Retired: 1999
Orig. Price: $25 • **Value: $28**

Emma
14" • #9101 • TJ
Issued: 1995 • Retired: 1997
Orig. Price: $27 • **Value: $55**

Bears

	Price Paid	Value
1.		
2.		
3.		
4.		
5.		
6.		
7.		
8.		
9.		
10.		
Totals		

Value Guide — Boyds Plush Animals

Emmett Elfberg
10" • #917305 • TJ
Issued: 1996 • Retired: 1999
Orig. Price: $21 • **Value: $28**

Emmy Lou
10" • #91001 • TJ
Issued: 1996 • Retired: 1999
Orig. Price: $24 • **Value: $35**

Erin K. Bear
7" • #91562 • TJ
Issued: 1996 • Retired: 1999
Orig. Price: $11 • **Value: $25**

Essex
12" • #5701-10 • AS
Issued: 1994 • Retired: 1996
Orig. Price: $20 • **Value: $45**

Ethan
9" • #917322 • TJ
Issued: 1998 • Retired: 1999
Orig. Price: $21 • **Value: $33**

Ethel B. Bruin
12" • #912051 • TJ
Issued: 1997 • Retired: 1998
Orig. Price: $25 • **Value: $45**

Eudemia Q. Quignapple
9" • #91006 • TJ
Issued: 1997 • Retired: 1999
Orig. Price: $16 • **Value: $28**

Eugenia
16" • #9120 • TJ
Issued: 1994 • Retired: 1996
Orig. Price: $45 • **Value: $92**

Eugenia The Apple Seller
16" • #9120-01 • AS
Issued: 1995 • Retired: 1995
Orig. Price: $53 • **Value: $135**

Bears

	Price Paid	Value
1.		
2.		
3.		
4.		
5.		
6.		
7.		
8.		
9.		

Totals

Value Guide — Boyds Plush Animals

1

Eunice P. Snowbeary
9" • #9137-01 • TJ
Issued: 1997 • Retired: 1999
Orig. Price: $20 • **Value: N/E**

2

Evelyn
10" • #91614 • TJ
Issued: 1997 • Retired: 1998
Orig. Price: $24 • **Value: $40**

3

Everest
8.5" • #5844-05 • GB
Issued: 1996 • Retired: 1999
Orig. Price: $17 • **Value: $33**

4

Ewell
8" • #9127 • TJ
Issued: 1994 • Retired: 1999
Orig. Price: $17 • **Value: $25**

5

Father Chrisbear
info unavailable
Orig. Price: N/A • **Value: $190**

6

Father Christmas
info unavailable
Orig. Price: N/A • **Value: N/E**

7

Father Christmas
info unavailable
Orig. Price: N/A • **Value: N/E**

8

Federico
11" • #1100-08 • CC
Issued: 1993 • Retired: 1997
Orig. Price: $10 • **Value: $38**

9

Federico
11" • #98039 • TJ
Issued: 1996 • Retired: 1997
Orig. Price: $21 • **Value: $45**

10

Felicity S. Elfberg
5.5" • #917300 • TJ
Issued: 1997 • Retired: 1998
Orig. Price: $13 • **Value: $26**

Bears

	Price Paid	Value
1.		
2.		
3.		
4.		
5.		
6.		
7.		
8.		
9.		
10.		

Totals

1

Fidelity B. Morgan IV
17" • #5110-05 • JB
Issued: 1997 • Retired: 1999
Orig. Price: $29 • **Value: $35**

2

Fiona Fitzbruin
14" • #91203 • TJ
Issued: 1997 • Retired: 1998
Orig. Price: $26 • **Value: $40**

3

Fitzgerald D. Bearington
12" • #590040-03 • MB
Issued: 1997 • Retired: 1997
Orig. Price: $48 • **Value: $77**

4

Fitzgerald O'Bruin
6" • #91802 • TJ
Issued: 1995 • Retired: 1997
Orig. Price: $12 • **Value: $32**

5

Fitzroy
N/A • #5795 • TJ
Issued: 1992 • Retired: 1992
Orig. Price: $18 • **Value: $76**

6

Fitzroy
7.5" • #9195 • TJ
Issued: 1992 • Retired: 1994
Orig. Price: $16 • **Value: $65**

Bears

	Price Paid	Value
1.		
2.		
3.		
4.		
5.		
6.		
7.		
8.		
9.		
10.		

Totals

7

Fleurette
12" • #6103B • AS
Issued: 1991 • Retired: 1991
Orig. Price: N/A • **Value: N/E**

8

Floyd
9" • #917321 • TJ
Issued: 1998 • Retired: 1999
Orig. Price: $21 • **Value: $30**

9

Foodle McDoodle
9" • #51710-05 • BY
Issued: 1999 • Current
Orig. Price: $8 • **Value: $8**

10

Forrest B. Bearsley
10" • #91744 • TJ
Issued: 1999 • Current
Orig. Price: $20 • **Value: $20**

1
Franklin
8" • #1050-06 • DB
Issued: 1995 • Retired: 1996
Orig. Price: $11 • **Value: $58**

2
Franz Von Bruin
6" • #5010-06 • WB
Issued: 1994 • Retired: 1995
Orig. Price: $10 • **Value: $53**

3
Freddy Beanberger
10" • #911901 • TJ
Issued: 1998 • Retired: 1998
Orig. Price: $27 • **Value: $40**

4
Gabriel
9" • #5825 • CB
Issued: 1991 • Retired: 1997
Orig. Price: $14 • **Value: $52**

5
Gardner
N/A • #6162B • TJ
Issued: 1991 • Retired: 1991
Orig. Price: $63 • **Value: N/E**

6
Gary M. Bearenthal
16" • #912500 • TJ
Issued: 1999 • Current
Orig. Price: $53 • **Value: $53**

7
Geneva
8" • #9162 • TJ
Issued: 1994 • Retired: 1994
Orig. Price: $18 • **Value: $118**

8
George
11" • #1100-03 • CC
Issued: 1996 • Retired: 1997
Orig. Price: $10 • **Value: $30**

9
Geraldo
8" • #912441 • TJ
Issued: 1996 • Retired: 1997
Orig. Price: $19 • **Value: $38**

10
New!
Ginnie Higgenthorpe
6" • #918442 • TJ
Issued: 2000 • Current
Orig. Price: $10 • **Value: $10**

Bears

	Price Paid	Value
1.		
2.		
3.		
4.		
5.		
6.		
7.		
8.		
9.		
10.		

Totals

1

Gladstone
12" • #5701 • AS
Issued: 1990 • Retired: 1993
Orig. Price: $20 • **Value: $87**

2

Glenda
12" • #91891-04 • TJ
Issued: 1998 • Retired: 1999
Orig. Price: $21 • **Value: N/E**

3

Glynnis
8" • #918910-02 • TJ
Issued: 1998 • Retired: 1999
Orig. Price: $17 • **Value: N/E**

4

Goober Padoodle
6" • #517010-05 • BY
Issued: 1999 • Current
Orig. Price: $5 • **Value: $5**

5

Gorden B. Bean
10" • #5105 • JB
Issued: pre-1990 • Retired: 1998
Orig. Price: $14 • **Value: $48**

6

Grace
N/A • #6163B • TJ
Issued: 1991 • Retired: 1991
Orig. Price: $63 • **Value: N/E**

7

Grace
10" • #91742 • TJ
Issued: 1997 • Retired: 1998
Orig. Price: $20 • **Value: $30**

8

Grace Bedlington
16" • #912072 • TJ
Issued: 1999 • Current
Orig. Price: $40 • **Value: $40**

9

Gram
18" • #5775 • HD
Issued: 1991 • Retired: 1991
Orig. Price: $39 • **Value: $300**

10

Gramps
18" • #5770 • HD
Issued: 1991 • Retired: 1991
Orig. Price: $39 • **Value: $340**

Bears

	Price Paid	Value
1.		
2.		
3.		
4.		
5.		
6.		
7.		
8.		
9.		
10.		

Totals

1

Grandma Bearburg
14" • N/A • N/A
Issued: 1992 • Retired: 1992
Orig. Price: N/A • **Value: N/E**

2

Grenville
16" • #5715 • AS
Issued: 1992 • Retired: 1999
Orig. Price: $32 • **Value: $80**

3

Grover
8" • #91739 • TJ
Issued: 1997 • Retired: 1998
Orig. Price: $12 • **Value: $23**

4

Grumps
9" • #5766 • HD
Issued: 1991 • Retired: 1994
Orig. Price: $14 • **Value: $76**

5

Guinevere
12" • #91891-09 • TJ
Issued: 1996 • Retired: 1999
Orig. Price: $21 • **Value: $30**

6

Gunnar
8" • #9123 • TJ
Issued: 1995 • Retired: 1996
Orig. Price: $24 • **Value: $40**

7

Gunther Von Bruin
6" • #5012 • WB
Issued: 1993 • Retired: 1994
Orig. Price: N/A • **Value: $135**

8

Gus Ghoulie
12" • #919640 • TJ
Issued: 1999 • Retired: 1999
Orig. Price: $20 • **Value: $48**

9

Gustav Von Bruin
10" • #5011 • WB
Issued: 1993 • Retired: 1994
Orig. Price: $21 • **Value: $60**

10

Gwain
12" • #91891-06 • TJ
Issued: 1997 • Retired: 1999
Orig. Price: $21 • **Value: N/E**

Bears

	Price Paid	Value
1.		
2.		
3.		
4.		
5.		
6.		
7.		
8.		
9.		
10.		
Totals		

Gwendina
11" • #91891-12 • TJ
Issued: 1999 • Retired: 1999
Orig. Price: $21 • **Value: N/E**

Gwendolyn
12" • #91891-02 • TJ
Issued: 1997 • Retired: 1999
Orig. Price: $21 • **Value: $27**

Gwinton
8" • #918910-06 • TJ
Issued: 1998 • Retired: 1999
Orig. Price: $17 • **Value: N/E**

Gwynda
8" • #918910-09 • TJ
Issued: 1998 • Retired: 1999
Orig. Price: $17 • **Value: N/E**

Hadley Flatski
8" • #5680-05 • FL
Issued: 1994 • Retired: 1997
Orig. Price: $12 • **Value: $37**

New!

PHOTO UNAVAILABLE

Hampton T. Bearington
10" • #590052-08 • MB
Issued: 2000 • To Be Retired: 2000
Orig. Price: $36 • **Value: $36**

Bears

	Price Paid	Value
1.		
2.		
3.		
4.		
5.		
6.		
7.		
8.		
9.		
Totals		

Hancock
8" • #1050-11 • DB
Issued: 1995 • Retired: 1996
Orig. Price: $11 • **Value: $43**

Hans Q. Berriman
6" • #91392 • TJ
Issued: 1997 • Retired: 1999
Orig. Price: $13 • **Value: $32**

Harding
8" • #1051-06 • DB
Issued: 1996 • Retired: 1998
Orig. Price: $13 • **Value: $29**

1

Harding G. Bearington
10" • #590051-01 • MB
Issued: 1999 • Retired: 1999
Orig. Price: $28 • **Value: $39**

2

Harrison
10" • #9176 • TJ
Issued: 1993 • Retired: 1997
Orig. Price: $20 • **Value: $36**

3

Harry S. Pattington
16" • #92001-01 • AR
Issued: 1999 • Retired: 1999
Orig. Price: $45 • **Value: N/E**

4

Hartley B. Mine
8.5" • #91521 • TJ
Issued: 1999 • To Be Retired: 2000
Orig. Price: $14 • **Value: $14**

5

New!

Hastings P. Bearsford
6" • #57250-11 • AS
Issued: 2000 • Current
Orig. Price: $7 • **Value: $7**

6

Hattie & Annie
info unavailable
Orig. Price: N/A • **Value: N/E**

7

Hawley Flatski
8" • #56801-03 • FL
Issued: 1998 • Retired: 1999
Orig. Price: $13 • **Value: N/E**

8

New!

Hayden T. Bearsford
6" • #57250-10 • AS
Issued: 2000 • Current
Orig. Price: $7 • **Value: $7**

9

Hazel
8" • #1000-03 • CC
Issued: 1993 • Retired: 1996
Orig. Price: $6 • **Value: $38**

10

New!

Hazelnut B. Bean
8.25" • #500100-05 • JB
Issued: 2000 • Current
Orig. Price: $7 • **Value: $7**

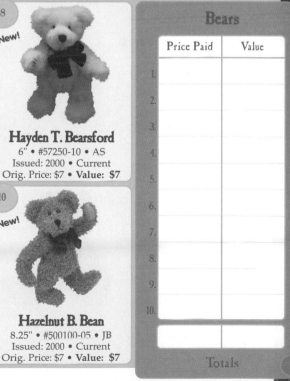

Bears

	Price Paid	Value
1.		
2.		
3.		
4.		
5.		
6.		
7.		
8.		
9.		
10.		

Totals

Heath
10" • #5703 • AS
Issued: 1990 • Retired: 1992
Orig. Price: $18 • **Value: $85**

Heath II
10" • #5703N • AS
Issued: 1992 • Retired: 1997
Orig. Price: $18 • **Value: $33**

Hemingway K. Grizzman
14" • #91263 • TJ
Issued: 1999 • Current
Orig. Price: $40 • **Value: $40**

Henley Fitzhampton
6" • #912034 • TJ
Issued: 1999 • Current
Orig. Price: $13 • **Value: $13**

Henry
8" • #1000-05 • CC
Issued: 1993 • Retired: 1995
Orig. Price: $6 • **Value: $45**

Henson
10" • #58011-05 • SB
Issued: 1998 • Current
Orig. Price: $20 • **Value: $20**

Bears	
Price Paid	Value
1.	
2.	
3.	
4.	
5.	
6.	
7.	
8.	
9.	
10.	
Totals	

Herbert Henry Jodibear
9" • #92000-05 • AR
Issued: 1999 • Current
Orig. Price: $20 • **Value: $20**

Hermine Grisslin
16" • #91206 • TJ
Issued: 1995 • Retired: 1997
Orig. Price: $45 • **Value: $62**

Hershal
16" • #5125 • JB
Issued: 1991 • Retired: 1992
Orig. Price: $27 • **Value: $145**

Hillary B. Bean
14" • #5123-10 • JB
Issued: 1993 • Retired: 1998
Orig. Price: $20 • **Value: $33**

1

Hockley
16" • #5640 • BA
Issued: 1992 • Retired: 1996
Orig. Price: $21 • **Value: $52**

2

Homer
14" • #5760 • HD
Issued: 1991 • Retired: 1994
Orig. Price: $27 • **Value: $200**

3

PHOTO UNAVAILABLE

Homer
N/A • #6166B • TJ
Issued: 1991 • Retired: 1991
Orig. Price: $63 • **Value: $200**

4

Homer
8" • #9177 • TJ
Issued: 1993 • Retired: 1996
Orig. Price: $26 • **Value: $55**

5

Honey P. Snicklefritz (musical)
8" • #51760-08 • BY
Issued: 1999 • Retired: 1999
Orig. Price: $12 • **Value: $20**

6

Honeypot
14" • #5761 • HD
Issued: 1991 • Retired: 1994
Orig. Price: $27 • **Value: $180**

7

Hsing-Hsing Wongbruin
14" • #51540-07 • JB
Issued: 1999 • Current
Orig. Price: $20 • **Value: $20**

8

Hubbard W. Growler
12" • #5721-01 • AS
Issued: 1997 • Retired: 1998
Orig. Price: $21 • **Value: $42**

9

Huck
6" • #918051 • TJ
Issued: 1996 • Retired: 1998
Orig. Price: $12 • **Value: $26**

10

Humboldt
6" • #5840-05 • GB
Issued: 1996 • Current
Orig. Price: $9 • **Value: $9**

Bears	
Price Paid	Value
1.	
2.	
3.	
4.	
5.	
6.	
7.	
8.	
9.	
10.	

Totals

1

Hume
info unavailable
Orig. Price: N/A • **Value: N/E**

2

New!

Huney B. Keeper
9" • #91774 • TJ
Issued: 2000 • Current
Orig. Price: $24 • **Value: $24**

3

New!

Hunter Bearsdale With Greenspan
14" & 5" • #912625 • TJ
Issued: 2000 • Current
Orig. Price: $32 • **Value: $32**

4

Hurshel
12" • #5639-05 • BA
Issued: 1996 • Retired: 1999
Orig. Price: $16 • **Value: N/E**

5

Isaiah
10" • #917304 • TJ
Issued: 1996 • Retired: 1998
Orig. Price: $19 • **Value: $37**

6

J.B. Bean
10" • #5106 • JB
Issued: pre-1990 • Retired: 1997
Orig. Price: $14 • **Value: $38**

Bears

	Price Paid	Value
1.		
2.		
3.		
4.		
5.		
6.		
7.		
8.		
9.		
10.		
Totals		

7

J.P. Huttin III
17" • #5110-08 • JB
Issued: 1995 • Retired: 1998
Orig. Price: $29 • **Value: $42**

8

J.P. Locksley
12" • #57002-08 • AS
Issued: 1999 • Current
Orig. Price: $20 • **Value: $20**

9

Jackson R. Bearington
16" • #590021-05 • MB
Issued: 1998 • Retired: 1999
Orig. Price: $100 • **Value: $160**

10

Jameson J. Bearsford
6" • #57251-10 • AS
Issued: 1999 • Current
Orig. Price: $8 • **Value: $8**

Value Guide — Boyds Plush Animals

Jed Bruin
14" • #5123W • JB
Issued: 1992 • Retired: 1992
Orig. Price: $20 • **Value: $108**

Jefferson
8" • #1050-02 • DB
Issued: 1995 • Retired: 1996
Orig. Price: $11 • **Value: $50**

Jesse
11" • #1100-05 • CC
Issued: 1993 • Retired: 1995
Orig. Price: $10 • **Value: $60**

Jethro
9" • #5630 • BA
Issued: 1995 • Retired: 1997
Orig. Price: $10 • **Value: $35**

Jody
16" • #5641-09 • BA
Issued: 1995 • Retired: 1996
Orig. Price: $24 • **Value: $44**

John
13" • #5828 • CB
Issued: 1992 • Retired: 1997
Orig. Price: $20 • **Value: $42**

Joshua
9" • #5826 • CB
Issued: 1992 • Retired: 1997
Orig. Price: $14 • **Value: $34**

New!

Juliet S. Bearlove
12" • #912651 • TJ
Issued: 2000 • Current
Orig. Price: $24 • **Value: $24**

Karla Mulbeary
8" • #915500 • TJ
Issued: 1999 • Current
Orig. Price: $18 • **Value: $18**

Katie B. Berrijam
10" • #910062 • TJ
Issued: 1999 • Current
Orig. Price: $23 • **Value: $23**

Bears	Price Paid	Value
1.		
2.		
3.		
4.		
5.		
6.		
7.		
8.		
9.		
10.		
Totals		

1

Katy Bear
info unavailable
Orig. Price: N/A • **Value: N/E**

2

Kayla Mulbeary
6" • #913941 • TJ
Issued: 1999 • Current
Orig. Price: $14 • **Value: $14**

3

Kelsey M. Jodibear With Arby B. Tugalong
7.5" • #900209 • UB
Issued: 1999 • To Be Retired: 2000
Orig. Price: $61 • **Value: $61**

4

New!

Kevin G. Bearsley
10" • #917362 • TJ
Issued: 2000 • Current
Orig. Price: $23 • **Value: $23**

5

Kip
8" • #5642-08 • BA
Issued: 1993 • Retired: 1997
Orig. Price: $11 • **Value: $33**

6

Klaus Von Fuzzner
14" • #91262 • TJ
Issued: 1998 • Current
Orig. Price: $40 • **Value: $40**

Bears

	Price Paid	Value
1.		
2.		
3.		
4.		
5.		
6.		
7.		
8.		
9.		
10.		

Totals

7

Knut V. Berriman
8" • #91231 • TJ
Issued: 1997 • Retired: 1999
Orig. Price: $24 • **Value: $30**

8

New!

Kookie Snicklefritz
10" • #51770-12 • BY
Issued: 2000 • Current
Orig. Price: $14 • **Value: $14**

9

Kringle Bear
10" • #9163 • TJ
Issued: 1993 • Retired: 1996
Orig. Price: $19 • **Value: $48**

10

Kringle Bear
14" • #9191 • TJ
Issued: 1993 • Retired: 1996
Orig. Price: $27 • **Value: $62**

Kyle L. Berriman
10" • #917401 • TJ
Issued: 2000 • Current
Orig. Price: $20 • **Value: $20**

Lacy
10" • #6100B • TJ
Issued: pre-1990 • Retired: 1992
Orig. Price: $16 • **Value: $115**

Lacy
10" • #6100DB • TJ
Issued: pre-1990 • Retired: 1991
Orig. Price: N/A • **Value: $122**

Lacy
14" • #6101B • TJ
Issued: pre-1990 • Retired: 1992
Orig. Price: $21 • **Value: $140**

Lacy
14" • #6101DB • TJ
Issued: pre-1990 • Retired: 1991
Orig. Price: N/A • **Value: $135**

Lady B. Bug
10" • #91775 • TJ
Issued: 2000 • Current
Orig. Price: $20 • **Value: $20**

Lancaster
8" • #57051-08 • AS
Issued: 1998 • Current
Orig. Price: $13 • **Value: $13**

Lancelot
21" • #5722-11 • AS
Issued: 1996 • Retired: 1999
Orig. Price: $53 • **Value: N/E**

Lars
8" • #91735 • TJ
Issued: 1996 • Retired: 1997
Orig. Price: $18 • **Value: $34**

Laurel S. Berrijam
6" • #913954 • TJ
Issued: 1999 • Current
Orig. Price: $13 • **Value: $13**

Bears		
	Price Paid	Value
1.		
2.		
3.		
4.		
5.		
6.		
7.		
8.		
9.		
10.		
Totals		

Lem Bruin
14" • #5123 • JB
Issued: pre-1990 • Retired: 1993
Orig. Price: $20 • **Value: $90**

Leo Bruinski
10" • #918320 • TJ
Issued: 1998 • Current
Orig. Price: $31 • **Value: $31**

Leon
8" • #1001-08 • CC
Issued: 1993 • Retired: 1999
Orig. Price: $6 • **Value: $22**

Lillian K. Bearsley
10" • #91743 • TJ
Issued: 1998 • Current
Orig. Price: $20 • **Value: $20**

Lincoln B. Bearington
16" • #590022-08 • MB
Issued: 1999 • Retired: 1999
Orig. Price: $100 • **Value: $130**

Linkin
6" • #5811 • SB
Issued: 1992 • Retired: 1995
Orig. Price: $7 • **Value: $50**

Bears

	Price Paid	Value
1.		
2.		
3.		
4.		
5.		
6.		
7.		
8.		
9.		

Totals

Lisa T. Bearringer
16" • #911950 • TJ
Issued: 1998 • Current
Orig. Price: $58 • **Value: $58**

Liza J. Berrijam
10" • #910061 • TJ
Issued: 1999 • Current
Orig. Price: $17 • **Value: $17**

Lizzie McBee
8" • #91005 • TJ
Issued: 1996 • Retired: 1997
Orig. Price: $20 • **Value: $40**

Value Guide — Boyds Plush Animals

1

Lloyd
10" • #5714 • AS
Issued: 1991 • Retired: 1992
Orig. Price: $18 • **Value: $175**

2

Logan Fremont
8" • #919611 • TJ
Issued: 1999 • Current
Orig. Price: $13 • **Value: $13**

3
New!

Lois B. Bearlove
6" • #913956 • TJ
Issued: 2000 • Current
Orig. Price: $13 • **Value: $13**

4

Lou Bearig
6" • #91771-06 • TJ
Issued: 1998 • Current
Orig. Price: $14 • **Value: $14**

5

Louella
10" • #91242 • TJ
Issued: 1996 • Retired: 1998
Orig. Price: $24 • **Value: $42**

6

Louie B. Bear
16" • #5114-11 • JB
Issued: 1995 • Retired: 1997
Orig. Price: $27 • **Value: $48**

7

Lydia Fitzbruin
14" • #9182 • TJ
Issued: 1993 • Retired: 1996
Orig. Price: $27 • **Value: $85**

8

MacMillan
8" • #5705-10 • AS
Issued: 1995 • Retired: 1997
Orig. Price: $13 • **Value: $28**

9

Madeline Willoughby
10" • #918333 • TJ
Issued: 1999 • Current
Orig. Price: $30 • **Value: $30**

10

Madison L. Bearington
6" • #590080 08 • MB
Issued: 1997 • Retired: 1997
Orig. Price: $18 • **Value: $35**

Bears

	Price Paid	Value
1.		
2.		
3.		
4.		
5.		
6.		
7.		
8.		
9.		
10.		

Totals

1

Major
10" • #5717 • AS
Issued: 1991 • Retired: 1992
Orig. Price: $18 • **Value: $95**

2

Major II
10" • #5703B • AS
Issued: 1992 • Retired: 1995
Orig. Price: $18 • **Value: $44**

3

Malcolm
16" • #5711 • AS
Issued: 1992 • Retired: 1999
Orig. Price: $32 • **Value: $50**

4

Margaret T. Pattington
12" • #92001-03 • AR
Issued: 1999 • Retired: 1999
Orig. Price: $32 • **Value: $38**

5

Margarita
14" • #911062 • TJ
Issued: 1998 • To Be Retired: 2000
Orig. Price: $20 • **Value: $20**

6

Marlowe Snoopstein
11" • #91871 • TJ
Issued: 1999 • Current
Orig. Price: $23 • **Value: $23**

Bears	
Price Paid	Value
1.	
2.	
3.	
4.	
5.	
6.	
7.	
8.	
9.	
10.	
Totals	

7

Marvin P. Snowbeary
6" • #9136-01 • TJ
Issued: 1997 • Current
Orig. Price: $12 • **Value: $12**

8

Matilda
N/A • #6161B • TJ
Issued: 1991 • Retired: 1991
Orig. Price: $63 • **Value: N/E**

9

Matthew (Fall 1996)
8" • #91756 • TJ
Issued: 1996 • Retired: 1997
Orig. Price: $26 • **Value: $42**

10

Matthew (Fall 1997)
8" • #91756-08 • TJ
Issued: 1997 • Retired: 1998
Orig. Price: $26 • **Value: $36**

Value Guide — Boyds Plush Animals

1

Matthew *(Fall 1998)*
8" • #91756-10 • TJ
Issued: 1998 • Retired: 1999
Orig. Price: $27 • **Value: $35**

2

Matthew *(Fall 1999)*
8" • #91756-12 • TJ
Issued: 1999 • Retired: 1999
Orig. Price: $26 • **Value: N/E**

3

PHOTO UNAVAILABLE

Matthew Bear
10" • #5070 • N/A
Issued: N/A • Retired: N/A
Orig. Price: N/A • **Value: N/E**

4

Matthew H. Growler
12" • #5721 • AS
Issued: 1996 • Retired: 1999
Orig. Price: $21 • **Value: $33**

5

Maya Berriman
6" • #91394 • TJ
Issued: 1999 • Current
Orig. Price: $14 • **Value: $14**

6

McKenzie
6" • #5840-03 • GB
Issued: 1997 • To Be Retired: 2000
Orig. Price: $9 • **Value: $9**

7

McKinley
12" • #5848-05 • GB
Issued: 1996 • Retired: 1999
Orig. Price: $21 • **Value: $27**

8

McMullen
12" • #5702 • AS
Issued: 1990 • Retired: 1991
Orig. Price: $20 • **Value: $120**

9

McShamus O'Growler
9" • #91732 • TJ
Issued: 1997 • Retired: 1998
Orig. Price: $21 • **Value: $42**

10

New!

Megan Berriman
14" • #912623 • TJ
Issued: 2000 • Current
Orig. Price: $32 • **Value: $32**

Bears

	Price Paid	Value
1.		
2.		
3.		
4.		
5.		
6.		
7.		
8.		
9.		
10.		

Totals

1

Melbourne
12" • #5719 • AS
Issued: 1992 • Retired: 1994
Orig. Price: $20 • **Value: $83**

2

New!

Melinda S. Willoughby
6" • #913961 • TJ
Issued: 2000 • Current
Orig. Price: $12 • **Value: $12**

3

Memsy
12" • N/A • N/A
Issued: N/A • Retired: N/A
Orig. Price: N/A • **Value: $440**

4

Mercedes Fitzbruin
8" • #91204 • TJ
Issued: 1998 • Current
Orig. Price: $19 • **Value: $19**

5

Meredith K. Pattington
14" • #900204 • UB
Issued: 1999 • To Be Retired: 2000
Orig. Price: $116 • **Value: $116**

6

Merlin
N/A • #6167B • TJ
Issued: 1991 • Retired: 1991
Orig. Price: $63 • **Value: N/E**

Bears

	Price Paid	Value
1.		
2.		
3.		
4.		
5.		
6.		
7.		
8.		
9.		
10.		

7

Mickey
8" • #9157-01 • TJ
Issued: 1993 • Retired: 1994
Orig. Price: $14 • **Value: $65**

8

New!

Mikayla Springbeary
14" • #912624 • TJ
Issued: 2000 • Current
Orig. Price: $32 • **Value: $32**

9

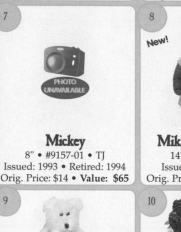

Milo
9" • #5767 • HD
Issued: 1992 • Retired: 1994
Orig. Price: $14 • **Value: $92**

10

Minnie Higgenthorpe
6" • #918441 • TJ
Issued: 1999 • Retired: 1999
Orig. Price: $10 • **Value: $22**

Totals

Value Guide — Boyds Plush Animals

1

Miss Ashley
info unavailable
Orig. Price: N/A • **Value: N/E**

2

Missy
8" • #5642-10 • BA
Issued: 1995 • Retired: 1996
Orig. Price: $11 • **Value: $45**

3

Mistle
8.5" • #5151-04 • JB
Issued: 1994 • Retired: 1997
Orig. Price: $12 • **Value: $36**

4

Mitchell Bearsdale
14" • #912615 • TJ
Issued: 1999 • Current
Orig. Price: $40 • **Value: $40**

5

Mohley
N/A • #5771 • HD
Issued: 1992 • Retired: 1992
Orig. Price: N/A • **Value: $135**

6

**Momma McBear
And Delmar**
10" & 6" • #91007 • TJ
Issued: 1997 • To Be Retired: 2000
Orig. Price: $25 • **Value: $25**

7

Monroe J. Bearington
16" • #590023-11 • MB
Issued: 1999 • To Be Retired: 2000
Orig. Price: $100 • **Value: $100**

8

Moriarity
11" • #9171 • TJ
Issued: 1993 • Retired: 1995
Orig. Price: $21 • **Value: $95**

9

Morris
8" • #1003-05 • CC
Issued: 1997 • Retired: 1999
Orig. Price: $7 • **Value: $20**

10
New!

Mr. BoJingles
14" • #91264 • TJ
Issued: 2000 • Current
Orig. Price: $20 • **Value: $20**

Bears

	Price Paid	Value
1.		
2.		
3.		
4.		
5.		
6.		
7.		
8.		
9.		
10.		

Totals

1

Mr. Jones
16" • #5869-08 • AR
Issued: 1997 • Retired: 1998
Orig. Price: $37 • **Value: $52**

2

Mr. Smythe
12" • #58691-05 • AR
Issued: 1998 • Retired: 1998
Orig. Price: $27 • **Value: $42**

3

Mr. Trumbull
10" • #918330 • TJ
Issued: 1998 • Current
Orig. Price: $28 • **Value: $28**

4

Mrs. Bearberry
info unavailable
Orig. Price: N/A • **Value: N/E**

5

Mrs. Bearburg
info unavailable
Orig. Price: N/A • **Value: N/E**

6

Mrs. Fiedler
info unavailable
Orig. Price: N/A • **Value: N/E**

7

Mrs. Mertz
10" • #918331 • TJ
Issued: 1999 • Current
Orig. Price: $30 • **Value: $30**

8

Mrs. Northstar
13" • #917303-03 • TJ
Issued: 1999 • Retired: 1999
Orig. Price: $31 • **Value: N/E**

9

Mrs. Trumbull
10" • #91833 • TJ
Issued: 1998 • Current
Orig. Price: $30 • **Value: $30**

Bears

	Price Paid	Value
1.		
2.		
3.		
4.		
5.		
6.		
7.		
8.		
9.		

Totals

Value Guide — Boyds Plush Animals

1

Muffin
8" • #56421-03 • BA
Issued: 1998 • Current
Orig. Price: $11 • **Value: $11**

2

Nadia Berriman
10" • #917420 • TJ
Issued: 1999 • Current
Orig. Price: $30 • **Value: $30**

3

Nana
14" • #5765 • HD
Issued: 1991 • Retired: 1992
Orig. Price: $27 • **Value: $510**

4 New!

Nanette Dubeary
6" • #918432 • TJ
Issued: 2000 • Current
Orig. Price: $10 • **Value: $10**

5

Nanny Bear
info unavailable
Orig. Price: N/A • **Value: N/E**

6 New!

Nantucket P. Bearington
4.5" • #590102 • MB
Issued: 2000 • Current
Orig. Price: $11 • **Value: $11**

7 New!

Naomi Bearlove
6" • #913957 • TJ
Issued: 2000 • Current
Orig. Price: $14 • **Value: $14**

8

Natasha Berriman
6" • #918050 • TJ
Issued: 1998 • Current
Orig. Price: $12 • **Value: $12**

9

Nellie
14" • #91105 • TJ
Issued: 1995 • Retired: 1997
Orig. Price: $20 • **Value: $46**

10

Nelson
16" • #91261 • TJ
Issued: 1997 • Retired: 1999
Orig. Price: $45 • **Value: $60**

Bears

	Price Paid	Value
1.		
2.		
3.		
4.		
5.		
6.		
7.		
8.		
9.		
10.		

Totals

Neville
5.5" • #5707 • AS
Issued: 1990 • Retired: 1999
Orig. Price: $7 • **Value: N/E**

Newton
8" • #9133 • TJ
Issued: 1994 • Retired: 1996
Orig. Price: $25 • **Value: $52**

Nicholas
8" • #9173 • TJ
Issued: 1993 • Retired: 1997
Orig. Price: $20 • **Value: $40**

Niki
6" • #91730 • TJ
Issued: 1996 • Retired: 1997
Orig. Price: $13 • **Value: $32**

Niki II
6" • #91730-1 • TJ
Issued: 1998 • Current
Orig. Price: $13 • **Value: $13**

Nod
6" • #5810 • SB
Issued: 1991 • Retired: 1992
Orig. Price: $7 • **Value: $56**

Bears

	Price Paid	Value
1.		
2.		
3.		
4.		
5.		
6.		
7.		
8.		
9.		
10.		

Totals

Nod II
6" • #5810 • SB
Issued: 1992 • Retired: 1999
Orig. Price: $7 • **Value: N/E**

North Pole Bear
info unavailable
Orig. Price: N/A • **Value: N/E**

Ogden B. Bean
8" • #5153 • JB
Issued: 1994 • Retired: 1999
Orig. Price: $12 • **Value: $28**

Olaf
12" • #9138 • TJ
Issued: 1994 • Retired: 1996
Orig. Price: $27 • **Value: $52**

Value Guide — Boyds Plush Animals

1

Omega T. Legacy & Alpha
16" & 5" • #900099 • N/A
Issued: 1999 • Retired: 1999
Orig. Price: $70 • **Value: N/E**

2

Ophelia
16" • #91207-01 • TJ
Issued: 1997 • Retired: 1997
Orig. Price: $40 • **Value: $63**

3

Ophelia W. Witebred
16" • #91207 • TJ
Issued: 1996 • Retired: 1998
Orig. Price: $40 • **Value: $55**

4

Orville Bearington
4.5" • #590085-03 • MB
Issued: 1998 • Retired: 1999
Orig. Price: $10 • **Value: $23**

5

Otis B. Bean
14" • #5107 • JB
Issued: pre-1990 • Retired: 1997
Orig. Price: $20 • **Value: $52**

6

Otto Von Bruin
6" • #5010 • WB
Issued: 1992 • Retired: 1994
Orig. Price: $9 • **Value: $48**

7

Oxford T. Bearrister
12" • #57001-05 • AS
Issued: 1999 • Retired: 1999
Orig. Price: $20 • **Value: N/E**

8

Paddy McDoodle
9" • #51710 • BY
Issued: 1998 • Current
Orig. Price: $8 • **Value: $8**

9 New!

Paige Willoughby
8" • #918351 • TJ
Issued: 2000 • Current
Orig. Price: $19 • **Value: $19**

10 New!

Patches B. Beariluved
10" • #51000 • JB
Issued: 2000 • Current
Orig. Price: $18 • **Value: $18**

Bears

	Price Paid	Value
1.		
2.		
3.		
4.		
5.		
6.		
7.		
8.		
9.		
10.		
Totals		

Patrick
8" • #9901 • TJ
Issued: 1995 • Retired: 1995
Orig. Price: $18 • **Value: $65**

Patsy
10" • #9100 • TJ
Issued: 1995 • Retired: 1996
Orig. Price: $20 • **Value: $56**

Paxton P. Bean
10" • #510300-05 • JB
Issued: 1998 • Current
Orig. Price: $14 • **Value: $14**

Peary
16" • #5807-10 • SB
Issued: 1998 • Current
Orig. Price: $29 • **Value: $29**

Pendleton J. Bruin
16" • #510400-11 • JB
Issued: 1998 • Current
Orig. Price: $27 • **Value: $26**

Perceval
10" • #5703-08 • AS
Issued: 1992 • Retired: 1999
Orig. Price: $18 • **Value: $30**

Bears

	Price Paid	Value
1.		
2.		
3.		
4.		
5.		
6.		
7.		
8.		
9.		
10.		
Totals		

Percy
5.5" • #5725-11 • AS
Issued: 1994 • Current
Orig. Price: $7 • **Value: $7**

Perriwinkle P. Snicklefritz (musical)
8" • #51760-06 • BY
Issued: 1999 • Retired: 1999
Orig. Price: $12 • **Value: N/E**

Perry
8" • #1000-11 • CC
Issued: 1994 • Retired: 1997
Orig. Price: $6 • **Value: $32**

Phillip Bear Hop
11" • #9189 • TJ
Issued: 1991 • Retired: 1992
Orig. Price: $27 • **Value: $355**

Value Guide — Boyds Plush Animals

1

Philomena
14" • #91106 • TJ
Issued: 1995 • Retired: 1997
Orig. Price: $20 • **Value: $44**

2

Pinecone
info unavailable
Orig. Price: N/A • **Value: N/E**

3

Pohley
9" • #5768 • HD
Issued: 1991 • Retired: 1994
Orig. Price: $14 • **Value: $130**

4

Polly Quignapple
10" • #910020 • TJ
Issued: 1999 • Current
Orig. Price: $27 • **Value: $27**

5

New!

Poof Pufflebeary & Blankie
15" • #51780-03 • BY
Issued: 2000 • Current
Orig. Price: $24 • **Value: $24**

6

Pop Bruin
16" • #5124 • JB
Issued: pre-1990 • Retired: 1995
Orig. Price: $27 • **Value: $88**

7

Poppa Bear & Noelle
10" & 5.5" • #917302 • JB
Issued: 1997 • Retired: 1999
Orig. Price: $27 • **Value: $42**

8

Prudence Bearimore
12" • #912053 • TJ
Issued: 1999 • Current
Orig. Price: $31 • **Value: $31**

9

Puck
8" • #9172 • TJ
Issued: 1993 • Retired: 1997
Orig. Price: $17 • **Value: $42**

10

Punkie Boobear
10" • #919630 • TJ
Issued: 1999 • Current
Orig. Price: $24 • **Value: $24**

Bears

	Price Paid	Value
1.		
2.		
3.		
4.		
5.		
6.		
7.		
8.		
9.		
10.		

Totals

1

Quincy B. Bibbly
8.5" • #915611 • TJ
Issued: 1999 • Retired: 1999
Orig. Price: $12 • **Value: N/E**

2 New!

Radcliffe Fitzbruin
16" • #912020 • TJ
Issued: 2000 • Current
Orig. Price: $45 • **Value: $45**

3

Raleigh
10" • #5703M • AS
Issued: 1994 • Retired: 1997
Orig. Price: $18 • **Value: $37**

4

Reagan V. Bearington
8" • #590070-05 • MB
Issued: 1997 • Retired: 1997
Orig. Price: $24 • **Value: $56**

5

Remington Braveheart
18" • #57210-05 • AS
Issued: 1999 • Retired: 1999
Orig. Price: $42 • **Value: N/E**

6

Reva
9" • #5630-02 • BA
Issued: 1995 • Retired: 1997
Orig. Price: $10 • **Value: $30**

Bears

	Price Paid	Value
1.		
2.		
3.		
4.		
5.		
6.		
7.		
8.		
9.		
10.		

Totals

7

Rex
8" • #912440 • TJ
Issued: 1996 • Retired: 1998
Orig. Price: $18 • **Value: $30**

8 New!

Rockwell B. Bruin
18" • #57211-05 • AS
Issued: 2000 • Current
Orig. Price: $41 • **Value: $41**

9

Rohley
9" • #5769 • HD
Issued: 1991 • Retired: 1992
Orig. Price: $14 • **Value: $165**

10

Roosevelt
14" • #6108B • JB
Issued: 1991 • Retired: 1992
Orig. Price: $27 • **Value: $240**

Value Guide — Boyds Plush Animals

1

Roosevelt
8" • #9902 • TJ
Issued: 1995 • Retired: 1996
Orig. Price: $18 • **Value: $52**

2

Roosevelt P. Bearington
16" • #590020-08 • MB
Issued: 1997 • Retired: 1997
Orig. Price: $100 • **Value: $165**

3

New!

PHOTO UNAVAILABLE

Ross G. Jodibear
9" • #92000-08 • AR
Issued: 2000 • Current
Orig. Price: $21 • **Value: $21**

4

Roxanne K. Bear
10" • #91741 • TJ
Issued: 1996 • Retired: 1998
Orig. Price: $20 • **Value: $30**

5

Royce
14" • #6107B • TJ
Issued: 1990 • Retired: 1992
Orig. Price: $32 • **Value: $280**

6

Rudolf
18" • #5807B • SB
Issued: 1992 • Retired: 1992
Orig. Price: N/A • **Value: $540**

7

Rufus Bear
16" • #5111 • JB
Issued: pre-1990 • Retired: 1998
Orig. Price: $27 • **Value: $47**

8

Rupert
8" • #9142 • TJ
Issued: 1994 • Retired: 1996
Orig. Price: $18 • **Value: $53**

9

Rutherford
16" • #912610 • TJ
Issued: 1998 • To Be Retired: 2000
Orig. Price: $58 • **Value: $58**

10

S.C. Northstar
14" • #917303 • TJ
Issued: 1997 • Retired: 1999
Orig. Price: $27 • **Value: $47**

Bears

	Price Paid	Value
1.		
2.		
3.		
4.		
5.		
6.		
7.		
8.		
9.		
10.		
Totals		

1

St. Niklas
10" • #917311 • TJ
Issued: 1998 • Current
Orig. Price: $21 • **Value: $21**

2

New!

Sally Quignapple And Annie
10" & 5" • #91009 • TJ
Issued: 2000 • Current
Orig. Price: $25 • **Value: $25**

3

Samuel
6" • #918052 • TJ
Issued: 1998 • Current
Orig. Price: $12 • **Value: $12**

4

New!

Samuel Adams
8.5" • #915210 • TJ
Issued: 2000 • Current
Orig. Price: $14 • **Value: $14**

5

Sandy Claus
16" • #91731 • TJ
Issued: 1995 • Retired: 1998
Orig. Price: $29 • **Value: $62**

6

Sandy Claus II
16" • #917310 • TJ
Issued: 1998 • Current
Orig. Price: $29 • **Value: $29**

7

Santa Bear
info unavailable
Orig. Price: N/A • **Value: N/E**

8

Sarah Beth Jodibear
9" • #92000-04 • AR
Issued: 1999 • Current
Orig. Price: $20 • **Value: $20**

9

Sasha
10" • #9174 • TJ
Issued: 1995 • Retired: 1998
Orig. Price: $20 • **Value: $35**

10

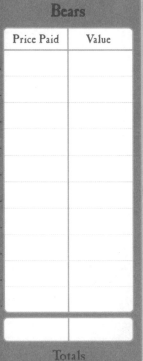

Scooter
8" • #5642-03 • BA
Issued: 1993 • Retired: 1995
Orig. Price: $11 • **Value: $50**

Bears

	Price Paid	Value
1.		
2.		
3.		
4.		
5.		
6.		
7.		
8.		
9.		
10.		

Totals

Sebastian
13" • #5827 • CB
Issued: 1991 • Retired: 1997
Orig. Price: $20 • **Value: $47**

Seymour P. Snowbeary
12" • #9138-01 • TJ
Issued: 1997 • Retired: 1999
Orig. Price: $27 • **Value: $33**

Sheldon Bearchild
6" • #918061 • TJ
Issued: 1998 • Current
Orig. Price: $8 • **Value: $8**

Sherlock
11" • #5821 • TJ
Issued: 1992 • Retired: 1992
Orig. Price: $20 • **Value: $115**

Sherlock
11" • #9188 • TJ
Issued: 1993 • Retired: 1997
Orig. Price: $21 • **Value: $48**

Sigmund Von Bruin
6" • #5010-08 • WB
Issued: 1994 • Retired: 1995
Orig. Price: $10 • **Value: $60**

Simone de Bearvoir
6" • #9180 • TJ
Issued: 1993 • Retired: 1996
Orig. Price: $9 • **Value: $37**

New!

Sinclair Bearsford
16" • #57150-03 • AS
Issued: 2000 • Current
Orig. Price: $32 • **Value: $32**

Sinkin
18" • #5808 • SB
Issued: 1991 • Retired: 1992
Orig. Price: $32 • **Value: $94**

Sinkin II
18" • #5808 • SB
Issued: 1992 • Retired: 1997
Orig. Price: $32 • **Value: $49**

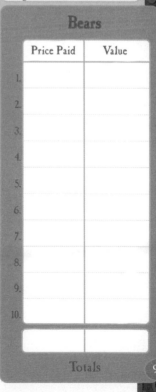

Bears		
	Price Paid	Value
1.		
2.		
3.		
4.		
5.		
6.		
7.		
8.		
9.		
10.		
Totals		

Sir Henry
12" • #5720 • AS
Issued: 1991 • Retired: 1992
Orig. Price: $20 • **Value: $118**

Skidoo
11" • #9193 • TJ
Issued: 1992 • Retired: 1998
Orig. Price: $24 • **Value: $40**

Skip
12" • #5638 • BA
Issued: 1992 • Retired: 1996
Orig. Price: $16 • **Value: $42**

Skylar Thistlebeary
16" • #911951 • TJ
Issued: 1999 • Current
Orig. Price: $45 • **Value: $45**

Slugger
8" • #9177-01 • TJ
Issued: 1996 • Retired: 1999
Orig. Price: $26 • **Value: $40**

Smith Witter II
17" • #5110 • JB
Issued: 1994 • Retired: 1998
Orig. Price: $29 • **Value: $44**

Bears

	Price Paid	Value
1.		
2.		
3.		
4.		
5.		
6.		
7.		
8.		
9.		
10.		

Totals

Sniffles
9" • #5773 • HD
Issued: 1991 • Retired: 1992
Orig. Price: $14 • **Value: $158**

New!

Snookie Snicklefritz
10" • #51770-09 • BY
Issued: 2000 • Current
Orig. Price: $14 • **Value: $14**

Snowball
14" • #5123W • JB
Issued: 1992 • Retired: 1993
Orig. Price: N/A • **Value: $98**

Spencer
5.5" • #5725 • AS
Issued: 1993 • Current
Orig. Price: $7 • **Value: $7**

Value Guide — Boyds Plush Animals

1

Squeeky
8" • #5615 • SQ
Issued: 1991 • Retired: 1991
Orig. Price: $10 • **Value: $105**

2

Squeeky
8" • #5616 • SQ
Issued: 1992 • Retired: 1992
Orig. Price: $10 • **Value: $130**

3

Stella Seamstress
info unavailable
Orig. Price: N/A • **Value: N/E**

4

Stevenson Q. Bearitage
10" • #91736 • TJ
Issued: 1999 • Current
Orig. Price: $24 • **Value: $24**

5

Stilton
info unavailable
Orig. Price: N/A • **Value: N/E**

6

Stonewall Bear
info unavailable
Orig. Price: N/A • **Value: N/E**

7

Sven
8" • #9122 • TJ
Issued: 1994 • Retired: 1996
Orig. Price: $18 • **Value: $48**

8

T. Farley Wuzzie
5" • #595100-11 • TF
Issued: 1998 • Retired: 1999
Orig. Price: $9 • **Value: $19**

9

T. Frampton Wuzzie
5" • #595100-05 • TF
Issued: 1999 • Current
Orig. Price: $9 • **Value: $9**

10

T. Frasier Wuzzie
5" • #595100-08 • TF
Issued: 1998 • Current
Orig. Price: $9 • **Value: $9**

Bears

	Price Paid	Value
1.		
2.		
3.		
4.		
5.		
6.		
7.		
8.		
9.		
10.		

Totals

Value Guide — Boyds Plush Animals

1

T. Fulton Wuzzie
5" • #595100-06 • TF
Issued: 1998 • Current
Orig. Price: $9 • **Value: $9**

2

Tabitha J. Spellbinder With Midnight Sneakypuss
16" & 6" • #900201 • UB
Issued: 1999 • To Be Retired: 2000
Orig. Price: $69 • **Value: $69**

3

Tasha B. Frostbeary
14" & 6" & 3" • #900205 • UB
Issued: 1999 • Current
Orig. Price: $69 • **Value: $69**

4

Tassel F. Wuzzie
3" • #596004 • TF
Issued: 1999 • Retired: 1999
Orig. Price: $8 • **Value: $16**

5

Tatum F. Wuzzie
3" • #596001 • TF
Issued: 1999 • Retired: 1999
Orig. Price: $8 • **Value: $16**

6

Ted
8" • #9156 • TJ
Issued: 1993 • Retired: 1996
Orig. Price: $16 • **Value: $50**

7

Teddy Beanberger
(formerly "Teddy Beanbauer")
16" • #9118 • TJ
Issued: 1995 • Retired: 1997
Orig. Price: $53 • **Value: $82**

8

Thatcher
5.5" • #5706 • AS
Issued: 1990 • Retired: 1997
Orig. Price: $7 • **Value: $34**

9

Thayer
8.5" • #91570 • TJ
Issued: 1997 • Current
Orig. Price: $18 • **Value: $18**

10

Theodore
7.5" • #9196 • TJ
Issued: 1992 • Retired: 1994
Orig. Price: $16 • **Value: $64**

Bears

	Price Paid	Value
1.		
2.		
3.		
4.		
5.		
6.		
7.		
8.		
9.		
10.		

Totals

Thinkin
6" • #5809 • SB
Issued: 1991 • Retired: 1994
Orig. Price: $7 • **Value: $75**

Thisbey F. Wuzzie
2.5" • #595160-02 • TF
Issued: 1999 • Current
Orig. Price: $7 • **Value: $7**

Thor M. Berriman
12" • #91734 • TJ
Issued: 1998 • Retired: 1998
Orig. Price: $30 • **Value: $50**

Tilly F. Wuzzie
3" • #596000 • TF
Issued: 1999 • Current
Orig. Price: $8 • **Value: $8**

Timothy F. Wuzzie
3.5" • #595140 • TF
Issued: 1998 • Current
Orig. Price: $8 • **Value: $8**

Ting F. Wuzzie
2.5" • #595161 • TF
Issued: 1999 • Current
Orig. Price: $7 • **Value: $7**

Tinkin
10" • #5801 • SB
Issued: 1991 • Retired: 1992
Orig. Price: $20 • **Value: $70**

Tinkin II
10" • #5801 • SB
Issued: 1992 • Retired: 1997
Orig. Price: $20 • **Value: $46**

Tipton F. Wuzzie
2.5" • #595160-07 • TF
Issued: 1999 • Current
Orig. Price: $7 • **Value: $7**

Toe
8.5" • #5151-02 • JB
Issued: 1994 • Retired: 1997
Orig. Price: $12 • **Value: $45**

Bears

	Price Paid	Value
1.		
2.		
3.		
4.		
5.		
6.		
7.		
8.		
9.		
10.		

Totals

Value Guide — Boyds Plush Animals

Tomba Bearski
14" • #912620 • TJ
Issued: 1999 • Current
Orig. Price: $42 • **Value: $42**

Toodle Padoodle
6" • #517010-03 • BY
Issued: 1999 • Current
Orig. Price: $5 • **Value: $5**

Tootie F. Wuzzie
2.5" • #595160-01 • TF
Issued: 1999 • Current
Orig. Price: $7 • **Value: $7**

Townsend Q. Bearrister
12" • #57001-03 • AS
Issued: 1999 • To Be Retired: 2000
Orig. Price: $20 • **Value: $20**

Travis B. Bean
16" • #5114-05 • JB
Issued: 1993 • Retired: 1998
Orig. Price: $27 • **Value: $50**

Travis Bear
info unavailable
Orig. Price: N/A • **Value: N/E**

Tremont
16" • #56411-08 • BA
Issued: 1997 • Current
Orig. Price: $26 • **Value: $26**

Trevor F. Wuzzie
2.5" • #595160-08 • TF
Issued: 1997 • Retired: 1999
Orig. Price: $7 • **Value: $12**

Truman S. Bearington
18" • #590010-05 • MB
Issued: 1998 • Retired: 1998
Orig. Price: $126 • **Value: $165**

New!

Tumble F. Wuzzie
3" • #596005 • TF
Issued: 2000 • Current
Orig. Price: $8 • **Value: $8**

Bears

	Price Paid	Value
1.		
2.		
3.		
4.		
5.		
6.		
7.		
8.		
9.		
10.		

Totals

Value Guide — Boyds Plush Animals

1

Tundra Northpole
12" • #912810 • TJ
Issued: 1999 • Current
Orig. Price: $24 • **Value: $24**

2

Tutu
16" • #6169B • TJ
Issued: 1991 • Retired: 1991
Orig. Price: $63 • **Value: N/E**

3

Twas F. Wuzzie
3" • #596003 • TF
Issued: 1999 • Retired: 1999
Orig. Price: $8 • **Value: $12**

4

Twila Higgenthorpe
6" • #91843 • TJ
Issued: 1997 • Current
Orig. Price: $10 • **Value: $10**

5

Twilight F. Wuzzie
2.5" • #595160-06 • TF
Issued: 1999 • Current
Orig. Price: $7 • **Value: $7**

6

Twizzle F. Wuzzie
3.5" • #595141 • TF
Issued: 1998 • Retired: 1999
Orig. Price: $8 • **Value: $12**

7

Tylar F. Wuzzie
2.5" • #595160-11 • TF
Issued: 1997 • Retired: 1999
Orig. Price: $7 • **Value: $12**

8

Tyler Summerfield
12" • #9124 • TJ
Issued: 1996 • Retired: 1997
Orig. Price: $37 • **Value: $60**

9

Tyrone F. Wuzzie
2.5" • #595160-05 • TF
Issued: 1997 • Current
Orig. Price: $7 • **Value: $7**

10

New!

Uncle Ben Bearington
4.5" • #590103 • MB
Issued: 2000 • Current
Orig. Price: $11 • **Value: $11**

Bears

	Price Paid	Value
1.		
2.		
3.		
4.		
5.		
6.		
7.		
8.		
9.		
10.		
Totals		

Value Guide — Boyds Plush Animals

1

Ursa
14" • #5720-07 • AS
Issued: 1995 • Retired: 1998
Orig. Price: $24 • **Value: $37**

2

Varsity Bear
info unavailable
Orig. Price: N/A • **Value: $140**

3

Varsity Bear
N/A • #9198 • N/A
Issued: 1992 • Retired: 1992
Orig. Price: N/A • **Value: $275**

4

Vincent
11" • #1100-11 • CC
Issued: 1995 • Retired: 1997
Orig. Price: $10 • **Value: $40**

5

Waldo Bearsworth
11" • #912045 • TJ
Issued: 1999 • Current
Orig. Price: $27 • **Value: $27**

6

Walpole
8" • #5705M • AS
Issued: 1993 • Retired: 1997
Orig. Price: $13 • **Value: $32**

7

Walton
11" • #9128 • TJ
Issued: 1994 • Retired: 1997
Orig. Price: $21 • **Value: $48**

8

Warren
8" • #1002-01 • CC
Issued: 1993 • Retired: 1997
Orig. Price: $6 • **Value: $35**

9

Watson
8" • #9187 • TJ
Issued: 1993 • Retired: 1999
Orig. Price: $17 • **Value: $27**

10

Wayfer North
10" • #917360 • TJ
Issued: 1999 • Current
Orig. Price: $26 • **Value: $26**

Bears

	Price Paid	Value
1.		
2.		
3.		
4.		
5.		
6.		
7.		
8.		
9.		
10.		

Totals

1
Weaver Berrybrook
12" • #911930 • TJ
Issued: 1999 • Retired: 1999
Orig. Price: $20 • **Value: $30**

2
New!
Webber Vanguard
16" • #51100-07 • JB
Issued: 2000 • Current
Orig. Price: $29 • **Value: $29**

3
Wellington
21" • #5722 • AS
Issued: 1992 • Retired: 1997
Orig. Price: $53 • **Value: $75**

4
Werner Von Bruin
6" • #5010-11 • WB
Issued: 1993 • Retired: 1995
Orig. Price: $10 • **Value: $50**

5
Wheaton Flatski
8" • #5680-10 • FL
Issued: 1996 • Retired: 1996
Orig. Price: $13 • **Value: $52**

6
Whitaker Q. Bruin
5.5" • #91806 • TJ
Issued: 1996 • Retired: 1998
Orig. Price: $11 • **Value: $25**

7

PHOTO UNAVAILABLE
White Bean Bear
info unavailable
Orig. Price: N/A • **Value: N/E**

8
Wilbur Bearington
4.5" • #590085-10 • MB
Issued: 1998 • Retired: 1999
Orig. Price: $10 • **Value: $17**

9
Wilcox J. Beansford
14" • #51081-05 • JB
Issued: 1999 • Current
Orig. Price: $20 • **Value: $20**

10
Willa Bruin
11" • #91205 • TJ
Issued: 1995 • Retired: 1997
Orig. Price: $30 • **Value: $46**

	Price Paid	Value
1.		
2.		
3.		
4.		
5.		
6.		
7.		
8.		
9.		
10.		

Bears

Totals

William P.
12" • #1107-03 • CC
Issued: 1998 • Retired: 1999
Orig. Price: $12 • **Value: $15**

Willmar Flatski
8" • #56801-05 • FL
Issued: 1998 • Retired: 1999
Orig. Price: $13 • **Value: $16**

Wilson
8" • #5705 • AS
Issued: 1990 • Retired: 1997
Orig. Price: $12 • **Value: $32**

Winifred Witebred
14" • #912071 • TJ
Issued: 1998 • Current
Orig. Price: $34 • **Value: $34**

Winkie II
12" • #5639-08 • BA
Issued: 1992 • Retired: 1998
Orig. Price: $16 • **Value: $28**

Winkin
10" • #5800 • SB
Issued: 1991 • Retired: 1993
Orig. Price: $20 • **Value: $100**

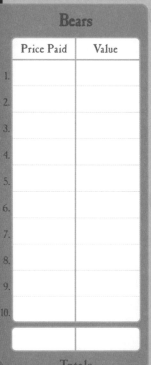

Winnie II
14" • #912071-01 • TJ
Issued: 1998 • Current
Orig. Price: $34 • **Value: $34**

Winnie Wuzzwhite
14" • #912071-02 • TJ
Issued: 1999 • Retired: 1999
Orig. Price: $34 • **Value: $38**

Winstead P. Bear
15" • #515210-03 • JB
Issued: 1998 • To Be Retired: 2000
Orig. Price: $24 • **Value: $24**

Winston B. Bean
10" • #5104 • JB
Issued: pre-1990 • Retired: 1996
Orig. Price: $14 • **Value: $39**

Bears		
	Price Paid	Value
1.		
2.		
3.		
4.		
5.		
6.		
7.		
8.		
9.		
10.		
Totals		

1

Witch-A-Ma-Call-It
info unavailable
Orig. Price: N/A • **Value: N/E**

2

Woodrow T. Bearington
12" • #590041-03 • MB
Issued: 1999 • Retired: 1999
Orig. Price: $48 • **Value: $60**

3

Woodruff K. Bearsford
6" • #57251-05 • AS
Issued: 1999 • Current
Orig. Price: $8 • **Value: $8**

4

New!

Wookie Snicklefritz
10" • #51770-06 • BY
Issued: 2000 • Current
Orig. Price: $14 • **Value: $14**

5

Worthington Fitzbruin
8.5" • #912032 • TJ
Issued: 1997 • To Be Retired: 2000
Orig. Price: $14 • **Value: $14**

6

Yardley Fitzhampton
14" • #912030 • TJ
Issued: 1999 • Current
Orig. Price: $27 • **Value: $27**

7

Yeager Bearington
4.5" • #590085-05 • MB
Issued: 1999 • Current
Orig. Price: $10 • **Value: $10**

8

Yogi
6" • #91771-02 • TJ
Issued: 1997 • Current
Orig. Price: $14 • **Value: $14**

9

Yolanda Panda
6" • #57701 • AS
Issued: 1998 • Current
Orig. Price: $9 • **Value: $9**

10

York
8" • #57051-05 • AS
Issued: 1998 • Current
Orig. Price: $13 • **Value: $13**

Bears	
Price Paid	Value
1.	
2.	
3.	
4.	
5.	
6.	
7.	
8.	
9.	
10.	

Totals

Yvette Dubeary
6" • #918431 • TJ
Issued: 1999 • Current
Orig. Price: $10 • **Value: $10**

Zazu
16" • #5641-05 • BA
Issued: 1996 • Current
Orig. Price: $26 • **Value: $26**

Ziggy Bear
12" • #5060 • N/A
Issued: N/A • Retired: N/A
Orig. Price: N/A • **Value: N/E**

CATS

Whether you are a cat lover or not, you are sure to find one here that suits your fancy in this season's new group of 11 felines, which consists of everything from the common household tabby to the "purr-fect" purebred Persian.

Allie Fuzzbucket
9" • #51720 • BY
Issued: 1998 • Current
Orig. Price: $8 • **Value: $8**

Bears

	Price Paid	Value
1.		
2.		
3.		

Cats

4.		
5.		
6.		
7.		

Totals

Armstrong Cattington
4.5" • #590087-07 • MB
Issued: 1999 • Current
Orig. Price: $10 • **Value: $10**

Baby
11" • #6105C • TJ
Issued: 1990 • Retired: 1990
Orig. Price: N/A • **Value: $280**

New!

Blake B. Wordsworth
5.5" • #5745-06 • AS
Issued: 2000 • Current
Orig. Price: $8 • **Value: $8**

Value Guide — Boyds Plush Animals

1

Boots Alleyruckus
14" • #5308-07 • JB
Issued: 1999 • Current
Orig. Price: $20 • **Value: $20**

2

Bronte
5.5" • #5742-10 • AS
Issued: 1994 • Retired: 1996
Orig. Price: $8 • **Value: $58**

3

Browning
8" • #5741 • AS
Issued: 1992 • Retired: 1999
Orig. Price: $12 • **Value: $25**

4

Byron
8" • #5740 • AS
Issued: 1992 • Retired: 1999
Orig. Price: $12 • **Value: $25**

5

Cabin Cat
info unavailable
Orig. Price: N/A • **Value: N/E**

6
Callaway Flatcat
8" • #56951-06 • FL
Issued: 1998 • Retired: 1999
Orig. Price: $13 • **Value: $20**

7
New!

Callie Fuzzbucket
6" • #517020-06 • BY
Issued: 2000 • Current
Orig. Price: $5 • **Value: $5**

8
Candy Corn Cat
8" • #91971 • TJ
Issued: 1995 • Retired: 1997
Orig. Price: $18 • **Value: $50**

9

Catherine Q. Fuzzberg
8" • #5303-08 • JB
Issued: 1997 • Current
Orig. Price: $10 • **Value: $10**

10

Chaucer
8" • #9135 • TJ
Issued: 1994 • Retired: 1995
Orig. Price: $20 • **Value: $59**

Cats

	Price Paid	Value
1.		
2.		
3.		
4.		
5.		
6.		
7.		
8.		
9.		
10.		

Totals

Value Guide — Boyds Plush Animals

1

Chaucer
8" • #9135-01 • TJ
Issued: 1994 • Retired: 1995
Orig. Price: $20 • **Value: $52**

2

Claudine de la Plumtete
6" • #91710 • TJ
Issued: 1999 • Current
Orig. Price: $9 • **Value: $9**

3

Cleo P. Pussytoes
16" • #91209 • TJ
Issued: 1997 • Retired: 1999
Orig. Price: $40 • **Value: $48**

4

Cookie Grimilkin
11" • #5306 • JB
Issued: 1991 • Current
Orig. Price: $14 • **Value: $14**

5

Cuthbert Catberg
16" • #5314 • JB
Issued: 1992 • Retired: 1993
Orig. Price: N/A • **Value: $112**

6

Dewey Q. Grimilkin
info unavailable
Orig. Price: N/A • **Value: $117**

Cats

	Price Paid	Value
1.		
2.		
3.		
4.		
5.		
6.		
7.		
8.		
9.		

7

Dewey R. Cat
11" • #5302T • JB
Issued: 1990 • Retired: 1990
Orig. Price: N/A • **Value: $135**

8

New!

Dickens Q. Wordsworth
5.5" • #5745-03 • AS
Issued: 2000 • Current
Orig. Price: $8 • **Value: $8**

9

New!

Dorchester Catsworth With Artie
10" • #919760 • TJ
Issued: 2000 • Current
Orig. Price: $30 • **Value: $30**

1

Eleanor
info unavailable
Orig. Price: N/A • **Value: N/E**

2

Ellsworth Flatcat II
8" • #5695-08 • FL
Issued: 1994 • Retired: 1999
Orig. Price: $12 • **Value: $24**

3

New!

Emerson T. Penworthy
8" • #57410-03 • AS
Issued: 2000 • Current
Orig. Price: $12 • **Value: $12**

4

Ernest Q. Grimilkin
11" • #5304 • JB
Issued: pre-1990 • Current
Orig. Price: $14 • **Value: $14**

5

Felina B. Catterwall
8" • #919701 • TJ
Issued: 1998 • Retired: 1999
Orig. Price: $12 • **Value: $22**

6

Felina B. Catterwall
8" • #919701-01 • TJ
Issued: 1999 • Current
Orig. Price: $14 • **Value: $14**

7

Fraid E. Cat
5.5" • #9198 • TJ
Issued: 1994 • Retired: 1997
Orig. Price: $12 • **Value: $36**

8

Gae Q. Grimilkin
14" • #5324 • JB
Issued: pre-1990 • Retired: 1992
Orig. Price: $20 • **Value: $135**

9

Gardner
info unavailable
Orig. Price: $63 • **Value: N/E**

10

Garner J. Cattington
10" • #590250-11 • MB
Issued: 1998 • Retired: 1998
Orig. Price: $31 • **Value: $50**

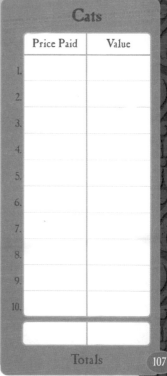

	Price Paid	Value
1.		
2.		
3.		
4.		
5.		
6.		
7.		
8.		
9.		
10.		

Cats

Totals

1

Glenwood Flatcat
8" • #56951-08 • FL
Issued: 1998 • Retired: 1999
Orig. Price: $13 • **Value: $18**

2

Grace
info unavailable
Orig. Price: $63 • **Value: N/E**

3

Greybeard
16" • #5312 • JB
Issued: 1991 • Retired: 1993
Orig. Price: $29 • **Value: $165**

4

Hattie
6" • #9105 • TJ
Issued: 1995 • Retired: 1997
Orig. Price: $12 • **Value: $32**

5

Heranamous
16" • #5311-07 • JB
Issued: 1996 • Retired: 1999
Orig. Price: $29 • **Value: $32**

6

Holloway Flatcat
8" • #5695-07 • FL
Issued: 1994 • Retired: 1999
Orig. Price: $12 • **Value: $25**

7

Inky Catterwall
8" • #91972 • TJ
Issued: 1998 • Retired: 1999
Orig. Price: $18 • **Value: $25**

8

New!

Java B. Bean
8.25" • #500102-07 • JB
Issued: 2000 • Current
Orig. Price: $7 • **Value: $7**

9

Kattelina Purrsley
11" • #91978 • TJ
Issued: 1999 • To Be Retired: 2000
Orig. Price: $20 • **Value: $20**

Cats

	Price Paid	Value
1.		
2.		
3.		
4.		
5.		
6.		
7.		
8.		
9.		
Totals		

Value Guide — Boyds Plush Animals

1

Keats
5.5" • #5743 • AS
Issued: 1992 • Current
Orig. Price: $8 • **Value: $8**

2

Kitt Purrsley
8" • #91711 • TJ
Issued: 1999 • Current
Orig. Price: $18 • **Value: $18**

3

Lacy
10" • #6100C • TJ
Issued: 1990 • Retired: 1992
Orig. Price: $16 • **Value: $120**

4

Lacy
14" • #6101C • TJ
Issued: 1990 • Retired: 1991
Orig. Price: $21 • **Value: $98**

5

Lindbergh Cattington
4.5" • #590087-03 • MB
Issued: 1999 • Current
Orig. Price: $10 • **Value: $10**

6

Lindsey P. Pussytoes
12" • #912091 • TJ
Issued: 1998 • To Be Retired: 2000
Orig. Price: $31 • **Value: $31**

7

Lola Ninelives
9" • #919751 • TJ
Issued: 1999 • Current
Orig. Price: $24 • **Value: $24**

8

Marissa P. Pussyfoot
14" • #912093 • TJ
Issued: 1999 • Current
Orig. Price: $36 • **Value: $36**

9

Millicent P. Pussytoes
11" • #91976 • TJ
Issued: 1997 • Retired: 1998
Orig. Price: $20 • **Value: $34**

10

New!

Milton R. Penworthy
8" • #57410-07 • AS
Issued: 2000 • Current
Orig. Price: $12 • **Value: $12**

Cats	Price Paid	Value
1.		
2.		
3.		
4.		
5.		
6.		
7.		
8.		
9.		
10.		
Totals		

Value Guide — Boyds Plush Animals

1
New!

Miss Prissy Fussybuns
14" • #912094 • TJ
Issued: 2000 • Current
Orig. Price: $30 • **Value: $30**

2
New!

Momma McFuzz And Missy
12" & 5" • #910080 • TJ
Issued: 2000 • Current
Orig. Price: $30 • **Value: $30**

3

Mondale W. Cattington
10" • #590250-05 • MB
Issued: 1999 • Retired: 1999
Orig. Price: $29 • **Value: N/E**

4

Mrs. Partridge
9" • #919750 • TJ
Issued: 1998 • To Be Retired: 2000
Orig. Price: $30 • **Value: $30**

5

Mrs. Petrie
9" • #919752 • TJ
Issued: 1999 • Current
Orig. Price: $30 • **Value: $30**

6

Ned
12" • #5656-03 • BA
Issued: 1993 • Retired: 1995
Orig. Price: $16 • **Value: $70**

7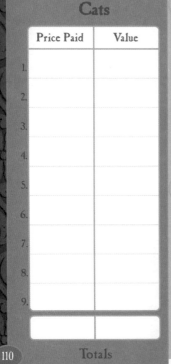

Opel Catberg
14" • #5324-10 • JB
Issued: 1995 • Retired: 1999
Orig. Price: $20 • **Value: $33**

8

Ophilia Q. Grimilkin
14" • #5323 • JB
Issued: pre-1990 • Retired: 1990
Orig. Price: $20 • **Value: $180**

9

Pearl Catberg
14" • #5324-01 • JB
Issued: 1994 • Retired: 1995
Orig. Price: $20 • **Value: $88**

Cats

	Price Paid	Value
1.		
2.		
3.		
4.		
5.		
6.		
7.		
8.		
9.		
Totals		

Value Guide — Boyds Plush Animals

1

New!

Phoebe Purrsmore
5.5" • #917101 • TJ
Issued: 2000 • Current
Orig. Price: $12 • **Value: $12**

2

Poe
5.5" • #5742-07 • AS
Issued: 1993 • Retired: 1999
Orig. Price: $8 • **Value: $25**

3

Punkin Puss
8" • #9197 • TJ
Issued: 1992 • Retired: 1997
Orig. Price: $18 • **Value: $46**

4

Puss N. Boo
8" • #9164 • TJ
Issued: 1993 • Retired: 1995
Orig. Price: $18 • **Value: $55**

5

Quayle D. Cattington
6" • #590270-07 • MB
Issued: 1999 • Retired: 1999
Orig. Price: $16 • **Value: $22**

6

New!

Robyn Purrsmore
8" • #915600 • TJ
Issued: 2000 • Current
Orig. Price: $12 • **Value: $12**

7

Royce
info unavailable
Orig. Price: $32 • **Value: N/E**

8

Sabrina P. Catterwall
8" • #919700 • TJ
Issued: 1998 • Retired: 1999
Orig. Price: $12 • **Value: N/E**

9

Sabrina P. Catterwall
8" • #919700-01 • TJ
Issued: 1999 • Current
Orig. Price: $14 • **Value: $14**

10

Samantha Sneakypuss
11" • #91979 • TJ
Issued: 1999 • Current
Orig. Price: $20 • **Value: $20**

	Cats	
	Price Paid	Value
1.		
2.		
3.		
4.		
5.		
6.		
7.		
8.		
9.		
10.		
	Totals	

Value Guide — Boyds Plush Animals

1

PHOTO UNAVAILABLE

Samuel Catberg
info unavailable
Orig. Price: N/A • **Value: N/E**

2

Shelly
5.5" • #5742 • AS
Issued: 1992 • Current
Orig. Price: $8 • **Value: $8**

3

Socks Grimilkin
14" • #5324-07 • JB
Issued: 1993 • Retired: 1998
Orig. Price: $20 • **Value: $40**

4

Spiro T. Cattington
12" • #590240-07 • MB
Issued: 1998 • Retired: 1998
Orig. Price: $51 • **Value: N/E**

5

Spooky Tangaween
11" • #91975 • TJ
Issued: 1996 • Retired: 1998
Orig. Price: $20 • **Value: $35**

6

Suzie Purrkins
11" • #91977 • TJ
Issued: 1998 • Retired: 1998
Orig. Price: $20 • **Value: $31**

Cats

	Price Paid	Value
1.		
2.		
3.		
4.		
5.		
6.		
7.		
8.		
9.		
Totals		

7

Sweetpea Catberg
11" • #5305 • JB
Issued: pre-1990 • Retired: 1992
Orig. Price: $14 • **Value: $69**

8

Sweetpea Catberg
11" • #5307 • JB
Issued: 1992 • Retired: 1998
Orig. Price: $14 • **Value: $32**

9

T. Frankel Wuzzie
5" • #595103 • TF
Issued: 1999 • Current
Orig. Price: $9 • **Value: $9**

Value Guide — Boyds Plush Animals

Tabby F. Wuzzie
3" • #595240-07 • TF
Issued: 1999 • Current
Orig. Price: $7 • **Value: $7**

Tennyson
5.5" • #5744 • AS
Issued: 1992 • Retired: 1999
Orig. Price: $8 • **Value: $20**

New!

Tessa Fluffypaws
14" • #5309-01 • JB
Issued: 2000 • Current
Orig. Price: $20 • **Value: $20**

Thom
12" • #5656-07 • BA
Issued: 1993 • Retired: 1995
Orig. Price: $16 • **Value: $46**

Thoreau
8" • #5740-08 • AS
Issued: 1995 • Retired: 1999
Orig. Price: $12 • **Value: $23**

Tigerlily
16" • #5311 • JB
Issued: pre-1990 • Retired: 1995
Orig. Price: $29 • **Value: $45**

Treat F. Wuzzie
3" • #596002 • TF
Issued: 1999 • Retired: 1999
Orig. Price: $8 • **Value: N/E**

Turner F. Wuzzie
3" • #595240-06 • TF
Issued: 1998 • Current
Orig. Price: $7 • **Value: $7**

Walter Q. Fuzzberg
8" • #5303-07 • JB
Issued: 1997 • Current
Orig. Price: $10 • **Value: $10**

Zachariah Alleyruckus
14" • #5308-06 • JB
Issued: 1999 • Current
Orig. Price: $20 • **Value: $20**

Cats

	Price Paid	Value
1.		
2.		
3.		
4.		
5.		
6.		
7.		
8.		
9.		
10.		
Totals		

Value Guide — Boyds Plush Animals

1

Zap Catberg
14" • #5325 • JB
Issued: 1992 • Retired: 1992
Orig. Price: $20 • **Value: N/E**

2

Zelda Catberg
14" • #5324-06 • JB
Issued: 1993 • Retired: 1993
Orig. Price: N/A • **Value: $85**

3

Zenus W. Grimilkin
11" • #5303 • JB
Issued: pre-1990 • Retired: 1991
Orig. Price: $14 • **Value: $175**

4

Zip Catberg
14" • #5325 • JB
Issued: pre-1990 • Retired: 1992
Orig. Price: $20 • **Value: $130**

5

Zoe R. Grimilkin
11" • #5304-07 • JB
Issued: 1994 • Retired: 1999
Orig. Price: $14 • **Value: $22**

6

Zoom Catberg
14" • #5326 • JB
Issued: 1992 • Retired: 1993
Orig. Price: $20 • **Value: $138**

Cats

	Price Paid	Value
1.		
2.		
3.		
4.		
5.		
6.		

Cows

7.		

Totals

COWS

"Elford Bullsworth" and "T. Fodder Wuzzie" join the herd this season, taking the place of "Sadie Utterburg" on the shelves, who headed in search of greener pastures after her retirement in 1999.

7

Angus MacMoo
11" • #91341 • TJ
Issued: 1999 • To Be Retired: 2000
Orig. Price: $20 • **Value: $20**

Value Guide — Boyds Plush Animals

1

Bertha Utterberg
8" • #5758 • AS
Issued: 1996 • Retired: 1996
Orig. Price: $13 • **Value: $48**

2

Bessie Moostein
11" • #5532 • AM
Issued: 1991 • Current
Orig. Price: $14 • **Value: $14**

3
New!

Elford Bullsworth
14" • #55330-05 • AM
Issued: 2000 • Current
Orig. Price: $19 • **Value: $19**

4

Elmer Beefcake
14" • #5535-11 • AM
Issued: 1995 • Retired: 1996
Orig. Price: $20 • **Value: $63**

5

Elmo Beefcake
11" • #5532-03 • AM
Issued: 1993 • To Be Retired: 2000
Orig. Price: $14 • **Value: $35**

6

Ernestine Vanderhoof
8" • #55312-05 • AM
Issued: 1999 • Current
Orig. Price: $11 • **Value: $11**

7

Herman Beefcake
16" • #5534 • AM
Issued: 1992 • Retired: 1994
Orig. Price: $27 • **Value: $250**

8

Hester
12" • #5660-10 • BA
Issued: 1996 • Retired: 1997
Orig. Price: $16 • **Value: $34**

9

Hortense Moostein
16" • #5533 • AM
Issued: 1992 • Retired: 1995
Orig. Price: $29 • **Value: $120**

Cows

	Price Paid	Value
1.		
2.		
3.		
4.		
5.		
6.		
7.		
8.		
9.		

Totals

Value Guide — Boyds Plush Animals

1

Ida Moostein
14" • #5535-10 • AM
Issued: 1994 • Retired: 1996
Orig. Price: $20 • **Value: $50**

2

Sadie Utterburg
16" • #5533-10 • AM
Issued: 1996 • Retired: 1999
Orig. Price: $29 • **Value: $39**

3

Silo Q. Vanderhoof
8" • #55312-07 • AM
Issued: 1999 • Current
Orig. Price: $11 • **Value: $11**

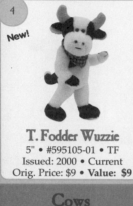

4

New!

T. Fodder Wuzzie
5" • #595105-01 • TF
Issued: 2000 • Current
Orig. Price: $9 • **Value: $9**

CROWS

Claire Herz designed these flighty members of the Boyds family. "Edgar" and "Hank Krow Jr." were both members of the *Artisan Series*, and both headed south in 1997 where they settled into the retired life.

Cows

Price Paid	Value
1.	
2.	
3.	
4.	

Crows

5.	
6.	

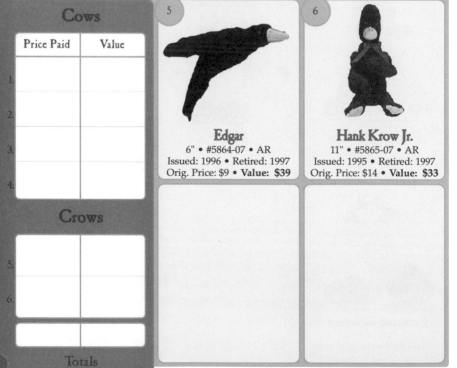

5

Edgar
6" • #5864-07 • AR
Issued: 1996 • Retired: 1997
Orig. Price: $9 • **Value: $39**

6

Hank Krow Jr.
11" • #5865-07 • AR
Issued: 1995 • Retired: 1997
Orig. Price: $14 • **Value: $33**

Dogs

Five playful puppies bound into the line this season, bringing the total number to 32. However, new collectors may face a challenge in getting their paws on some of the older dogs, as only 10 of the canines are current.

Arno-w-ld
12" • #5655-07 • BA
Issued: 1996 • Retired: 1997
Orig. Price: $16 • **Value: $50**

Bagley Flatberg
8" • #5690-03 • FL
Issued: 1996 • Retired: 1999
Orig. Price: $13 • **Value: $25**

Barkley McFarkle
9" • #51750 • BY
Issued: 1999 • Current
Orig. Price: $8 • **Value: $8**

Betty Biscuit
10" • #5402-08 • JB
Issued: 1995 • Retired: 1997
Orig. Price: $14 • **Value: $35**

Beulah Canine
11" • #5403 • JB
Issued: pre-1990 • Retired: 1991
Orig. Price: $14 • **Value: N/E**

New!

Binky McFarkle
6" • #517050-03 • BY
Issued: 2000 • Current
Orig. Price: $5 • **Value: $5**

Bunky McFarkle
9" • #51750-07 • BY
Issued: 1999 • Current
Orig. Price: $8 • **Value: $8**

New!

Carson B. Barker
16" • #540300-05 • JB
Issued: 2000 • Current
Orig. Price: $30 • **Value: $30**

Dogs

	Price Paid	Value
1.		
2.		
3.		
4.		
5.		
6.		
7.		
8.		

Totals

1

Clancy G. Hydrant, Jr.
10" • #5404 • JB
Issued: 1998 • To Be Retired: 2000
Orig. Price: $14 • **Value: $15**

2

Collier P. Hydrant II
16" • #5403 • JB
Issued: 1997 • Retired: 1999
Orig. Price: $29 • **Value: $35**

3

Fritz Von Bruin
6" • #5014 • WB
Issued: 1992 • Retired: 1992
Orig. Price: N/A • **Value: $180**

4

Hector Flatberg
8" • #5690-07 • FL
Issued: 1995 • Retired: 1996
Orig. Price: $13 • **Value: $35**

5

Hercules Von Mutt
6" • #5014-01 • WB
Issued: 1993 • Retired: 1994
Orig. Price: $10 • **Value: $68**

6

Indy *(Fall 1997)*
5.5" • #91757 • TJ
Issued: 1997 • Retired: 1998
Orig. Price: $12 • **Value: $26**

Dogs

	Price Paid	Value
1.		
2.		
3.		
4.		
5.		
6.		
7.		
8.		
9.		

Totals

7

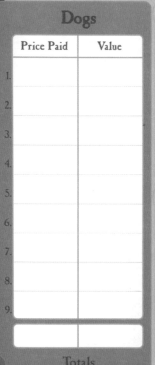

Indy *(Fall 1998)*
5.5" • #91757-10 • TJ
Issued: 1998 • Retired: 1999
Orig. Price: $12 • **Value: $20**

8

Indy *(Fall 1999)*
5" • #91757-12 • TJ
Issued: 1999 • Retired: 1999
Orig. Price: $12 • **Value: N/E**

9

New!

PHOTO UNAVAILABLE

Indy *(Spring 2000)*
5" • #91757-14 • TJ
Issued: 2000 • To Be Retired: 2000
Orig. Price: $12 • **Value: $12**

Irving Poochberg
14" • #5420 • JB
Issued: pre-1990 • Retired: 1992
Orig. Price: $16 • **Value: $150**

Martin Muttski
11" • #5400 • JB
Issued: pre-1990 • Retired: 1992
Orig. Price: $14 • **Value: $125**

Merritt M. Mutt
11" • #5401 • JB
Issued: pre-1990 • Retired: 1991
Orig. Price: $14 • **Value: $120**

Merton Flatberg
8" • #5690-08 • FL
Issued: 1994 • Retired: 1997
Orig. Price: $12 • **Value: $32**

Northrop Flatberg
8" • #5690-01 • FL
Issued: 1994 • Retired: 1999
Orig. Price: $12 • **Value: $28**

Philo Puddlemaker
12" • #56551-07 • BA
Issued: 1999 • Current
Orig. Price: $16 • **Value: $16**

Preston
12" • #56961-01 • FL
Issued: 1996 • Retired: 1996
Orig. Price: N/A • **Value: $35**

Ralph Poochstein
10" • #5400-10 • JB
Issued: 1995 • Retired: 1997
Orig. Price: $14 • **Value: $36**

Roosevelt
15" • #6108D • TJ
Issued: pre-1990 • Retired: 1991
Orig. Price: $27 • **Value: $165**

Dogs

	Price Paid	Value
1.		
2.		
3.		
4.		
5.		
6.		
7.		
8.		
9.		
Totals		

Value Guide — Boyds Plush Animals

Snuffy B. Barker
10" • #5405 • JB
Issued: 2000 • Current
Orig. Price: $15 • **Value: $15**

Speed Poochberg
11" • #5402 • JB
Issued: pre-1990 • Retired: 1992
Orig. Price: $14 • **Value: $130**

T. Foley Wuzzie
5" • #595104-05 • TF
Issued: 2000 • Current
Orig. Price: $9 • **Value: $9**

Toby F. Wuzzie
3" • #595500-08 • TF
Issued: 1999 • Current
Orig. Price: $7 • **Value: $7**

Unidentified Dog
10" • N/A • N/A
Issued: N/A • Retired: N/A
Orig. Price: N/A • **Value: N/E**

Walker
12" • #5655-08 • BA
Issued: 1994 • Retired: 1997
Orig. Price: $16 • **Value: $35**

Dogs

Price Paid	Value
1.	
2.	
3.	
4.	
5.	
6.	

Donkeys

7.	

Totals

DONKEYS

Donkeys aren't known for their speed, but "Brayburn" made a speedy exit in 1997, honored with retirement only one year after his introduction.

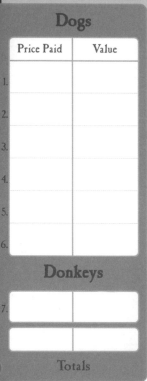

Brayburn
8" • #5670 • FL
Issued: 1996 • Retired: 1997
Orig. Price: $13 • **Value: $40**

ELEPHANTS

You'd think it would be hard to miss an elephant, but that isn't the case with these pachyderms who sauntered out of the collection within one year of their production. "Newton," who retired in 1997, was the last elephant from the collection to be available.

Newton
8" • #5665 • FL
Issued: 1996 • Retired: 1997
Orig. Price: $13 • **Value: $42**

Nicolai A. Pachydermsky
16" • #5528-06 • AM
Issued: 1993 • Retired: 1994
Orig. Price: $28 • **Value: $230**

Olivia A. Pachydermsky
10" • #5527-06 • AM
Issued: 1993 • Retired: 1994
Orig. Price: $14 • **Value: $145**

Omar A. Pachydermsky
7.5" • #5526-06 • AM
Issued: 1993 • Retired: 1994
Orig. Price: $8 • **Value: $95**

FOXES

"Reggie Foxworthy" became the first fox worthy of joing the line, creating a new branch of the Boyds family tree. With his dapper good looks, this critter is sure to be followed by more of his "foxy" friends in the future.

Reggie Foxworthy
8" • #55210 • AM
Issued: 1999 • Current
Orig. Price: $12 • **Value: $12**

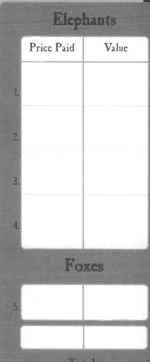

Elephants	
Price Paid	Value
1.	
2.	
3.	
4.	

Foxes	
5.	

Totals

121

FROGS

"Jeremiah B. Ribbit" and "S.C. Ribbit" hopped off their lilypads and into retirement in 1999. "Racheal Q. Ribbit" was green with envy so she will retire in 2000, leaving only two of her amphibious friends available.

Ezra R. Ribbit
6" • #566470 • BA
Issued: 1998 • Current
Orig. Price: $5 • **Value: $5**

G. Kelly Ribbit (musical)
9" • #91320 • TJ
Issued: 1999 • Current
Orig. Price: $25 • **Value: $25**

Jacque Le Grenouille
8" • #5018 • WB
Issued: 1993 • Retired: 1995
Orig. Price: $10 • **Value: $65**

Jeremiah B. Ribbit
9.5" • #566450 • BA
Issued: 1997 • Retired: 1999
Orig. Price: $12 • **Value: $18**

Frogs

	Price Paid	Value
1.		
2.		
3.		
4.		
5.		
6.		
Totals		

Racheal Q. Ribbit
12" • #566340 • BA
Issued: 1997 • To Be Retired: 2000
Orig. Price: $21 • **Value: $21**

S.C. Ribbit (musical)
12" • #917309 • TJ
Issued: 1998 • Retired: 1999
Orig. Price: $25 • **Value: $30**

GORILLAS

The 1998 retirement of "Joe Magilla" prompted his friends "Mike Magilla" and "Viola Magillacuddy" to follow his lead in 1999, leaving no current gorillas in the collection.

Joe Magilla
11" • #5525 • AM
Issued: 1995 • Retired: 1998
Orig. Price: $14 • **Value: $30**

Mike Magilla
8" • #55251 • AM
Issued: 1998 • Retired: 1999
Orig. Price: $12 • **Value: $18**

Viola Magillacuddy
8" • #91351 • TJ
Issued: 1999 • Retired: 1999
Orig. Price: $14 • **Value: $16**

HARES

Hares run a close second to the bears in popularity, and bunny lovers have a wide selection of hopping honeys to choose from. Twenty-six hares jump into the line this season, while seven are expected to hop into retirement by the end of 2000.

Alexandra
14" • #5730 • AS
Issued: 1991 • Retired: 1995
Orig. Price: $20 • **Value: $114**

Alice
7.5" • #5750 • AS
Issued: 1992 • Retired: 1999
Orig. Price: $7 • **Value: $22**

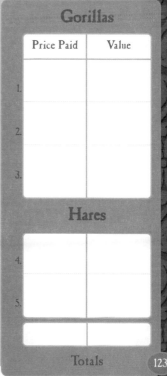

Gorillas	
Price Paid	Value
1.	
2.	
3.	

Hares	
4.	
5.	
Totals	

Value Guide — Boyds Plush Animals

1

Allison Babbit
14" • #9166 • TJ
Issued: 1994 • Retired: 1998
Orig. Price: $20 • **Value: $30**

2

Amarretto
17" • #9110 • TJ
Issued: 1995 • Retired: 1997
Orig. Price: $19 • **Value: $32**

3

Amelia R. Hare
12" • #5203 • JB
Issued: pre-1990 • Retired: 1998
Orig. Price: $14 • **Value: $26**

4

Anastasia
14" • #5876 • HT
Issued: 1992 • Retired: 1992
Orig. Price: $32 • **Value: $84**

5

Anastasia
12" • #912081 • TJ
Issued: 1998 • Current
Orig. Price: $26 • **Value: $26**

6

Anisette
12" • #9109-07 • TJ
Issued: 1996 • Retired: 1996
Orig. Price: $12 • **Value: $42**

Hares

	Price Paid	Value
1.		
2.		
3.		
4.		
5.		
6.		
7.		
8.		
9.		
10.		

Totals

7

Anna
6" • #5870 • HT
Issued: 1992 • Retired: 1993
Orig. Price: $9 • **Value: $100**

8

Anne
7.5" • #5734 • AS
Issued: 1991 • Retired: 1997
Orig. Price: $7 • **Value: $33**

9

Archer
10" • #91544 • TJ
Issued: 1996 • Retired: 1998
Orig. Price: $24 • **Value: $42**

10

Ashley
12" • #9132 • TJ
Issued: 1995 • Retired: 1998
Orig. Price: $20 • **Value: $32**

Value Guide — Boyds Plush Animals

Aubergine
7.5" • #9107 • TJ
Issued: 1995 • Retired: 1998
Orig. Price: $12 • **Value: $24**

Auntie Adina (LE-500)
14" • N/A • N/A
Issued: N/A • Retired: N/A
Orig. Price: N/A • **Value: $230**

Auntie Babbit
12" • #91660 • JB
Issued: 1996 • Retired: 1998
Orig. Price: $30 • **Value: $48**

Auntie Harestein
14" • N/A • N/A
Issued: 1993 • Retired: 1993
Orig. Price: N/A • **Value: N/E**

Babs
12" • #5650-09 • BA
Issued: 1994 • Retired: 1998
Orig. Price: $16 • **Value: $35**

Baby
14" • #6105H • TJ
Issued: 1990 • Retired: 1991
Orig. Price: N/A • **Value: $280**

Beatrice
14" • #6168H • TJ
Issued: 1991 • Retired: 1991
Orig. Price: $63 • **Value: N/E**

Bedford Boneah
17" • #58291-05 • CH
Issued: 1998 • Retired: 1999
Orig. Price: $23 • **Value: N/E**

New!

Bedford Boneah II
14" • #582910-05 • CH
Issued: 2000 • Current
Orig. Price: $24 • **Value: $24**

Beecher B. Bunny
10" • #5250-10 • JB
Issued: 1996 • Retired: 1998
Orig. Price: $16 • **Value: $35**

Hares

	Price Paid	Value
1.		
2.		
3.		
4.		
5.		
6.		
7.		
8.		
9.		
10.		
Totals		

Value Guide — Boyds Plush Animals

1. Bixie
12" • #56501-10 • BA
Issued: 1998 • Current
Orig. Price: $16 • **Value: $16**

2. Bopper
14" • #5748 • HD
Issued: 1991 • Retired: 1992
Orig. Price: $27 • **Value: $145**

3. Brigette Delapain
10" • #91691 • TJ
Issued: 1996 • Retired: 1998
Orig. Price: $21 • **Value: $45**

4. Brigham Boneah
15" • #58291 • CH
Issued: 1997 • Retired: 1999
Orig. Price: $23 • **Value: N/E**

New!

5. Brigham Boneah II
14" • #582910 • CH
Issued: 2000 • Current
Orig. Price: $24 • **Value: $24**

6. Briton R. Hare
15" • #5204 • JB
Issued: pre-1990 • Retired: 1991
Orig. Price: $20 • **Value: $115**

New!

7. Buffie Bunnyhop
8" • #522700-03 • JB
Issued: 2000 • Current
Orig. Price: $10 • **Value: $10**

8. Bumpus
9" • #5746 • HD
Issued: 1991 • Retired: 1992
Orig. Price: $14 • **Value: $108**

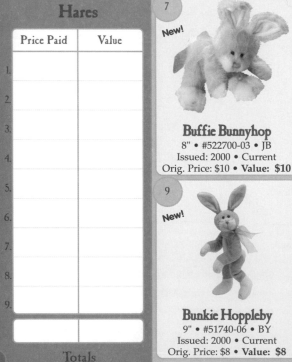

New!

9. Bunkie Hoppleby
9" • #51740-06 • BY
Issued: 2000 • Current
Orig. Price: $8 • **Value: $8**

Hares

	Price Paid	Value
1.		
2.		
3.		
4.		
5.		
6.		
7.		
8.		
9.		
Totals		

1

Bunnylove Rarebit
9" • #91314 • TJ
Issued: 1996 • Retired: 1998
Orig. Price: $20 • **Value: $40**

2

Camilla
7.5" • #5732 • AS
Issued: 1993 • Retired: 1998
Orig. Price: $7 • **Value: $20**

3

New!

Cara Z. Bunnyhugs
9" • #91649 • TJ
Issued: 2000 • Current
Orig. Price: $14 • **Value: $14**

4

Carlin Wabbit
8" • #9115 • TJ
Issued: 1995 • Retired: 1998
Orig. Price: $13 • **Value: $30**

5

New!

Cathy J. Hiphop
6" • #917030 • TJ
Issued: 2000 • Current
Orig. Price: $12 • **Value: $12**

6

Cecilia
8" • #5648-01 • BA
Issued: 1993 • Retired: 1998
Orig. Price: $11 • **Value: $22**

7

Chardonnay
7.5" • #9106 • TJ
Issued: 1995 • Retired: 1998
Orig. Price: $12 • **Value: $30**

8

Charlotte R. Hare
14" • #5224 • JB
Issued: 1992 • Retired: 1998
Orig. Price: $20 • **Value: $38**

9

Chelsea R. Hare
14" • #5217-01 • JB
Issued: 1993 • Retired: 1998
Orig. Price: $20 • **Value: $32**

10

Chesterfield Q. Burpee
8" • #91546 • TJ
Issued: 1996 • Retired: 1998
Orig. Price: $21 • **Value: $40**

Hares

	Price Paid	Value
1.		
2.		
3.		
4.		
5.		
6.		
7.		
8.		
9.		
10.		
Totals		

Value Guide — Boyds Plush Animals

Chloe Fitzhare
17" • #5240-03 • JB
Issued: 1996 • Retired: 1998
Orig. Price: $29 • **Value: $38**

Clara R. Hare
8" • #5227-08 • JB
Issued: 1994 • Retired: 1998
Orig. Price: $10 • **Value: $22**

Clarisse
16" • #91208 • TJ
Issued: 1997 • Retired: 1998
Orig. Price: $40 • **Value: $55**

Columbine Dubois
6" • #91402 • TJ
Issued: 1996 • Retired: 1998
Orig. Price: $12 • **Value: $30**

Cora B. Bunny
20" • #5212 • JB
Issued: pre-1990 • Retired: 1994
Orig. Price: $29 • **Value: $140**

Cordillia R. Hare
15" • #5205 • JB
Issued: pre-1990 • Retired: 1992
Orig. Price: $20 • **Value: $120**

Hares

Price Paid	Value
1.	
2.	
3.	
4.	
5.	
6.	
7.	
8.	
9.	
10.	

Totals

Cosette D. Lapine
10" • #916601 • TJ
Issued: 1997 • Retired: 1999
Orig. Price: $27 • **Value: $34**

Cousin Rose Anjanette
7.5" • #91112-01 • TJ
Issued: 1998 • To Be Retired: 2000
Orig. Price: $12 • **Value: $12**

Curly Lapin
14" • #5207 • JB
Issued: pre-1990 • Retired: 1995
Orig. Price: $14 • **Value: $63**

Daffodil de la Hoppsack
8" • #91404 • TJ
Issued: 1998 • Retired: 1999
Orig. Price: $13 • **Value: $25**

Value Guide — Boyds Plush Animals

1

Daisey
12" • #9109 • TJ
Issued: 1995 • Retired: 1998
Orig. Price: $12 • **Value: $24**

2

Daphne R. Hare
14" • #5225 • JB
Issued: 1992 • Retired: 1998
Orig. Price: $20 • **Value: $35**

3

Darcy Babbit
14" • #9178 • TJ
Issued: 1993 • Retired: 1995
Orig. Price: $18 • **Value: $130**

4

Darcy Babbit II
info unavailable
Orig. Price: N/A • **Value: $135**

5

Delia R. Hare
12" • #5202 • JB
Issued: 1992 • Retired: 1992
Orig. Price: $14 • **Value: $130**

6

Demi
10.5" • #9112 • TJ
Issued: 1995 • Retired: 1998
Orig. Price: $20 • **Value: $40**

7

Demi II
12" • #9112-00 • TJ
Issued: 1995 • Retired: 1995
Orig. Price: $21 • **Value: $38**

8

Diana
10.5" • #5738 • AS
Issued: 1991 • Retired: 1997
Orig. Price: $14 • **Value: $42**

9

Diana
8" • #9181-01 • TJ
Issued: 1996 • Retired: 1997
Orig. Price: $21 • **Value: $33**

10

Diana
(also known as "Elizabeth")
7.5" • #98041 • TJ
Issued: 1996 • Retired: 1996
Orig. Price: $12 • **Value: $30**

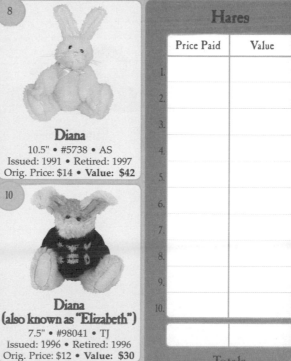

Hares

	Price Paid	Value
1.		
2.		
3.		
4.		
5.		
6.		
7.		
8.		
9.		
10.		
Totals		

Dixie
16" • #56541-08 • BA
Issued: 1996 • Retired: 1998
Orig. Price: $24 • **Value: $30**

Dolly Q. Bunnycombe
10" • #590150-01 • MB
Issued: 1998 • Retired: 1998
Orig. Price: $24 • **Value: $45**

Donna
8" • #1200-01 • CC
Issued: 1994 • Retired: 1998
Orig. Price: $7 • **Value: $21**

Dora B. Bunny
20" • #5211 • JB
Issued: pre-1990 • Retired: 1994
Orig. Price: $29 • **Value: $160**

Dudley Hopson
8" • #91663 • TJ
Issued: 1999 • To Be Retired: 2000
Orig. Price: $12 • **Value: $12**

Earhart Harington
4.5" • #590086-01 • MB
Issued: 1999 • Current
Orig. Price: $10 • **Value: $10**

Edina Flatstein
8" • #5685-05 • FL
Issued: 1996 • Current
Orig. Price: $13 • **Value: $13**

Edith Q. Harington
9" • #590160-03 • MB
Issued: 1999 • Retired: 1999
Orig. Price: $26 • **Value: $30**

New!

PHOTO UNAVAILABLE

Edith Q. Harington II
9" • #5901600-03 • MB
Issued: 2000 • To Be Retired: 2000
Orig. Price: $31 • **Value: $31**

Eleanor
10.5" • #5737-01 • AS
Issued: 1995 • Retired: 1997
Orig. Price: $14 • **Value: $37**

Hares

	Price Paid	Value
1.		
2.		
3.		
4.		
5.		
6.		
7.		
8.		
9.		
10.		

Totals

Elizabeth
7.5" • #5733 • AS
Issued: 1991 • Retired: 1999
Orig. Price: $7 • **Value: $19**

Eloise R. Hare
8.5" • #5230-10 • JB
Issued: 1994 • Retired: 1999
Orig. Price: $12 • **Value: $20**

Elsinore
7.5" • #5732-05 • AS
Issued: 1996 • Retired: 1999
Orig. Price: $7 • **Value: $15**

PHOTO UNAVAILABLE

Emily Babbit *(Spring 1993)*
8" • #9150 • TJ
Issued: 1993 • Retired: 1994
Orig. Price: $20 • **Value: $225**

Emily Babbit *(Fall 1993)*
8" • #9158 • TJ
Issued: 1993 • Retired: 1994
Orig. Price: $24 • **Value: $180**

Emily Babbit *(Spring 1994)*
10.5" • #9150 • TJ
Issued: 1994 • Retired: 1995
Orig. Price: $27 • **Value: $62**

Emily Babbit *(Spring 1995)*
10.5" • #9150-01 • TJ
Issued: 1995 • Retired: 1996
Orig. Price: $20 • **Value: $55**

Emily Babbit *(Fall 1995)*
10.5" • #9150-04 • TJ
Issued: 1995 • Retired: 1996
Orig. Price: $20 • **Value: $52**

Emily Babbit *(Spring 1996)*
10.5" • #9150-05 • TJ
Issued: 1996 • Retired: 1997
Orig. Price: $24 • **Value: $42**

Emily Babbit *(Fall 1996)*
8" • #9150-06 • TJ
Issued: 1996 • Retired: 1997
Orig. Price: $24 • **Value: $40**

Hares

Price Paid	Value
1.	
2.	
3.	
4.	
5.	
6.	
7.	
8.	
9.	
10.	

Totals

Emily Babbit *(Spring 1997)*
10.5" • #9150-07 • TJ
Issued: 1997 • Retired: 1998
Orig. Price: $24 • **Value: $36**

Emily Babbit *(Fall 1997)*
10.5" • #9150-08 • TJ
Issued: 1997 • Retired: 1998
Orig. Price: $25 • **Value: $35**

Emily Babbit *(Spring 1998)*
8" • #9150-09 • TJ
Issued: 1998 • Retired: 1999
Orig. Price: $27 • **Value: $33**

Emily Babbit *(Fall 1998)*
10" • #9150-10 • TJ
Issued: 1998 • Retired: 1999
Orig. Price: $27 • **Value: $33**

Emily Babbit *(Spring 1999)*
8" • #9150-11 • TJ
Issued: 1999 • Retired: 1999
Orig. Price: $27 • **Value: N/E**

Emily Babbit *(Fall 1999)*
8" • #9150-12 • TJ
Issued: 1999 • Retired: 1999
Orig. Price: $27 • **Value: N/E**

Hares

Price Paid	Value
1.	
2.	
3.	
4.	
5.	
6.	
7.	
8.	
9.	
10.	

Totals

New!

Emily Babbit *(Spring 2000)*
8" • #9150-14 • TJ
Issued: 2000 • To Be Retired: 2000
Orig. Price: $27 • **Value: $27**

Emily R. Hare
14" • #5226 • JB
Issued: 1992 • Retired: 1993
Orig. Price: $20 • **Value: $110**

Emma R. Hare
14" • #5225-08 • JB
Issued: 1994 • Retired: 1996
Orig. Price: $20 • **Value: $60**

Farnsworth Jr.
9.5" • #5870-08 • AR
Issued: 1995 • Retired: 1998
Orig. Price: $12 • **Value: $28**

Value Guide — Boyds Plush Animals

1

Farnsworth Sr.
15" • #5875-08 • AR
Issued: 1995 • Retired: 1998
Orig. Price: $20 • **Value: $37**

2

Fergie
7.5" • #5735 • AS
Issued: 1991 • Retired: 1992
Orig. Price: $7 • **Value: $80**

3

Fern Blumenshine
6" • #91692 • TJ
Issued: 1999 • Current
Orig. Price: $12 • **Value: $12**

4

Fleurette Hare
info unavailable
Orig. Price: N/A • **Value: N/E**

5

Flora B. Bunny
20" • #5210 • JB
Issued: 1990 • Retired: 1994
Orig. Price: $29 • **Value: $145**

6

Flossie B. Hopplebuns
8" • #56481-10 • BA
Issued: 1999 • Retired: 1999
Orig. Price: $11 • **Value: N/E**

7
New!

Fluffie Bunnyhop
8" • #522700-01 • JB
Issued: 2000 • Current
Orig. Price: $10 • **Value: $10**

8

Frangelica
12" • #9109-10 • TJ
Issued: 1996 • Retired: 1998
Orig. Price: $12 • **Value: $30**

9

G.G. Willikers
8" • #91162 • TJ
Issued: 1996 • Retired: 1998
Orig. Price: $20 • **Value: $38**

10

Gardner
N/A • #6162H • TJ
Issued: 1991 • Retired: 1991
Orig. Price: $63 • **Value: N/E**

Hares

	Price Paid	Value
1.		
2.		
3.		
4.		
5.		
6.		
7.		
8.		
9.		
10.		
Totals		

Value Guide — Boyds Plush Animals

1

Giselle de la Fleur
6" • #91703 • TJ
Issued: 1998 • Retired: 1999
Orig. Price: $10 • **Value: $17**

2

Golda
10.5" • #9146 • TJ
Issued: 1994 • Retired: 1995
Orig. Price: $20 • **Value: $44**

3

Grace
N/A • #6163H • TJ
Issued: 1991 • Retired: 1991
Orig. Price: $63 • **Value: N/E**

4

Grace Agnes
11" • #5830-01 • CB
Issued: 1994 • Retired: 1995
Orig. Price: $21 • **Value: $75**

5

Grayson R. Hare
9" • #5230-06 • JB
Issued: 1997 • Retired: 1999
Orig. Price: $12 • **Value: $24**

6

Greta de la Fleur
6" • #91704 • TJ
Issued: 1999 • Retired: 1999
Orig. Price: $9 • **Value: $17**

Hares

	Price Paid	Value
1.		
2.		
3.		
4.		
5.		
6.		
7.		
8.		
9.		
10.		
Totals		

7

Gretchen
10" • #911210 • TJ
Issued: 1998 • Retired: 1999
Orig. Price: $17 • **Value: $23**

8

Hailey
8" • #9168 • TJ
Issued: 1995 • Retired: 1998
Orig. Price: $11 • **Value: $25**

9

Hannah
7.5" • #91111 • TJ
Issued: 1997 • Retired: 1999
Orig. Price: $12 • **Value: $22**

10

Harriett R. Hare
12" • #5200-08 • JB
Issued: 1994 • Retired: 1996
Orig. Price: $14 • **Value: $43**

Value Guide — Boyds Plush Animals

1

Harry Lapin II
14" • #5217 • JB
Issued: 1992 • Retired: 1993
Orig. Price: N/A • **Value: $205**

2

Harry R. Hare
17" • #5217-03 • JB
Issued: 1993 • Retired: 1994
Orig. Price: $20 • **Value: $115**

3

Harvey P. Hoppleby
9" • #51740 • BY
Issued: 1999 • Current
Orig. Price: $8 • **Value: $8**

4

Hedy
10.5" • #9186-01 • TJ
Issued: 1994 • Retired: 1998
Orig. Price: $20 • **Value: $38**

5

Higgins
10" • #5877-06 • AR
Issued: 1995 • Retired: 1997
Orig. Price: $21 • **Value: $48**

6

Higgy
7" • #5876-03 • AR
Issued: 1996 • Retired: 1997
Orig. Price: $20 • **Value: $34**

7

Homer
N/A • #6166H • TJ
Issued: 1991 • Retired: 1991
Orig. Price: $63 • **Value: N/E**

8

Hopkins
10.5" • #91121 • TJ
Issued: 1998 • Retired: 1999
Orig. Price: $18 • **Value: $25**

9

Iris Rosenbunny
10" • #91651 • TJ
Issued: 1999 • To Be Retired: 2000
Orig. Price: $20 • **Value: $20**

10

Jack
20" • #5215 • JB
Issued: 1991 • Retired: 1992
Orig. Price: $29 • **Value: $235**

Hares

	Price Paid	Value
1.		
2.		
3.		
4.		
5.		
6.		
7.		
8.		
9.		
10.		
Totals		

Value Guide — Boyds Plush Animals

1
Jane
14" • #5732 • AS
Issued: 1992 • Retired: 1992
Orig. Price: $20 • **Value: $250**

2
Jane
10.5" • #5737-05 • AS
Issued: 1994 • Retired: 1998
Orig. Price: $14 • **Value: $26**

3

Janet
8" • #1200-03 • CC
Issued: 1994 • Retired: 1997
Orig. Price: $7 • **Value: $32**

4
New!

Jenna D. Lapinne
8.5" • #916630 • TJ
Issued: 2000 • Current
Orig. Price: $16 • **Value: $16**

5
Jessica
8" • #9168-02 • TJ
Issued: 1997 • Current
Orig. Price: $12 • **Value: $12**

6

Jill
20" • #5216 • JB
Issued: 1991 • Retired: 1992
Orig. Price: $29 • **Value: $220**

Hares

	Price Paid	Value
1.		
2.		
3.		
4.		
5.		
6.		
7.		
8.		
9.		
10.		

Totals

7

Josephine
6" • #91701 • TJ
Issued: 1996 • Retired: 1998
Orig. Price: $9 • **Value: $20**

8

Juliana Hopkins
8" • #91122 • TJ
Issued: 1999 • Retired: 1999
Orig. Price: $17 • **Value: $20**

9
New!

Juliana Hopkins II
8" • #911220 • TJ
Issued: 2000 • Current
Orig. Price: $15 • **Value: $15**

10
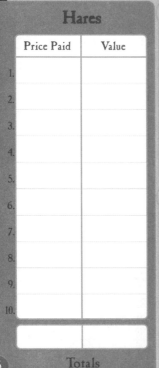

Julip O'Harea
12" • #91664 • TJ
Issued: 1996 • Retired: 1998
Orig. Price: $23 • **Value: $32**

4

Value Guide — Boyds Plush Animals

1

Katerina
10" • #5874 • HT
Issued: 1992 • Retired: 1993
Orig. Price: $20 • **Value: $92**

2

Kathryn
7.5" • #5732-01 • AS
Issued: 1994 • Retired: 1998
Orig. Price: $7 • **Value: $24**

3

Kerry Q. Hopgood
17" • #52401-03 • JB
Issued: 1999 • Current
Orig. Price: $29 • **Value: $29**

4

Lacy
14" • #6100H • TJ
Issued: 1990 • Retired: 1994
Orig. Price: $16 • **Value: $105**

5

Lacy
17" • #6101H • TJ
Issued: 1990 • Retired: 1992
Orig. Price: $21 • **Value: $125**

6

Lady Harriwell
11" • #91892-14 • TJ
Issued: 1999 • Retired: 1999
Orig. Price: $21 • **Value: $23**

7

Lady Payton
10.5" • #918921-09 • TJ
Issued: 1998 • Retired: 1999
Orig. Price: $17 • **Value: $25**

8

Lady Pembrooke
15" • #91892-09 • TJ
Issued: 1997 • Retired: 1999
Orig. Price: $21 • **Value: $25**

9

Lana
10.5" • #9186 • TJ
Issued: 1993 • Retired: 1994
Orig. Price: $20 • **Value: $60**

10

Larry Lapin
17" • #5209 • JB
Issued: pre-1990 • Retired: 1991
Orig. Price: $20 • **Value: $168**

Hares

	Price Paid	Value
1.		
2.		
3.		
4.		
5.		
6.		
7.		
8.		
9.		
10.		

Totals

1

Larry Too
17" • #5217 • JB
Issued: 1992 • Retired: 1992
Orig. Price: $20 • **Value: N/E**

2

Lauren
8" • #9168-01 • TJ
Issued: 1996 • Retired: 1998
Orig. Price: $11 • **Value: $25**

3

Lavinia V. Hariweather
10" • #91661 • TJ
Issued: 1997 • Retired: 1999
Orig. Price: $20 • **Value: $26**

4

Lenora Flatstein
8" • #5685-08 • FL
Issued: 1994 • Retired: 1998
Orig. Price: $12 • **Value: $27**

5

Leona B. Bunny
20" • #5214 • JB
Issued: pre-1990 • Retired: 1992
Orig. Price: $29 • **Value: N/E**

6

Libby Lapinette
6" • #91681 • TJ
Issued: 1999 • Retired: 1999
Orig. Price: $11 • **Value: $13**

7

New!

Lila Hopkins
8" • #91124 • TJ
Issued: 2000 • Current
Orig. Price: $18 • **Value: $18**

8

Lily R. Hare
8" • #5227-01 • JB
Issued: 1994 • Current
Orig. Price: $10 • **Value: $10**

9

Livingston R. Hare
12" • #5200 • JB
Issued: pre-1990 • Retired: 1998
Orig. Price: $14 • **Value: $32**

Hares

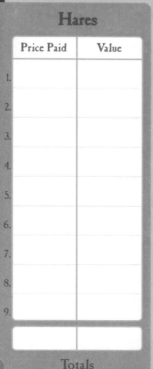

	Price Paid	Value
1.		
2.		
3.		
4.		
5.		
6.		
7.		
8.		
9.		

Totals

1

New!

Lottie de Lopear
9" • #91648 • TJ
Issued: 2000 • Current
Orig. Price: $15 • **Value: $15**

2

Lucille
13.5" • #91141 • TJ
Issued: 1997 • Retired: 1998
Orig. Price: $24 • **Value: $45**

3

Lucinda de la Fleur
6" • #91705 • TJ
Issued: 1999 • Current
Orig. Price: $9 • **Value: $9**

4

Lucy P. Blumenshine
6" • #91702 • TJ
Issued: 1997 • Retired: 1998
Orig. Price: $10 • **Value: $25**

5

Magnolia O'Harea
17" • #91667 • TJ
Issued: 1996 • Retired: 1998
Orig. Price: $31 • **Value: $43**

6

Mallory
info unavailable
Orig. Price: N/A • **Value: $40**

7

Margaret Mary
11" • #5830 • CB
Issued: 1992 • Retired: 1995
Orig. Price: $21 • **Value: $85**

8

Marigold McHare
8" • #52270-08 • JB
Issued: 1999 • Current
Orig. Price: $10 • **Value: $10**

9

Marlena
10.5" • #9154 • TJ
Issued: 1994 • Retired: 1997
Orig. Price: $20 • **Value: $40**

10

Marta M. Hare
12" • #5206 • JB
Issued: pre-1990 • Retired: 1992
Orig. Price: $14 • **Value: $130**

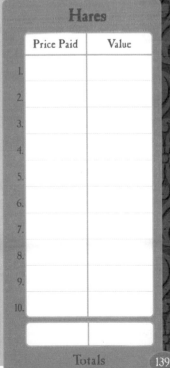

Hares

	Price Paid	Value
1.		
2.		
3.		
4.		
5.		
6.		
7.		
8.		
9.		
10.		

Totals

Value Guide — Boyds Plush Animals

1

Martha T. Bunnycombe
15.5" • #590140-03 • MB
Issued: 1998 • Retired: 1998
Orig. Price: $51 • **Value: $70**

2

Mary
10.5" • #5737 • AS
Issued: 1991 • Retired: 1997
Orig. Price: $14 • **Value: $32**

3

Mary Catherine
9" • #5829 • CB
Issued: 1992 • Retired: 1995
Orig. Price: $16 • **Value: $68**

4

Mary Regina
9" • #5829-01 • CB
Issued: 1994 • Retired: 1995
Orig. Price: $16 • **Value: $70**

5

Matilda
N/A • #6161H • TJ
Issued: 1991 • Retired: 1991
Orig. Price: $63 • **Value: N/E**

6

Merlin
N/A • #6167H • TJ
Issued: 1991 • Retired: 1991
Orig. Price: $63 • **Value: N/E**

Hares

	Price Paid	Value
1.		
2.		
3.		
4.		
5.		
6.		
7.		
8.		
9.		
10.		

Totals

7

Michelline
7.5" • #91815 • TJ
Issued: 1996 • Retired: 1997
Orig. Price: $13 • **Value: $27**

8

Mickey
8" • #1200-08 • CC
Issued: 1994 • Retired: 1995
Orig. Price: $7 • **Value: $50**

9

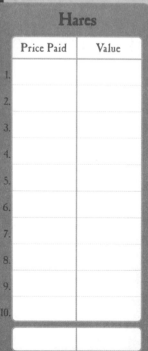

Mickie
16" • #5654 • BA
Issued: 1992 • Retired: 1998
Orig. Price: $21 • **Value: N/E**

10

Millie Hopkins
8" • #91123 • TJ
Issued: 1999 • To Be Retired: 2000
Orig. Price: $18 • **Value: $18**

Value Guide — Boyds Plush Animals

1

Mimi Delapain
8" • #9169 • JB
Issued: 1995 • Retired: 1998
Orig. Price: $9 • **Value: $23**

2

Mimosa
17" • #9110-10 • TJ
Issued: 1996 • Retired: 1998
Orig. Price: $19 • **Value: $32**

3

New!

Mipsie Blumenshine
6" • #917040 • TJ
Issued: 2000 • Current
Orig. Price: $12 • **Value: $12**

4

Miranda Blumenshine
10" • #91142 • TJ
Issued: 1999 • Current
Orig. Price: $23 • **Value: $23**

5

Moe Lapin
14" • #5208 • JB
Issued: 1990 • Retired: 1995
Orig. Price: $14 • **Value: $63**

6

Molly
14" • N/A • N/A
Issued: 1993 • Retired: 1993
Orig. Price: N/A • **Value: N/E**

7

**Momma O'Harea
& Bonnie Blue**
12" & 6" • #91008 • TJ
Issued: 1998 • Retired: 1998
Orig. Price: $29 • **Value: $36**

8

Montgomery Flatstein
8" • #5685-10 • FL
Issued: 1994 • Current
Orig. Price: $12 • **Value: $13**

9

Mrs. Harelwig
info unavailable
Orig. Price: N/A • **Value: N/E**

10

Mrs. Harestein
info unavailable
Orig. Price: N/A • **Value: N/E**

Hares

	Price Paid	Value
1.		
2.		
3.		
4.		
5.		
6.		
7.		
8.		
9.		
10.		

Totals

1

Nanny II
info unavailable
Orig. Price: N/A • **Value: N/E**

2

New!

Natalie Nibblenose
6" • #573300-01 • AS
Issued: 2000 • Current
Orig. Price: $7 • **Value: $7**

3

Natasha
10" • #5873 • HT
Issued: 1992 • Retired: 1994
Orig. Price: $20 • **Value: $80**

4

Nickie
16" • #5653 • BA
Issued: 1992 • Retired: 1993
Orig. Price: $21 • **Value: N/E**

5

New!

Nickie Nibblenose
6" • #573303-03 • AS
Issued: 2000 • Current
Orig. Price: $7 • **Value: $7**

6

Olga
6" • #5871 • HT
Issued: 1992 • Retired: 1992
Orig. Price: $9 • **Value: $110**

Hares

Price Paid	Value
1.	
2.	
3.	
4.	
5.	
6.	
7.	
8.	
9.	

Totals

7

Oliver
6" • #91110 • TJ
Issued: 1998 • Current
Orig. Price: $12 • **Value: $12**

8

Orchid de la Hoppsack
8" • #91405 • TJ
Issued: 1998 • Retired: 1999
Orig. Price: $13 • **Value: $20**

9

Pansy Rosenbunny
10" • #91652 • TJ
Issued: 1999 • Retired: 1999
Orig. Price: $20 • **Value: $22**

Value Guide — Boyds Plush Animals

1

New!

Paula Hoppleby
8" • #91125 • TJ
Issued: 2000 • Current
Orig. Price: $18 • **Value: $18**

2

Peapod
6" • #91071 • TJ
Issued: 1996 • Retired: 1997
Orig. Price: $12 • **Value: $35**

3

Penelope
14" • #5729 • AS
Issued: 1992 • Retired: 1995
Orig. Price: $20 • **Value: $70**

4

Peter
6" • #9111 • TJ
Issued: 1995 • Retired: 1997
Orig. Price: $11 • **Value: $28**

5

Pixie
12" • #5651 • BA
Issued: 1992 • Retired: 1993
Orig. Price: $16 • **Value: $54**

6

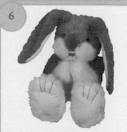

Pixie
12" • #56510-05 • BA
Issued: 1998 • Current
Orig. Price: $16 • **Value: $16**

7

New!

Pookie C. Hoppleby
6" • #517040-01 • BY
Issued: 2000 • Current
Orig. Price: $5 • **Value: $5**

8

Priscilla R. Hare
14" • #5217-08 • JB
Issued: 1995 • Retired: 1997
Orig. Price: $16 • **Value: $34**

9

Priscilla R. Hare
17" • #5217-12 • JB
Issued: 1993 • Retired: 1994
Orig. Price: $20 • **Value: N/E**

10

New!

Regena Haresford
13" • #916490 • TJ
Issued: 2000 • Current
Orig. Price: $30 • **Value: $30**

	Price Paid	Value
1.		
2.		
3.		
4.		
5.		
6.		
7.		
8.		
9.		
10.		

Hares

Totals

Value Guide — Boyds Plush Animals

1

Regina
14" • #5731 • AS
Issued: 1991 • Retired: 1993
Orig. Price: $20 • **Value: $135**

2

Regina
10.5" • #5737-08 • AS
Issued: 1998 • Retired: 1999
Orig. Price: $14 • **Value: $16**

3

Rita
11" • #1201-08 • CC
Issued: 1994 • Retired: 1995
Orig. Price: $10 • **Value: $60**

4

Rosalynn P. Harington
12" • #590140-01 • MB
Issued: 1999 • Retired: 1999
Orig. Price: $51 • **Value: $55**

5 New!

Rosalynn P. Harington II
12" • #5901400-01 • MB
Issued: 2000 • To Be Retired: 2000
Orig. Price: $56 • **Value: $56**

6

Roscoe P. Bumpercrop
17" • #912079 • TJ
Issued: 1999 • Current
Orig. Price: $40 • **Value: $40**

Hares

	Price Paid	Value
1.		
2.		
3.		
4.		
5.		
6.		
7.		
8.		
9.		
10.		

Totals

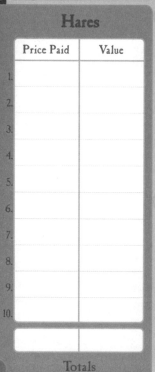

7

Rose
7.5" • #91112 • TJ
Issued: 1997 • Retired: 1998
Orig. Price: $12 • **Value: $22**

8 New!

Roslyn Hiphop
14" • #912080 • TJ
Issued: 2000 • Current
Orig. Price: $31 • **Value: $31**

9

Roxbunny R. Hare
14" • #5878-06 • AR
Issued: 1997 • Retired: 1998
Orig. Price: $14 • **Value: $32**

10

PHOTO UNAVAILABLE

Royce
N/A • #6107H • TJ
Issued: 1990 • Retired: 1992
Orig. Price: $32 • **Value: $300**

Value Guide — Boyds Plush Animals

Rumpus
9" • #5745 • HD
Issued: 1991 • Retired: 1992
Orig. Price: $14 • **Value: $155**

Ruth
11" • #1201-01 • CC
Issued: 1994 • Retired: 1995
Orig. Price: $10 • **Value: $62**

Sangria
17" • #9110-05 • TJ
Issued: 1998 • Retired: 1999
Orig. Price: $20 • **Value: $24**

Sara
7.5" • #9140 • TJ
Issued: 1994 • Retired: 1996
Orig. Price: $13 • **Value: $53**

Sara II
6" • #91401 • TJ
Issued: 1996 • Retired: 1998
Orig. Price: $13 • **Value: $23**

Sarah
10.5" • #5739 • AS
Issued: 1991 • Retired: 1993
Orig. Price: $14 • **Value: $80**

New!

Savannah Buttercup
10" • #91650 • TJ
Issued: 2000 • Current
Orig. Price: $27 • **Value: $27**

Sharona
10.5" • #5737-10 • AS
Issued: 1998 • Retired: 1999
Orig. Price: $14 • **Value: N/E**

Sophie
12" • #9114 • TJ
Issued: 1995 • Retired: 1998
Orig. Price: $20 • **Value: $40**

Sophie B. Bunny
20" • #5215 • JB
Issued: 1993 • Retired: 1994
Orig. Price: $29 • **Value: $225**

Hares

	Price Paid	Value
1.		
2.		
3.		
4.		
5.		
6.		
7.		
8.		
9.		
10.		
Totals		

145

Value Guide — Boyds Plush Animals

1

Squeeky
8" • #5620 • SQ
Issued: 1991 • Retired: 1992
Orig. Price: $10 • **Value: $95**

2

Squeeky
8" • #5621 • SQ
Issued: 1992 • Retired: 1992
Orig. Price: $10 • **Value: $98**

3

Stanley R. Hare
12" • #5201 • JB
Issued: 1991 • Retired: 1998
Orig. Price: $14 • **Value: $26**

4 New!

Stellina Hopswell
8" • #573700-01 • AS
Issued: 2000 • Current
Orig. Price: $14 • **Value: $14**

5 New!

Sterling Hopswell
8" • #573701-06 • AS
Issued: 2000 • Current
Orig. Price: $14 • **Value: $14**

6

Stewart Rarebit
8" • #9116 • TJ
Issued: 1995 • Retired: 1998
Orig. Price: $13 • **Value: $28**

Hares

Price Paid	Value
1.	
2.	
3.	
4.	
5.	
6.	
7.	
8.	
9.	

7 New!

T. Farrell Wuzzie
5" • #595101-06 • TF
Issued: 2000 • Current
Orig. Price: $9 • **Value: $9**

8 New!

T. Hopplewhite
12" • #52200-01 • JB
Issued: 2000 • Current
Orig. Price: $19 • **Value: $19**

9

Taffy C. Hopplebuns
8" • #56481-03 • BA
Issued: 1999 • Retired: 1999
Orig. Price: $11 • **Value: N/E**

Totals

Value Guide — Boyds Plush Animals

Tami F. Wuzzie
3" • #596100 • TF
Issued: 1999 • Current
Orig. Price: $8 • **Value: $8**

Tanner F. Wuzzie
4" • #595300-08 • TF
Issued: 1998 • Current
Orig. Price: $7 • **Value: $7**

Tapper F. Wuzzie
3" • #595300-06 • TF
Issued: 1999 • Current
Orig. Price: $7 • **Value: $7**

Tarragon
17" • #9110-07 • TJ
Issued: 1996 • Retired: 1997
Orig. Price: $19 • **Value: $49**

Tatiana
14" • #5877 • HT
Issued: 1992 • Retired: 1992
Orig. Price: $32 • **Value: $150**

Teddy Hare
info unavailable
Orig. Price: $13 • **Value: $225**

Teddy Hare
info unavailable
Orig. Price: N/A • **Value: $180**

Teddy Hare
info unavailable
Orig. Price: N/A • **Value: N/E**

Teddy Hare
info unavailable
Orig. Price: N/A • **Value: N/E**

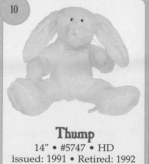

Thump
14" • #5747 • HD
Issued: 1991 • Retired: 1992
Orig. Price: $27 • **Value: $210**

Hares

	Price Paid	Value
1.		
2.		
3.		
4.		
5.		
6.		
7.		
8.		
9.		
10.		
Totals		

Value Guide — Boyds Plush Animals

1

Tipper
8" • #5648-08 • BA
Issued: 1993 • Retired: 1997
Orig. Price: $11 • **Value: $42**

2

Tippy F. Wuzzie
4" • #595300-01 • TF
Issued: 1998 • Current
Orig. Price: $7 • **Value: $7**

3

Trixie
16" • #5654-08 • BA
Issued: 1993 • Retired: 1996
Orig. Price: $24 • **Value: $85**

4

Tutu
N/A • #6169H • TJ
Issued: 1991 • Retired: 1991
Orig. Price: $63 • **Value: $175**

5

Vanessa D. LaPinne
10" • #91662 • TJ
Issued: 1999 • Current
Orig. Price: $27 • **Value: $27**

6

Veronica
10.5" • #9181 • TJ
Issued: 1994 • Retired: 1997
Orig. Price: $20 • **Value: $48**

Hares

Price Paid	Value
1.	
2.	
3.	
4.	
5.	
6.	
7.	
8.	
9.	
10.	

Totals

7

Victoria
7.5" • #5736 • AS
Issued: 1991 • Retired: 1999
Orig. Price: $7 • **Value: $17**

8

Violet Dubois
6" • #91403 • TJ
Issued: 1996 • Retired: 1998
Orig. Price: $12 • **Value: $26**

9

Wedgewood J. Hopgood
17" • #52401-10 • JB
Issued: 1999 • To Be Retired: 2000
Orig. Price: $29 • **Value: $29**

10

Whitney
12" • #9130 • TJ
Issued: 1995 • Retired: 1998
Orig. Price: $20 • **Value: $32**

Value Guide — Boyds Plush Animals

1

Wilhelm Von Bruin
6" • #5015 • WB
Issued: 1992 • Retired: 1995
Orig. Price: $9 • **Value: $45**

2

Wixie
12" • #5650 • BA
Issued: 1992 • Retired: 1998
Orig. Price: $16 • **Value: $32**

3

Zelda Fitzhare
17" • #5240-10 • JB
Issued: 1995 • Retired: 1998
Orig. Price: $29 • **Value: $40**

LAMBS

Twenty lambs have joined the Boyds family to date, including three that make their debut in 2000. These cuddly critters can all be easily recognized by their truly "ewe-nique" names, such as "Madabout Ewe" and "Dipsey Baadoodle."

4

Abbey Ewe
14" • #91311-01 • TJ
Issued: 1996 • Retired: 1998
Orig. Price: $29 • **Value: $46**

5

Daisy Ewe
10" • #5500 • AM
Issued: pre-1990 • Retired: 1994
Orig. Price: $14 • **Value: $52**

6

Dick Butkus
10" • #9155 • TJ
Issued: 1994 • Retired: 1994
Orig. Price: $20 • **Value: $140**

7

New!

Dipsey Baadoodle
9" • #51800-01 • BY
Issued: 2000 • Current
Orig. Price: $8 • **Value: $8**

8

Elspethe Ewe
8" • #91312 • TJ
Issued: 1997 • Retired: 1998
Orig. Price: $11 • **Value: $24**

Hares

	Price Paid	Value
1.		
2.		
3.		

Lambs

4.		
5.		
6.		
7.		
8.		

Totals

Value Guide — Boyds Plush Animals

1

New!

Embraceable Ewe
8" • #913121 • TJ
Issued: 2000 • Current
Orig. Price: $11 • **Value: $11**

2

Madabout Ewe
6" • #91312-01 • TJ
Issued: 1998 • Current
Orig. Price: $11 • **Value: $11**

3

Maisey Ewe
10" • #5501 • AM
Issued: pre-1990 • Retired: 1994
Orig. Price: $14 • **Value: $90**

4

New!

Matilda Baahead
10" • #55200-01 • AM
Issued: 2000 • Current
Orig. Price: $14 • **Value: $14**

5

Maude Ewe
7" • #5510-07 • AM
Issued: 1994 • Retired: 1996
Orig. Price: $7 • **Value: $45**

6

McNeil Mutton
14" • #91311-07 • TJ
Issued: 1996 • Retired: 1998
Orig. Price: $29 • **Value: $42**

7

Pansy
10" • #5501-01 • N/A
Issued: N/A • Retired: N/A
Orig. Price: N/A • **Value: $87**

8
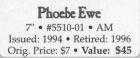

Phoebe Ewe
7" • #5510-01 • AM
Issued: 1994 • Retired: 1996
Orig. Price: $7 • **Value: $45**

9

Rose Mutton
15" • #5520 • AM
Issued: pre-1990 • Retired: 1994
Orig. Price: $20 • **Value: $120**

Lambs

	Price Paid	Value
1.		
2.		
3.		
4.		
5.		
6.		
7.		
8.		
9.		

Totals

150

Value Guide — Boyds Plush Animals

1

Sadie Ewe
7" • #5510-03 • AM
Issued: 1994 • Retired: 1994
Orig. Price: $7 • **Value: $92**

2

Squeeky
8" • #5622 • SQ
Issued: 1992 • Retired: 1992
Orig. Price: $10 • **Value: $85**

3

Tallulah Baahead
14" • #5520-01 • AM
Issued: 1995 • To Be Retired: 2000
Orig. Price: $20 • **Value: $20**

4

Tutu
N/A • #6169L • TJ
Issued: 1991 • Retired: 1991
Orig. Price: $63 • **Value: N/E**

5

Violet Ewe
10" • #5500-07 • AM
Issued: 1996 • Retired: 1998
Orig. Price: $14 • **Value: $30**

6

Wannabee Ewe-Too
8" • #91312-02 • TJ
Issued: 1999 • Retired: 1999
Orig. Price: $11 • **Value: N/E**

LIONS

With the introduction of a new millennium, a new generation of royalty prepares to take over the forest. Three "kings of the jungle" have been produced in 1999 and 2000 to take over the territory of their eight predecessors, all of whom have retired.

7

Butch
8" • #5861 • BB
Issued: 1994 • Retired: 1994
Orig. Price: $14 • **Value: $105**

8

Dickie The Lionheart
6" • #51700 • BY
Issued: 1997 • Retired: 1999
Orig. Price: $5 • **Value: N/E**

Lambs

	Price Paid	Value
1.		
2.		
3.		
4.		
5.		
6.		

Lions

7.		
8.		

Totals

Value Guide — Boyds Plush Animals

1

Elvis
12" • #5859 • AR
Issued: 1995 • Retired: 1996
Orig. Price: $20 • **Value: $47**

2
New!

I.M. Uproarius
11" • #55220 • AM
Issued: 2000 • Current
Orig. Price: $16 • **Value: $16**

3

Lance
8" • #51900 • BY
Issued: 1997 • Retired: 1999
Orig. Price: $8 • **Value: N/E**

4

Leopold Q. Lion
10" • #5530 • AM
Issued: pre-1990 • Retired: 1993
Orig. Price: $14 • **Value: $150**

5

Marley Dredlion
9" • #51735 • BY
Issued: 1999 • Current
Orig. Price: $8 • **Value: $8**

6

Merlin
info unavailable
Orig. Price: N/A • **Value: N/E**

7

Sampson T. Lion
14" • #5531 • AM
Issued: pre-1990 • Retired: 1992
Orig. Price: $29 • **Value: $285**

8

Spike T. Lion
14" • #5860 • BB
Issued: 1992 • Retired: 1994
Orig. Price: $20 • **Value: $110**

9
New!

Theo F. Wuzzie
3" • #596007 • TF
Issued: 2000 • Current
Orig. Price: $7 • **Value: $7**

Lions

	Price Paid	Value
1.		
2.		
3.		
4.		
5.		
6.		
7.		
8.		
9.		
Totals		

MICE

Since 1993, 16 mice have scurried into the collection, including one new introduction in 2000. Of these, eight can still be found munching on their favorite cheeses, while eight have quietly settled into retirement.

Bebe
6" • #9167 • TJ
Issued: 1994 • Retired: 1996
Orig. Price: $13 • **Value: $46**

Bebe
6" • #9167-01 • TJ
Issued: 1994 • Retired: 1995
Orig. Price: $13 • **Value: $46**

Brie
6" • #5756 • AS
Issued: 1993 • Current
Orig. Price: $8 • **Value: $8**

Chedda
6" • #5756-06 • AS
Issued: 1993 • Current
Orig. Price: $8 • **Value: $8**

Colby S. Mouski
6" • #91672 • TJ
Issued: 1998 • Retired: 1999
Orig. Price: $12 • **Value: $17**

Cottage McNibble
6" • #91673 • TJ
Issued: 1999 • Current
Orig. Price: $12 • **Value: $12**

Feta
6" • #91075 • TJ
Issued: 1995 • Retired: 1996
Orig. Price: $12 • **Value: $52**

Mice

	Price Paid	Value
1.		
2.		
3.		
4.		
5.		
6.		
7.		
Totals		

1

Gouda
6" • #91671 • TJ
Issued: 1998 • Current
Orig. Price: $12 • **Value: $12**

2

Joy
6" • #9165-06 • TJ
Issued: 1993 • Retired: 1996
Orig. Price: $12 • **Value: $42**

3

Monterey Mouski
6" • #91675 • TJ
Issued: 1999 • Current
Orig. Price: $12 • **Value: $12**

4

Noel
6" • #9165-01 • TJ
Issued: 1993 • Retired: 1996
Orig. Price: $12 • **Value: $43**

5

New!

Romano B. Grated
6" • #5755 • AS
Issued: 2000 • Current
Orig. Price: $8 • **Value: $8**

6

Roq
8" • #5757-01 • AS
Issued: 1994 • Retired: 1995
Orig. Price: $14 • **Value: $50**

Mice

	Price Paid	Value
1.		
2.		
3.		
4.		
5.		
6.		
7.		
8.		
9.		

Totals

7

Sharp McNibble
6" • #91674 • TJ
Issued: 1999 • Current
Orig. Price: $12 • **Value: $12**

8

Stilton
8" • #5757 • AS
Issued: 1993 • Retired: 1995
Orig. Price: $14 • **Value: $53**

9

Tidbit F. Wuzzie
2.5" • #595170 • TF
Issued: 1999 • Current
Orig. Price: $7 • **Value: $7**

MONKEYS

"Toodles F. Wuzzie" joins the Monkburys, the Tsuris and the Simianskys in the Boyds forest in 2000, becoming the seventh monkey to join the line and bringing some pint-sized "monkey fun" into the Boyds family.

Bertha S. Simiansky
10" • #5524-11 • AM
Issued: 1993 • Retired: 1996
Orig. Price: $14 • **Value: $42**

Dalton Monkbury
8" • #55242-08 • AM
Issued: 1998 • Current
Orig. Price: $12 • **Value: $12**

Darwin Monkbury
8" • #55242-05 • AM
Issued: 1998 • Current
Orig. Price: $12 • **Value: $12**

Finster R. Tsuris
10" • #55241-05 • AM
Issued: 1997 • Retired: 1999
Orig. Price: $14 • **Value: $35**

Imogene R. Tsuris
10" • #55241-11 • AM
Issued: 1997 • Retired: 1999
Orig. Price: $14 • **Value: $35**

Simon S. Simiansky
10" • #5524-10 • AM
Issued: 1993 • Retired: 1996
Orig. Price: $14 • **Value: $52**

New!

Toodles F. Wuzzie
3" • #596006 • TF
Issued: 2000 • Current
Orig. Price: $8 • **Value: $8**

Monkeys

	Price Paid	Value
1.		
2.		
3.		
4.		
5.		
6.		
7.		

MOOSE

The Von Hindenmoose family and their friends rule the northernmost branch of the Boyds family tree. To date, 39 moose have made their way into the collection, although only five have stayed in the area rather than heading back up north.

Beatrice Von Hindenmoose
17" • #5542 • NL
Issued: 1991 • Retired: 1997
Orig. Price: $16 • **Value: $55**

Bismark Von Hindenmoose
20" • #5545-05 • NL
Issued: 1995 • Retired: 1996
Orig. Price: $29 • **Value: $66**

Edwina
14" • #9144 • TJ
Issued: 1994 • Retired: 1997
Orig. Price: $20 • **Value: $37**

Egon Von Hindenmoose
6" • #5546 • NL
Issued: 1993 • Retired: 1997
Orig. Price: $8 • **Value: $40**

Euphoria
8" • #91446 • TJ
Issued: 1995 • Retired: 1998
Orig. Price: $14 • **Value: $28**

Father Krismoose
info unavailable
Orig. Price: N/A • **Value: N/E**

Father Moose Moss
info unavailable
Orig. Price: N/A • **Value: N/E**

Father Moosemas
info unavailable
Orig. Price: N/A • **Value: N/E**

Moose		
	Price Paid	Value
1.		
2.		
3.		
4.		
5.		
6.		
7.		
8.		
Totals		

Festus
14" • #91444 • TJ
Issued: 1995 • Retired: 1996
Orig. Price: $21 • **Value: $53**

Gertrude
17" • #6108 • TJ
Issued: 1993 • Retired: 1993
Orig. Price: N/A • **Value: $240**

Helmut
14" • #9145 • TJ
Issued: 1994 • Retired: 1995
Orig. Price: $27 • **Value: $65**
Variation: green sweater
Value: $80

Justina
(formerly "Philomena")
14" • #91443 • TJ
Issued: 1995 • Retired: 1997
Orig. Price: $27 • **Value: $50**

Kris Moose
(formerly "Father Krismoose")
14" • #9192 • JB
Issued: 1992 • Retired: 1996
Orig. Price: $27 • **Value: N/E**

Krismoose
info unavailable
Orig. Price: N/A • **Value: N/E**

Maddie LaMoose
6" • #517030-05 • BY
Issued: 1999 • Current
Orig. Price: $5 • **Value: $5**

Manheim Von Hindenmoose
20" • #5545 • NL
Issued: 1992 • Retired: 1996
Orig. Price: $29 • **Value: $66**

Martini
12" • #91109 • TJ
Issued: 1998 • Retired: 1999
Orig. Price: $12 • **Value: $28**

Maurice Von Hindenmoose
14" • #5540-05 • NL
Issued: 1996 • Retired: 1999
Orig. Price: $14 • **Value: $22**

Moose	
Price Paid	Value
1.	
2.	
3.	
4.	
5.	
6.	
7.	
8.	
9.	
10.	
Totals	157

Value Guide — Boyds Plush Animals

1

Maynard Von Hindenmoose
14" • #5541 • NL
Issued: 1992 • Retired: 1997
Orig. Price: $14 • **Value: $43**

2

Menachem
8.5" • #91212 • TJ
Issued: 1996 • Retired: 1998
Orig. Price: $20 • **Value: $34**

3

Mendel Von Hindenmoose
6" • #5547 • NL
Issued: 1996 • Current
Orig. Price: $8 • **Value: $8**

4

Milhous N. Moosington
14" • #590300 • MB
Issued: 1999 • Retired: 1999
Orig. Price: $84 • **Value: N/E**

5

Miliken Von Hindenmoose
17" • #55421-05 • NL
Issued: 1997 • Retired: 1999
Orig. Price: $20 • **Value: $32**

6

Millie LaMoose
9" • #51730 • BY
Issued: 1998 • Retired: 1999
Orig. Price: $8 • **Value: $16**

Moose

Price Paid	Value
1.	
2.	
3.	
4.	
5.	
6.	
7.	
8.	
9.	

Totals

7

Minney Moose
14" • #91108 • TJ
Issued: 1996 • Retired: 1998
Orig. Price: $20 • **Value: $34**

8

Montague
8" • #9121 • TJ
Issued: 1994 • Retired: 1996
Orig. Price: $20 • **Value: $43**

9

Montana Mooski
12" • #917295 • TJ
Issued: 1999 • Current
Orig. Price: $30 • **Value: $30**

Value Guide — Boyds Plush Animals

1

Monte Mooselton
12" • #917290 • TJ
Issued: 1998 • Retired: 1999
Orig. Price: $21 • **Value: $34**

2

Mortimer Von Hindenmoose
14" • #55411-05 • NL
Issued: 1997 • Retired: 1999
Orig. Price: $14 • **Value: $24**

3

Mother Moosemas
info unavailable
Orig. Price: N/A • **Value: N/E**

4

Murgatroyd Von Hindenmoose
14" • #5540 • NL
Issued: 1991 • Retired: 1994
Orig. Price: $14 • **Value: $45**

5

Murgatroyd Von Hindenmoose II
14" • #5540 • NL
Issued: 1993 • Retired: 1997
Orig. Price: $14 • **Value: $52**

6

Murphy Mooselfluff
10" • #917291 • TJ
Issued: 1999 • Current
Orig. Price: $24 • **Value: $24**

7

Myron Von Hindenmoose
10" • #912121 • TJ
Issued: 1997 • Retired: 1998
Orig. Price: $21 • **Value: $35**

8

Nadia Von Hindenmoose
17" • #5542-01 • NL
Issued: 1994 • Retired: 1996
Orig. Price: $20 • **Value: $82**

9

Siegfried Von Hindenmoose
20" • #5544 • NL
Issued: 1991 • Retired: 1995
Orig. Price: $29 • **Value: $185**

Moose

	Price Paid	Value
1.		
2.		
3.		
4.		
5.		
6.		
7.		
8.		
9.		
Totals		

1

T. Fargo Wuzzie
5" • #595102 • TF
Issued: 1999 • Current
Orig. Price: $9 • **Value: $9**

2

Talbot F. Wuzzie
3.5" • #595440 • TF
Issued: 1998 • Retired: 1999
Orig. Price: $7 • **Value: $10**

3

Windberg
8" • #5675-05 • FL
Issued: 1995 • Retired: 1999
Orig. Price: $13 • **Value: $22**

PENGUINS

"Tuxie Waddlewalk" has traveled all the way from the icy Arctic to become the first penguin in the Boyds family. A member of the Northern Lights collection, hopefully Tuxie will decide to stay a while before waddling away into retirement.

4

Tuxie Waddlewalk
8" • #55500 • NL
Issued: 1999 • Current
Orig. Price: $13 • **Value: $13**

Moose

	Price Paid	Value
1.		
2.		
3.		

Penguins

4.		

Pigs

5.		
Totals		

PIGS

Since 1992, 20 swine have been welcomed to the Boyds farm. Only 10 of these critters can still be found in their pigpen, including three new releases and two old-timers that are being honored with retirement in 2000.

5

Aphrodite
7" • #5537 • AM
Issued: 1994 • Retired: 1995
Orig. Price: $12 • **Value: $48**

Value Guide — Boyds Plush Animals

1

Aphrodite
7" • #5539 • AM
Issued: 1995 • Retired: 1996
Orig. Price: $12 • **Value: $43**

2

Erin O'Pigg
11" • #5536-09 • AM
Issued: 1996 • Retired: 1997
Orig. Price: $14 • **Value: $39**

3

Farland O'Pigg
16" • #5538 • AM
Issued: 1992 • Retired: 1997
Orig. Price: $29 • **Value: $75**

4

Kaitlin K. Trufflesnout
8" • #91601-03 • TJ
Issued: 1999 • Retired: 1999
Orig. Price: $12 • **Value: N/E**

5

Kaitlin McSwine
8" • #91601 • TJ
Issued: 1997 • Retired: 1999
Orig. Price: $12 • **Value: $23**

6

Kaitlin McSwine II
8" • #91601-01 • TJ
Issued: 1997 • Retired: 1999
Orig. Price: $14 • **Value: $18**

7

Kaitlin McSwine III
8" • #91601-02 • TJ
Issued: 1998 • Current
Orig. Price: $16 • **Value: $16**

8

Lofton Q. McSwine
8" • #55391-09 • AM
Issued: 1997 • To Be Retired: 2000
Orig. Price: $11 • **Value: $11**

9

Maggie O'Pigg
11" • #5536-07 • AM
Issued: 1993 • Retired: 1999
Orig. Price: $14 • **Value: $23**

10

New!

Mudpuddle P. Piglet
9" • #51790-09 • BY
Issued: 2000 • Current
Orig. Price: $8 • **Value: $8**

Pigs

	Price Paid	Value
1.		
2.		
3.		
4.		
5.		
6.		
7.		
8.		
9.		
10.		

Totals

Value Guide — Boyds Plush Animals

Primrose
11" • #9160 • TJ
Issued: 1993 • Retired: 1996
Orig. Price: $20 • **Value: $62**

Primrose II
11" • #9160-01 • TJ
Issued: 1997 • Retired: 1997
Orig. Price: $20 • **Value: $44**

Primrose III
11" • #9160-02 • TJ
Issued: 1998 • Current
Orig. Price: $23 • **Value: $23**

New!

Primrose IV
11" • #9160-04 • TJ
Issued: 2000 • Current
Orig. Price: $23 • **Value: $23**

Primrose P. Trufflesnout
11" • #9160-03 • TJ
Issued: 1999 • Retired: 1999
Orig. Price: $23 • **Value: N/E**

Reilly O'Pigg
16" • #5538-07 • AM
Issued: 1993 • Retired: 1995
Orig. Price: $29 • **Value: $80**

Pigs

	Price Paid	Value
1.		
2.		
3.		
4.		
5.		
6.		
7.		
8.		
9.		
Totals		

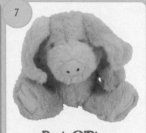

Rosie O'Pigg
11" • #5536 • AM
Issued: 1992 • Retired: 1998
Orig. Price: $14 • **Value: $35**

Sheffield O'Swine
8" • #55391-07 • AM
Issued: 1997 • To Be Retired: 2000
Orig. Price: $11 • **Value: $11**

New!

Truffles O' Pigg
9" • #916010-01 • TJ
Issued: 2000 • Current
Orig. Price: $16 • **Value: $16**

RACCOONS

"Bandit Bushytail," the first Boyds plush raccoon, slipped into the Boyds family in 2000. But his debut was not missed, as raccoon lovers everywhere flocked to stores to add the masked critter to their collections.

New!

Bandit Bushytail
6" • #55211 • AM
Issued: 2000 • Current
Orig. Price: $12 • **Value: $12**

ORNAMENTS

Spring is for hanging around and the 11 new ornaments for the 2000 season are perfect for just that. The Boyds ornaments feature a wide variety of animals and situations, which is further proof that these fluffy miniatures are not just for the holiday season.

Adrienne Berrifrost
5.5" • #56202-06 • OR
Issued: 1999 • Current
Orig. Price: $9 • **Value: $9**

Aimee Berrifrost
5.5" • #56202-04 • OR
Issued: 1999 • Current
Orig. Price: $9 • **Value: $9**

Alyssa Berrifrost
5.5" • #56202-02 • OR
Issued: 1999 • Current
Orig. Price: $9 • **Value: $9**

Angelica
7" • #5611-08 • OR
Issued: 1993 • Retired: 1997
Orig. Price: $12 • **Value: $22**

Angelina
5.5" • #5615-07 • OR
Issued: 1995 • Retired: 1997
Orig. Price: $7 • **Value: $18**

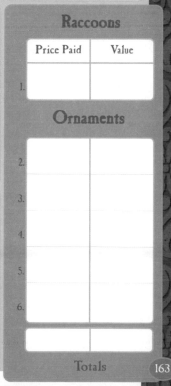

Raccoons	
Price Paid	Value

Ornaments	

Totals

163

Value Guide — Boyds Plush Animals

Angelina II
5.5" • #56151-07 • OR
Issued: 1998 • Current
Orig. Price: $7 • **Value: $7**

Ariel
5" • #5620-08 • OR
Issued: 1995 • Retired: 1999
Orig. Price: $7 • **Value: N/E**

Arinna Goodnight
5.5" • #56231-04 • OR
Issued: 1997 • Retired: 1999
Orig. Price: $7 • **Value: $10**

Athena
5.5" • #5617-01 • OR
Issued: 1995 • Retired: 1996
Orig. Price: $7 • **Value: $30**

Aurora Goodnight
5.5" • #56232-12 • OR
Issued: 1999 • Retired: 1999
Orig. Price: $7 • **Value: N/E**

Bernice Blizzard
3.5" • #56193 • OR
Issued: 1999 • Current
Orig. Price: $7 • **Value: $7**

Bert Blizzard
3.5" • #56192 • OR
Issued: 1999 • Current
Orig. Price: $7 • **Value: $7**

Bibi Buzzby
5.5" • #56220-12 • OR
Issued: 1999 • Current
Orig. Price: $8 • **Value: $8**

Billy Bob
5" • #56201-06 • OR
Issued: 1997 • Retired: 1999
Orig. Price: $7 • **Value: $12**

Ornaments

	Price Paid	Value
1.		
2.		
3.		
4.		
5.		
6.		
7.		
8.		
9.		

Totals

Value Guide — Boyds Plush Animals

1

Bud Buzzby
5.5" • #56220-08 • OR
Issued: 1999 • Current
Orig. Price: $8 • **Value: $8**

2

Cappuccino Frenzy
5.5" • #56271 • OR
Issued: 1999 • Current
Orig. Price: $7 • **Value: $7**

3

Cassie Goodnight
5.5" • #56232-01 • OR
Issued: 1998 • Retired: 1999
Orig. Price: $7 • **Value: $12**

4

Celeste
5" • #5609-01 • OR
Issued: 1994 • Retired: 1999
Orig. Price: $7 • **Value: N/E**

5

Celestina Goodnight
5.5" • #56231-02 • OR
Issued: 1997 • Retired: 1999
Orig. Price: $7 • **Value: $13**

6

Chilly Frostbite
3.5" • #56260 • OR
Issued: 1999 • Current
Orig. Price: $7 • **Value: $7**

7

Clarence
4.5" • #5608-08 • OR
Issued: 1993 • Retired: 1996
Orig. Price: $6 • **Value: $30**

8

Comet
5.5" • #5622 • OR
Issued: 1996 • Retired: 1999
Orig. Price: $7 • **Value: $16**

9

Corona Goodspeed
5.5" • #5624-09 • OR
Issued: 1998 • Current
Orig. Price: $7 • **Value: $7**

10

Country Angel
4.5" • #7401 • OR
Issued: 1993 • Retired: 1993
Orig. Price: N/A • **Value: $36**

Ornaments

	Price Paid	Value
1.		
2.		
3.		
4.		
5.		
6.		
7.		
8.		
9.		
10.		
Totals		

Value Guide — Boyds Plush Animals

1

Cowsies
5" • #5607 • OR
Issued: 1993 • Retired: 1994
Orig. Price: $5 • **Value: $45**

2

Deitrich
5.5" • #5608-06 • OR
Issued: 1996 • Retired: 1997
Orig. Price: $6 • **Value: N/E**

3 New!

Dinkle B. Bumbles
5.5" • #56221-12 • OR
Issued: 2000 • Current
Orig. Price: $8 • **Value: $8**

4

Dipper
7" • #5611-09 • OR
Issued: 1996 • Retired: 1998
Orig. Price: $12 • **Value: $20**

5

Echo Goodnight
5.5" • #56232-14 • OR
Issued: 1999 • Retired: 1999
Orig. Price: $7 • **Value: N/E**

6

Edna May
5" • #56201-02 • OR
Issued: 1997 • Retired: 1999
Orig. Price: $7 • **Value: $18**

Ornaments

	Price Paid	Value
1.		
2.		
3.		
4.		
5.		
6.		
7.		
8.		
9.		
10.		

Totals

7

Espresso Frisky
5.5" • #56272 • OR
Issued: 1999 • Current
Orig. Price: $7 • **Value: $7**

8

Gabriella
8" • #7408 • OR
Issued: 1994 • Retired: 1995
Orig. Price: $8 • **Value: N/E**

9

Gabriella
8" • #7408-08 • OR
Issued: 1996 • Retired: 1997
Orig. Price: $8 • **Value: N/E**

10

Galaxy
7" • #56111-01 • OR
Issued: 1998 • Retired: 1999
Orig. Price: $12 • **Value: N/E**

Value Guide — Boyds Plush Animals

1

New!

Gonna Luvya
5" • #56200-01 • OR
Issued: 2000 • Current
Orig. Price: $7 • **Value: $7**

2

Gweneth
5" • #56031 • OR
Issued: 1997 • Retired: 1999
Orig. Price: $6 • **Value: $18**

3

Immanuella
5" • #5609-09 • OR
Issued: 1996 • Retired: 1999
Orig. Price: $7 • **Value: N/E**

4

New!

Josanna Java
5.5" • #56273 • OR
Issued: 2000 • Current
Orig. Price: $7 • **Value: $7**

5

Juliette
4.5" • #5612-01 • OR
Issued: 1994 • Retired: 1999
Orig. Price: $7 • **Value: N/E**

6

Jupiter Goodspeed
5.5" • #5624-06 • OR
Issued: 1998 • Retired: 1999
Orig. Price: $7 • **Value: $15**

7
New!

Katalina Kafinata
5.5" • #56274 • OR
Issued: 2000 • Current
Orig. Price: $7 • **Value: $7**

8

New!

Lady B. Lovebug
5" • #595104 • TF
Issued: 2000 • Current
Orig. Price: $9 • **Value: $9**

9

Lambsies
4.5" • #5603 • OR
Issued: 1991 • Retired: 1995
Orig. Price: $5 • **Value: $28**

10

New!

Lilith Angel Ewe
5" • #56030-01 • OR
Issued: 2000 • Current
Orig. Price: $7 • **Value: $7**

	Price Paid	Value
1.		
2.		
3.		
4.		
5.		
6.		
7.		
8.		
9.		
10.		

Totals

Value Guide — Boyds Plush Animals

Lilly R. Ribbit
4" • #56194 • OR
Issued: 2000 • Current
Orig. Price: $7 • **Value: $7**

Linnea
7" • #5610-01 • OR
Issued: 1994 • Retired: 1997
Orig. Price: $12 • **Value: $20**

Lionsies
4.5" • #5604 • OR
Issued: 1991 • Retired: 1994
Orig. Price: $5 • **Value: $55**

Lorelei
5.5" • #56141 • OR
Issued: 1997 • Current
Orig. Price: $7 • **Value: $7**

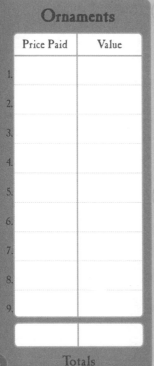

Luna
5" • #5621-10 • OR
Issued: 1996 • Retired: 1997
Orig. Price: $6 • **Value: N/E**

Mabel Witmoose
5" • #56172 • OR
Issued: 1999 • Current
Orig. Price: $8 • **Value: $8**

Ornaments

	Price Paid	Value
1.		
2.		
3.		
4.		
5.		
6.		
7.		
8.		
9.		
Totals		

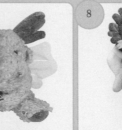

Matilda
5.5" • #5617-05 • OR
Issued: 1995 • Retired: 1999
Orig. Price: $7 • **Value: $12**

Mercer
5.5" • #56171-03 • OR
Issued: 1998 • Current
Orig. Price: $7 • **Value: $7**

Mercury
7" • #5610-09 • OR
Issued: 1996 • Retired: 1998
Orig. Price: $12 • **Value: $17**

Value Guide — Boyds Plush Animals

1

Mocha Mooseby
5.5" • #56270 • OR
Issued: 1999 • Current
Orig. Price: $7 • **Value: $7**

2

Moondust Goodspeed
5.5" • #5624-08 • OR
Issued: 1999 • Retired: 1999
Orig. Price: $7 • **Value: $12**

3

Moosies
6" • #5605 • OR
Issued: 1993 • Retired: 1996
Orig. Price: $5 • **Value: $29**

4

Narcissus
5" • #5621-08 • OR
Issued: 1996 • Retired: 1997
Orig. Price: $6 • **Value: $13**

5

Orion
5" • #5612-09 • OR
Issued: 1996 • Current
Orig. Price: $7 • **Value: $7**

6

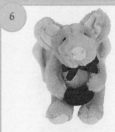

Ovid
4.5" • #5614 • OR
Issued: 1994 • Retired: 1996
Orig. Price: $7 • **Value: $35**

7

Pair O'Bears
info unavailable
Orig. Price: N/A • **Value: N/E**

8

Pair O'Bears
4.5" • #5601 • OR
Issued: pre-1990 • Retired: 1996
Orig. Price: $5 • **Value: $48**

9

Pair O'Hares
6" • #5600 • OR
Issued: 1991 • Retired: 1994
Orig. Price: $5 • **Value: $46**

10

Pair O'Hares
6" • #5602 • OR
Issued: 1990 • Retired: 1991
Orig. Price: $5 • **Value: N/E**

Ornaments

	Price Paid	Value
1.		
2.		
3.		
4.		
5.		
6.		
7.		
8.		
9.		
10.		

Totals

Value Guide — Boyds Plush Animals

1
Pair O'Highland Plaid Bears
5" • #5618-02 • OR
Issued: 1996 • Retired: 1998
Orig. Price: $4 • **Value: $12**

2
Pair O'Homespun Bears
5" • #5618 • OR
Issued: 1995 • Retired: 1996
Orig. Price: $4 • **Value: $35**

3
Pair O'Piggs
6" • #5606 • OR
Issued: 1993 • Retired: 1996
Orig. Price: $5 • **Value: $55**

4
New!
Pinkle B. Bumbles
5.5" • #56221-09 • OR
Issued: 2000 • Current
Orig. Price: $8 • **Value: $8**

5
Raggedy Twins
4.5" • #7400 • OR
Issued: 1993 • Retired: 1995
Orig. Price: $6 • **Value: $85**

6
Regulus P. Roar
5" • #56041 • OR
Issued: 1997 • Retired: 1999
Orig. Price: $6 • **Value: $12**

7
Seraphina
5" • #5615 • OR
Issued: 1994 • Retired: 1999
Orig. Price: $7 • **Value: $15**

8
Serena Goodnight
5.5" • #56232-08 • OR
Issued: 1998 • Current
Orig. Price: $7 • **Value: $7**

9
Silverton Snowbeary
5" • #56191 • OR
Issued: 1998 • Current
Orig. Price: $7 • **Value: $7**

Ornaments

	Price Paid	Value
1.		
2.		
3.		
4.		
5.		
6.		
7.		
8.		
9.		
Totals		

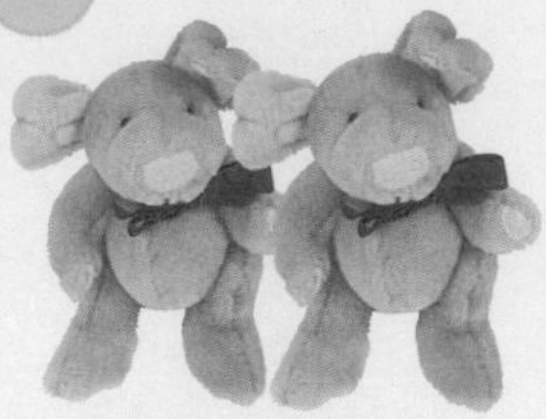

Value Guide — Boyds Plush Animals

Stardust Goodspeed
5.5" • #5624-01 • OR
Issued: 1999 • Current
Orig. Price: $7 • **Value: $7**

Stella Goodnight
5.5" • #5623-09 • OR
Issued: 1997 • Retired: 1999
Orig. Price: $7 • **Value: $18**

New!

T.F. Buzzie Wuzzie
2.5" • #595180 • TF
Issued: 2000 • Current
Orig. Price: $8 • **Value: $8**

New!

Tweedle F. Wuzzie
2.5" • #595181 • TF
Issued: 2000 • Current
Orig. Price: $8 • **Value: $8**

New!

Twiddle F. Wuzzie
2.5" • #595182 • TF
Issued: 2000 • Current
Orig. Price: $8 • **Value: $8**

Venus
4.5" • #5616 • OR
Issued: 1994 • Retired: 1996
Orig. Price: $7 • **Value: $29**

White Snowberry Bear
5" • #5619 • OR
Issued: 1995 • Retired: 1996
Orig. Price: $7 • **Value: N/E**

Willie S. Hydrant IV
5.5" • #5625 • OR
Issued: 1998 • Current
Orig. Price: $7 • **Value: $7**

New!

Winkle B. Bumbles
5.5" • #56221-06 • OR
Issued: 2000 • Current
Orig. Price: $8 • **Value: $8**

Zephyr Goodnight
5.5" • #5623-06 • OR
Issued: 1997 • Retired: 1999
Orig. Price: $7 • **Value: $12**

Ornaments

	Price Paid	Value
1.		
2.		
3.		
4.		
5.		
6.		
7.		
8.		
9.		
10.		

Totals

PINS

The *Wearable Wuzzies*, based on the *T.F. Wuzzies* collection, took the fashion world by storm with the debut of six pins in 1999 and three more in 2000. Although each is only 2" in height, each one makes a sticking impression on the hearts of collectors.

1

New!

Teedle F. Wuzzie
2" • #599911-02 • WW
Issued: 2000 • Current
Orig. Price: $6 • **Value: $6**

2

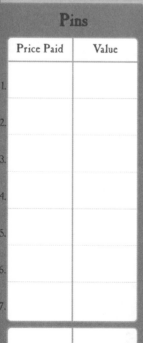

Tess F. Wuzzie
2" • #599901-06 • WW
Issued: 1999 • Current
Orig. Price: $5 • **Value: $5**

3

New!

Thistle F. Wuzzie
2" • #599912-07 • WW
Issued: 2000 • Current
Orig. Price: $6 • **Value: $6**

4

Thomas F. Wuzzie
2" • #599903-07 • WW
Issued: 1999 • Current
Orig. Price: $5 • **Value: $5**

5

New!

Tinger F. Wuzzie
2" • #599910-08 • WW
Issued: 2000 • Current
Orig. Price: $6 • **Value: $6**

6

Tinker F. Wuzzie
2" • #599900-02 • WW
Issued: 1999 • Current
Orig. Price: $6 • **Value: $6**

7

Tinsel F. Wuzzie
2" • #599900-08 • WW
Issued: 1999 • Current
Orig. Price: $6 • **Value: $6**

Pins

	Price Paid	Value
1.		
2.		
3.		
4.		
5.		
6.		
7.		
Totals		

1

Tucker F. Wuzzie
2" • #599902-08 • WW
Issued: 1999 • Current
Orig. Price: $5 • **Value: $5**

2

Twinkle F. Wuzzie
2" • #599900-01 • WW
Issued: 1999 • Current
Orig. Price: $6 • **Value: $6**

PUPPETS

The *ImagineBeary Friends* have been the talk of the town since their introduction in 1999. And they have been doing plenty of talking of their own as well! To date, three bears, one cat and one dog have been voicing their opinions and yammering up a storm!

3

Charlie P. Chatsworth
18" • #585000-08 • IF
Issued: 1999 • Current
Orig. Price: $40 • **Value: $40**

4

Fillabuster P. Chatsworth
18" • #585001-03 • IF
Issued: 1999 • Current
Orig. Price: $40 • **Value: $40**

5

New!

Howlin P. Chatsworth
18" • #585101-05 • IF
Issued: 2000 • Current
Orig. Price: $40 • **Value: $40**

6

New!

Katawalin P. Chatsworth
18" • #585200-07 • IF
Issued: 2000 • Current
Orig. Price: $40 • **Value: $40**

7

Wiley P. Chatsworth
18" • #585000-05 • IF
Issued: 1999 • Current
Orig. Price: $40 • **Value: $40**

Pins	
Price Paid	Value

Puppets	

Totals

173

TREE TOPPERS

"Ariella Angelfrost" heads this new category – and she wants to be at the head of your Christmas tree as well. The first tree topper to be produced by Boyds, Ariella makes a lovely companion not only during the holidays, but year round.

Ariella Angelfrost
10" • #744110 • TJ
Issued: 1999 • Current
Orig. Price: $15 • **Value: $15**

THE LOYAL ORDER OF FRIENDS OF BOYDS

The Loyal Order of Friends of Boyds celebrated its charter year in 1996. Since then, members have enjoyed several special benefits, including the 22 exclusive pieces that have been offered to them throughout the years.

1996

Raeburn
6" • #01996-31 • F.o.B.
Issued: 1996 • Retired: 1997
Membership Gift • **Value: $35**

Tree Toppers

Price Paid	Value
1.	

Collector's Club

2.	
3.	
4.	
5.	
6.	

Totals

174

1996

Uncle Elliot
pin • #01996-11 • F.o.B.
Issued: 1996 • Retired: 1997
Membership Gift • **Value: $26**

1996

Uncle Elliot ... The Head Bean Wants You
N/A • #01996-21 • F.o.B.
Issued: 1996 • Retired: 1997
Membership Gift • **Value: $95**

1997

Velma Q. Berriweather
11" • #01996-51 • F.o.B.
Issued: 1997 • Retired: 1997
Orig. Price: $29 • **Value: $70**

1997

Velma Q. Berriweather ... The Cookie Queen
N/A • #01996-41 • F.o.B.
Issued: 1997 • Retired: 1997
Orig. Price: $19 • **Value: $80**

1

1998

Eleanor
6" • #01998-31 • F.o.B.
Issued: 1998 • Retired: 1998
Membership Gift • **Value: N/E**

2

1998

Lady Libearty
pin • #01998-11 • F.o.B.
Issued: 1998 • Retired: 1998
Membership Gift • **Value: N/E**

3

1998

Lady Libearty
N/A • #01998-21 • F.o.B.
Issued: 1998 • Retired: 1998
Membership Gift • **Value: $45**

4

1998

Ms. Berriweather's Cottage
N/A • #01998-41 • F.o.B.
Issued: 1998 • Retired: 1998
Orig. Price: $21 • **Value: $50**

5

1998

Zelma G. Berriweather
11" • #01998-51 • F.o.B.
Issued: 1998 • Retired: 1998
Orig. Price: $32 • **Value: $60**

6

1999

Bloomin' F.o.B.
pin • #01999-11 • F.o.B.
Issued: 1999 • Retired: 1999
Membership Gift • **Value: N/E**

7

1999

Blossum B. Berriweather ...Bloom With Joy!
N/A • #01999-21 • F.o.B.
Issued: 1999 • Retired: 1999
Membership Gift • **Value: $30**

8

1999

Flora Mae Berriweather
6" • #01999-31 • F.o.B.
Issued: 1999 • Retired: 1999
Membership Gift • **Value: N/E**

9

1999

Noah's Genius At Work Table
Noah's Pageant Series
N/A • #2429 • F.o.B.
Issued: 1999 • Retired: 1999
Orig. Price: $11.50 • **Value: $50**

10

1999

Plant With Hope, Grow With Love, Bloom With Joy
6" & 6" & 6" • #01999-51 • F.o.B.
Issued: 1999 • Retired: 1999
Orig. Price: $25 • **Value: $46**

Collector's Club

	Price Paid	Value
1.		
2.		
3.		
4.		
5.		
6.		
7.		
8.		
9.		
10.		

Totals

175

1

1999

Sunny And Sally Berriweather... Plant With Hope
N/A • #01999-41 • F.o.B.
Issued: 1999 • Retired: 1999
Orig. Price: $23 • **Value: $45**

2
New!

"Brewin' F.o.B." Official Mini-Tea Set
N/A • #02000-65 • F.o.B.
Issued: 2000 • To Be Retired: 2000
Orig. Price: N/A • **Value: N/E**

3
New!

Caitlin Berriweather
pin • #02000-11 • F.o.B.
Issued: 2000 • To Be Retired: 2000
Membership Gift • **Value: N/E**

4
New!

Caitlin Berriweather
6" • #02000-31 • F.o.B.
Issued: 2000 • To Be Retired: 2000
Membership Gift • **Value: N/E**

5
New!

Catherine And Caitlin Berriweather... Fine Cup of Tea
N/A • #02000-21 • F.o.B.
Issued: 2000 • To Be Retired: 2000
Membership Gift • **Value: N/E**

6
New!

Catherine And Caitlin Berriweather With Little Scruff... Family Traditions
N/A • #02000-41 • F.o.B.
Issued: 2000 • To Be Retired: 2000
Orig. Price: $25• **Value: N/E**

7
New!

Catherine Berriweather And Little Scruff
11" & 3" • #02000-51 • F.o.B.
Issued: 2000 • To Be Retired: 2000
Orig. Price: $26 • **Value: N/E**

8
New!

Noah's Tool Box
N/A • #2434 • F.o.B.
Issued: 2000 • To Be Retired: 2000
Orig. Price: $12 • **Value: $12**

Collector's Club

	Price Paid	Value
1.		
2.		
3.		
4.		
5.		
6.		
7.		
8.		
Totals		

BOYDS PLUSH EXCLUSIVES

Several times a year, The Boyds Collection Ltd. offers exclusive pieces to select retail outlets throughout the United States and Canada. One of the largest dealers of exclusives and launches, or pieces that are produced before they are released in the regular line, is the television home shopping network QVC. Exclusives are often produced in very limited numbers and often disappear from shelves before most collectors are even aware of their existence.

EXCLUSIVE BEARS

Over the years, nearly 400 exclusive bears have marched into the collection. Like their counterparts in the regular line, these bears are immensely popular and often sell out quickly.

1

**AP Gold Bear
(LE-4,800)**
Canadian
10" • #BC94283
Issued: 1999
Value: $29.99 (Can.)

2

Aberdeen
QVC
Issued: 1994
Value: N/E

3

Abigail
Bon-Ton
Issued: 1996
Value: $50

4

Abigail
Elder-Beerman
Issued: 1998
Value: $50

5

Adkin
Frederick Atkins
10"
Issued: 1997
Value: $35

6

**Al'Berta B. Bear
(LE-10,000)**
Canadian
10" • #BC94277
Issued: 1998
Value: $42

7

Aldina
Dillard's
#94714DL
Issued: 1997
Value: $50

8

Alex Nicole
Dillard's
10" • #94743DL
Issued: 1999
Value: N/E

Bears

	Price Paid	Value
1.		
2.		
3.		
4.		
5.		
6.		
7.		
8.		
Totals		

177

Value Guide — Boyds Plush Animals

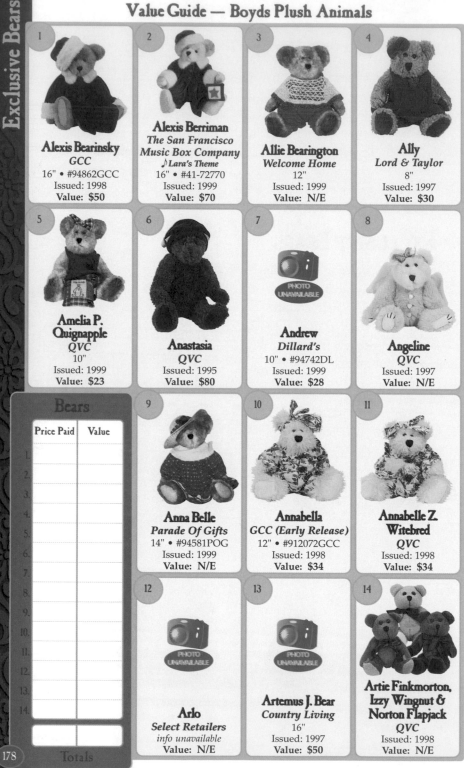

1

Alexis Bearinsky
GCC
16" • #94862GCC
Issued: 1998
Value: $50

2

Alexis Berriman
*The San Francisco
Music Box Company*
♪*Lara's Theme*
16" • #41-72770
Issued: 1999
Value: $70

3

Allie Bearington
Welcome Home
12"
Issued: 1999
Value: N/E

4

Ally
Lord & Taylor
8"
Issued: 1997
Value: $30

5

**Amelia P.
Quignapple**
QVC
10"
Issued: 1999
Value: $23

6

Anastasia
QVC
Issued: 1995
Value: $80

7

Andrew
Dillard's
10" • #94742DL
Issued: 1999
Value: $28

8

Angeline
QVC
Issued: 1997
Value: N/E

9

Anna Belle
Parade Of Gifts
14" • #94581POG
Issued: 1999
Value: N/E

10

Annabella
GCC (Early Release)
12" • #912072GCC
Issued: 1998
Value: $34

11

**Annabelle Z.
Witebred**
QVC
Issued: 1998
Value: $34

12

Arlo
Select Retailers
info unavailable
Value: N/E

13

Artemus J. Bear
Country Living
16"
Issued: 1997
Value: $50

14

**Artie Finkmorton,
Izzy Wingnut &
Norton Flapjack**
QVC
Issued: 1998
Value: N/E

Bears

	Price Paid	Value
1.		
2.		
3.		
4.		
5.		
6.		
7.		
8.		
9.		
10.		
11.		
12.		
13.		
14.		

Totals

Value Guide — Boyds Plush Animals

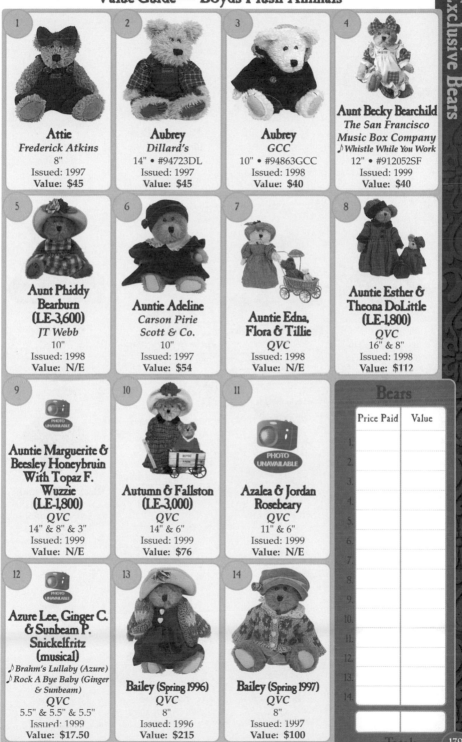

1

Attie
Frederick Atkins
8"
Issued: 1997
Value: $45

2

Aubrey
Dillard's
14" • #94723DL
Issued: 1997
Value: $45

3

Aubrey
GCC
10" • #94863GCC
Issued: 1998
Value: $40

4

Aunt Becky Bearchild
The San Francisco Music Box Company
♪ *Whistle While You Work*
12" • #912052SF
Issued: 1999
Value: $40

5

Aunt Phiddy Bearburn (LE-3,600)
JT Webb
10"
Issued: 1998
Value: N/E

6

Auntie Adeline
Carson Pirie Scott & Co.
10"
Issued: 1997
Value: $54

7

Auntie Edna, Flora & Tillie
QVC
Issued: 1998
Value: N/E

8

Auntie Esther & Theona DoLittle (LE-1,800)
QVC
16" & 8"
Issued: 1998
Value: $112

9

Auntie Marguerite & Beesley Honeybruin With Topaz F. Wuzzie (LE-1,800)
QVC
14" & 8" & 3"
Issued: 1999
Value: N/E

10

Autumn & Fallston (LE-3,000)
QVC
14" & 6"
Issued: 1999
Value: $76

11

Azalea & Jordan Rosebeary
QVC
11" & 6"
Issued: 1999
Value: N/E

12

Azure Lee, Ginger C. & Sunbeam P. Snickelfritz (musical)
♪ *Brahm's Lullaby (Azure)*
♪ *Rock A Bye Baby (Ginger & Sunbeam)*
QVC
5.5" & 5.5" & 5.5"
Issued: 1999
Value: $17.50

13

Bailey (Spring 1996)
QVC
8"
Issued: 1996
Value: $215

14

Bailey (Spring 1997)
QVC
8"
Issued: 1997
Value: $100

Bears

	Price Paid	Value
1.		
2.		
3.		
4.		
5.		
6.		
7.		
8.		
9.		
10.		
11.		
12.		
13.		
14.		
Totals		

179

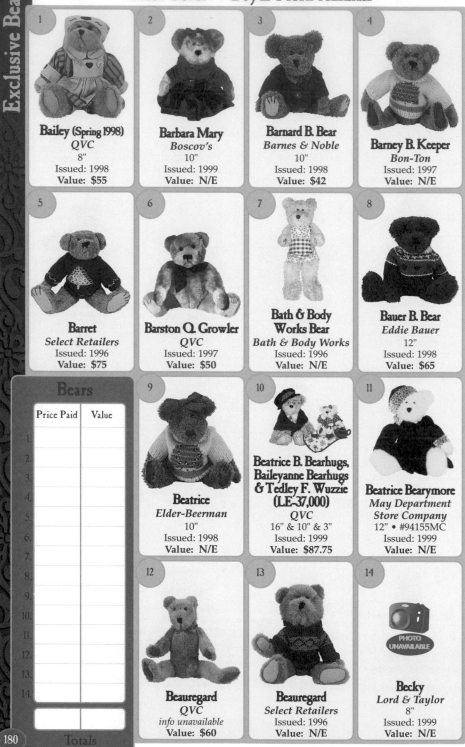

Exclusive Bears

1
Bailey (Spring 1998)
QVC
8"
Issued: 1998
Value: $55

2
Barbara Mary
Boscov's
10"
Issued: 1999
Value: N/E

3
Barnard B. Bear
Barnes & Noble
10"
Issued: 1998
Value: $42

4
Barney B. Keeper
Bon-Ton
Issued: 1997
Value: N/E

5
Barret
Select Retailers
Issued: 1996
Value: $75

6
Barston Q. Growler
QVC
Issued: 1997
Value: $50

7
**Bath & Body
Works Bear**
Bath & Body Works
Issued: 1996
Value: N/E

8
Bauer B. Bear
Eddie Bauer
12"
Issued: 1998
Value: $65

9
Beatrice
Elder-Beerman
10"
Issued: 1998
Value: N/E

10
**Beatrice B. Bearhugs,
Baileyanne Bearhugs
& Tedley F. Wuzzie
(LE-37,000)**
QVC
16" & 10" & 3"
Issued: 1999
Value: $87.75

11
Beatrice Bearymore
*May Department
Store Company*
12" • #94155MC
Issued: 1999
Value: N/E

12
Beauregard
QVC
info unavailable
Value: $60

13
Beauregard
Select Retailers
Issued: 1996
Value: N/E

14
Becky
Lord & Taylor
8"
Issued: 1999
Value: N/E

Bears		
	Price Paid	Value
1.		
2.		
3.		
4.		
5.		
6.		
7.		
8.		
9.		
10.		
11.		
12.		
13.		
14.		
Totals		

Value Guide — Boyds Plush Animals

1

Beezer B. Goodlebear
QVC
16"
Issued: 1999
Value: N/E

2

Belk Bear
Belk
Issued: 1997
Value: N/E

3

Benjamin Beanbeary
Belk
8"
Issued: 1998
Value: N/E

4

Benjamin Bear
*The San Francisco
Music Box Company*
♪ *Let Me Be Your Teddy Bear*
12" • #41-72142
Issued: 1998
Value: $40

5

Bernice B. Bear
Barnes & Noble
10"
Issued: 1999
Value: N/E

6

Berret
Select Retailers
8"
Issued: 1996
Value: N/E

7

Betty Lou
QVC
Issued: 1996
Value: $320

8

Bill
QVC
Issued: 1995
Value: N/E

9

Bingham
QVC
22"
Issued: 1998
Value: N/E

10

Blackstone
QVC
Issued: 1997
Value: $24

11

Boo Bear
Marshall Field's
Issued: 1994
Value: N/E

12

Boo B. Bear
QVC
Issued: 1997
Value: N/E

13

Boo-Boo
Select Retailers
Issued: 1998
Value: $32

14

Bosley & Chadwick
QVC
Issued: 1997
Value: N/E

Bears

	Price Paid	Value
1.		
2.		
3.		
4.		
5.		
6.		
7.		
8.		
9.		
10.		
11.		
12.		
13.		
14.		
Totals		

181

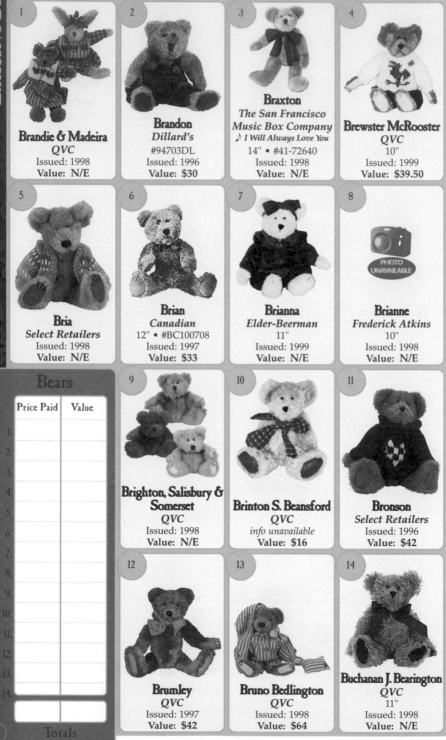

1

Brandie & Madeira
QVC
Issued: 1998
Value: N/E

2

Brandon
Dillard's
#94703DL
Issued: 1996
Value: $30

3

Braxton
*The San Francisco
Music Box Company*
♪ *I Will Always Love You*
14" • #41-72640
Issued: 1998
Value: N/E

4

Brewster McRooster
QVC
10"
Issued: 1999
Value: $39.50

5

Bria
Select Retailers
Issued: 1998
Value: N/E

6

Brian
Canadian
12" • #BC100708
Issued: 1997
Value: $33

7

Brianna
Elder-Beerman
11"
Issued: 1999
Value: N/E

8

PHOTO UNAVAILABLE

Brianne
Frederick Atkins
10"
Issued: 1998
Value: N/E

9

**Brighton, Salisbury &
Somerset**
QVC
Issued: 1998
Value: N/E

10

Brinton S. Beansford
QVC
info unavailable
Value: $16

11

Bronson
Select Retailers
Issued: 1996
Value: $42

12

Brumley
QVC
Issued: 1997
Value: $42

13

Bruno Bedlington
QVC
Issued: 1998
Value: $64

14

Buchanan J. Bearington
QVC
11"
Issued: 1998
Value: N/E

Bears

	Price Paid	Value
1.		
2.		
3.		
4.		
5.		
6.		
7.		
8.		
9.		
10.		
11.		
12.		
13.		
14.		
Totals		

Value Guide — Boyds Plush Animals

1

Buckles
Lord & Taylor
Issued: 1997
Value: N/E

2

Buffy
Victoria's Secret
Issued: 1996
Value: $43

3

Buford B.
QVC
Issued: 1997
Value: $58

4

Bunker Bedlington
GCC
8" • #94869GCC
Issued: 1999
Value: N/E

5

Burgess P. Bear
QVC
15"
info unavailable
Value: N/E

6

Burt
Select Retailers
info unavailable
Value: N/E

7

C. Elbert
Dillard's
17" • #94720DL
Issued: 1997
Value: $54

8

C.C. Goodbear
Country Clutter
10"
Issued: 1999
Value: N/E

9

Caledonia, Humboldt & Shasta
QVC
Issued: 1998
Value: N/E

10

Carlie
Proffitt's
12"
Issued: 1999
Value: N/E

11

Caroline
QVC
Issued: 1996
Value: $52

12

Casimir B. Bean
GCC
#94858GCC
Issued: 1998
Value: $38

13

Cass
Select Retailers
Issued: 1998
Value: N/E

14

Cassidy
QVC
Issued: 1997
Value: $80

Bears

	Price Paid	Value
1.		
2.		
3.		
4.		
5.		
6.		
7.		
8.		
9.		
10.		
11.		
12.		
13.		
14.		
Totals		

1
Ceylon Pekoe
QVC
Issued: 1997
Value: $60

2
Chamomille
The San Francisco Music Box Company
♪ *A Dream Is A Wish Your Heart Makes*
11" • #41-72645
Issued: 1998
Value: N/E

3
Chandler
Select Retailers
8"
Issued: 1997
Value: $35

4
Charlotte Tewksbeary With Hobbes
QVC
16" & 5"
Issued: 1999
Value: $47

5
Christian
Dillard's
12" • #94744DL
Issued: 1999
Value: $35

6
Christmas Bear
QVC
Issued: 1995
Value: $190

7
Cimmaron
QVC
Issued: 1997
Value: N/E

8
Clara
Bon-Ton
14"
Issued: 1996
Value: $45

9
Clara
Kirlin's
Issued: 1996
Value: $45

10
Clarissa
The San Francisco Music Box Company
♪ *Make Someone Happy*
15" • #41-72584
Issued: 1998
Value: $50

11
Clark
QVC
10"
Issued: 1998
Value: $35

12
Claudette
Country Gift
info unavailable
Value: N/E

13
Claudius B. Bean
Lord & Taylor
14"
Issued: 1998
Value: $50

14
Claudius B. Bean
QVC
Issued: 1997
Value: N/E

Bears

	Price Paid	Value
1.		
2.		
3.		
4.		
5.		
6.		
7.		
8.		
9.		
10.		
11.		
12.		
13.		
14.		
Totals		

Value Guide — Boyds Plush Animals

1

Clementine
Elder-Beerman
14"
Issued: 1997
Value: $50

2

Colleen
QVC
info unavailable
Value: N/E

3

Collette
Select Retailers
Issued: 1997
Value: N/E

4

Corliss & Quincy
QVC
8" & 8"
Issued: 1998
Value: $20

5

PHOTO UNAVAILABLE

Cosmos
Elder-Beerman
Issued: 1998
Value: N/E

6

Courtney
QVC
16"
Issued: 1998
Value: $50

7

Cranston
GCC
8.25" • #94855GCC
Issued: 1997
Value: $37

8

Cromwell
QVC
Issued: 1997
Value: $74

9

Cynthia Berrijam
QVC
16"
Issued: 1999
Value: $32

10

Danielle & Elizabieta de Bearvoire
QVC
Issued: 1997
Value: N/E

11

Daphne
Elder-Beerman
10" • #8155914EB
Issued: 1999
Value: N/E

12

Darbey & Daniel Bearimore
QVC
8" & 8"
Issued: 1999
Value: $30

13

Darby
Select Retailers
Issued: 1997
Value: N/E

14

Daria & Dickens
QVC
8" & 8"
Issued: 1998
Value: $60

Bears		
	Price Paid	Value
1.		
2.		
3.		
4.		
5.		
6.		
7.		
8.		
9.		
10.		
11.		
12.		
13.		
14.		
Totals		

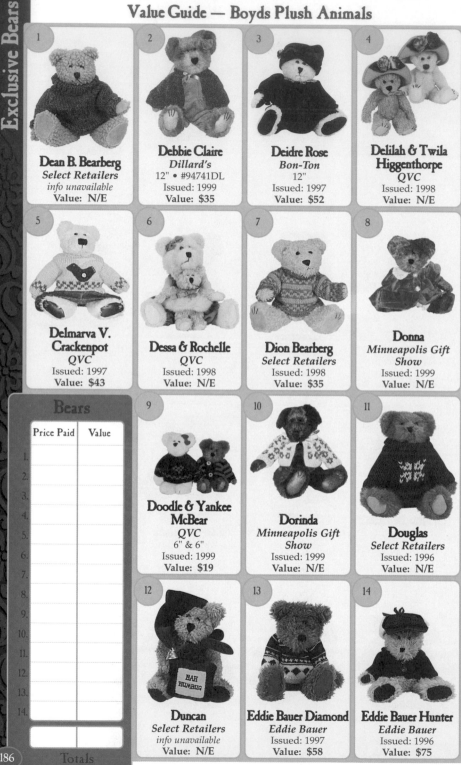

Exclusive Bears

1

Dean B. Bearberg
Select Retailers
info unavailable
Value: N/E

2

Debbie Claire
Dillard's
12" • #94741DL
Issued: 1999
Value: $35

3

Deidre Rose
Bon-Ton
12"
Issued: 1997
Value: $52

4

Delilah & Twila Higgenthorpe
QVC
Issued: 1998
Value: N/E

5

Delmarva V. Crackenpot
QVC
Issued: 1997
Value: $43

6

Dessa & Rochelle
QVC
Issued: 1998
Value: N/E

7

Dion Bearberg
Select Retailers
Issued: 1998
Value: $35

8

Donna
Minneapolis Gift Show
Issued: 1999
Value: N/E

9

Doodle & Yankee McBear
QVC
6" & 6"
Issued: 1999
Value: $19

10

Dorinda
Minneapolis Gift Show
Issued: 1999
Value: N/E

11

Douglas
Select Retailers
Issued: 1996
Value: N/E

12

Duncan
Select Retailers
info unavailable
Value: N/E

13

Eddie Bauer Diamond
Eddie Bauer
Issued: 1997
Value: $58

14

Eddie Bauer Hunter
Eddie Bauer
Issued: 1996
Value: $75

Bears

	Price Paid	Value
1.		
2.		
3.		
4.		
5.		
6.		
7.		
8.		
9.		
10.		
11.		
12.		
13.		
14.		
Totals		

Value Guide — Boyds Plush Animals

1

Edmund
Eddie Bauer
Issued: 1994
Value: N/E

2

Edward Q. Bearstone & Apopka
GCC
16" • #94874GCC
Issued: 1999
Value: N/E

3

Edwin R. Elfstein
Lord & Taylor
Issued: 1996
Value: N/E

4

Effie May
Bon-Ton
12"
Issued: 1998
Value: $54

5

Elisia P. Bearypoppin, Darrell & Ross
QVC
Issued: 1997
Value: $160

6

Ella
Dillard's
8" • #94724DL
Issued: 1997
Value: $40

7

Elliot
Select Retailers
info unavailable
Value: N/E

8

Elmore Elf Bear
QVC
Issued: 1996
Value: $36

9

Elsbeth
Dillard's
#94704DL
Issued: 1996
Value: N/E

10

Elton
QVC
Issued: 1996
Value: $77

11

Emily Claire
Welcome Home
Issued: 1998
Value: $50

12

Emily E. Dobbs
Coach House Gifts
10"
Issued: 1999
Value: N/E

13

Emma
Elder-Beerman
Issued: 1998
Value: $48

14

Englebert Q. Elfberg
GCC
10" • #94857GCC
Issued: 1998
Value: $36

Bears

	Price Paid	Value
1.		
2.		
3.		
4.		
5.		
6.		
7.		
8.		
9.		
10.		
11.		
12.		
13.		
14.		
Totals		

Value Guide — Boyds Plush Animals

1

Erin
Lord & Taylor
Issued: 1997
Value: $33

2

PHOTO UNAVAILABLE

Eugenia
Dillard's
Issued: 1997
Value: $75

3

Eugenia
The San Francisco Music Box Company
♪ *Can't Help Falling In Love*
16" • #56-66601
Issued: 1997
Value: N/E

4

Evan & Sheldon Bearchild
QVC
5.5" & 5.5"
Issued: 1998
Value: N/E

5

PHOTO UNAVAILABLE

Eve
Select Retailers
info unavailable
Value: N/E

6

Ewell Manitoba Mooselman (LE-2,400)
Canadian
#BC94275
Issued: 1997
Value: $62

7

Father Kristmas Bear & Northwind P. Bear
QVC
16" & 8"
Issued: 1999
Value: $43

8

Felicity
Lord & Taylor
Issued: 1997
Value: $20

9

PHOTO UNAVAILABLE

Fidelity
QVC
17"
Issued: 1999
Value: $23

10

Fidelity
The San Francisco Music Box Company
♪ *Love Will Keep Us Together*
17" • #41-72638
Issued: 1998
Value: N/E

11

Fillmore
QVC
Issued: 1998
Value: N/E

12

PHOTO UNAVAILABLE

Florence B. Bearhugs
QVC
12"
Issued: 1999
Value: $26

13

PHOTO UNAVAILABLE

Foodle, Bunky & Nat
QVC
10" & 10" & 10"
Issued: 1999
Value: $17.50

14

PHOTO UNAVAILABLE

Forrest B. Bruin
QVC
11"
Issued: 1999
Value: $16

Bears

	Price Paid	Value
1.		
2.		
3.		
4.		
5.		
6.		
7.		
8.		
9.		
10.		
11.		
12.		
13.		
14.		
Totals		

Value Guide — Boyds Plush Animals

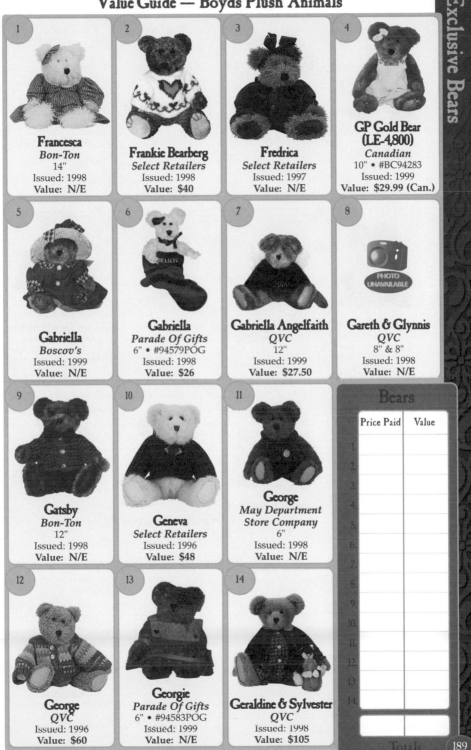

1

Francesca
Bon-Ton
14"
Issued: 1998
Value: N/E

2

Frankie Bearberg
Select Retailers
Issued: 1998
Value: $40

3

Fredrica
Select Retailers
Issued: 1997
Value: N/E

4

GP Gold Bear (LE-4,800)
Canadian
10" • #BC94283
Issued: 1999
Value: $29.99 (Can.)

5

Gabriella
Boscov's
Issued: 1999
Value: N/E

6

Gabriella
Parade Of Gifts
6" • #94579POG
Issued: 1998
Value: $26

7

Gabriella Angelfaith
QVC
12"
Issued: 1999
Value: $27.50

8

PHOTO UNAVAILABLE

Gareth & Glynnis
QVC
8" & 8"
Issued: 1998
Value: N/E

9

Gatsby
Bon-Ton
12"
Issued: 1998
Value: N/E

10

Geneva
Select Retailers
Issued: 1996
Value: $48

11

George
May Department Store Company
6"
Issued: 1998
Value: N/E

12

George
QVC
Issued: 1996
Value: $60

13

Georgie
Parade Of Gifts
6" • #94583POG
Issued: 1999
Value: N/E

14

Geraldine & Sylvester
QVC
Issued: 1998
Value: $105

Bears

	Price Paid	Value
1.		
2.		
3.		
4.		
5.		
6.		
7.		
8.		
9.		
10.		
11.		
12.		
13.		
14.		

Totals

Value Guide — Boyds Plush Animals

1
Getty Bearberg
Select Retailers
Issued: 1999
Value: N/E

2
Gideon
QVC
10"
Issued: 1998
Value: N/E

3
Glenna
Dillard's
7" • #94721DL
Issued: 1997
Value: $60

4
Gloria
QVC
14"
Issued: 1999
Value: N/E

5
Gomez
Select Retailers
10"
Issued: 1999
Value: N/E

6
Gourdie Frightmare
Select Retailers
8"
Issued: 1999
Value: N/E

7
Gracie
Dillard's
6"
Issued: 1999
Value: N/E

8
Gracie
May Department Store Company
6"
Issued: 1998
Value: N/E

9
Grandma Henrietta & Lizzie
QVC
Issued: 1997
Value: $128

10
Grant S. Bearington
Norm Thompson
Issued: 1997
Value: $76

11
Guilford
GCC
6" • #94852GCC
Issued: 1997
Value: $40

12
Guinella
Ideation
11"
Issued: 1999
Value: N/E

13
Guinevere
Lord & Taylor
Issued: 1996
Value: N/E

14
Guinevere
QVC
11"
Issued: 1997
Value: N/E

Bears

	Price Paid	Value
1.		
2.		
3.		
4.		
5.		
6.		
7.		
8.		
9.		
10.		
11.		
12.		
13.		
14.		
Totals		

Value Guide — Boyds Plush Animals

1

Guinevere
*The San Francisco
Music Box Company*
♪ *La Vie En Rose*
11" • #41-72139
Issued: 1998
Value: N/E

2

Gunnar
Select Retailers
info unavailable
Value: N/E

3

Gunter
Dillard's
10" • #94722DL
Issued: 1997
Value: $32

4

Guthrie P. Mussy
QVC
Issued: 1997
Value: N/E

5

Gwennora
QVC
11"
Issued: 1999
Value: $18

6

Hannah
Elder-Beerman
8" • #8242437EB
Issued: 1999
Value: N/E

7

Harry
Lord & Taylor
8"
Issued: 1997
Value: N/E

8

**Hayes R. Bearrington
(LE-2,000)**
*The San Francisco
Music Box Company*
♪ *What A Feeling*
15" • #41-72766
Issued: 1999
Value: $125

9

Heathcliff
QVC
Issued: 1997
Value: N/E

10

Hedda
QVC
Issued: 1996
Value: $85

11

**Heidi & Bethany
Thistlebeary**
QVC
9" & 6"
Issued: 1999
Value: N/E

12

Henry
Dillard's
14" • #94726DL
Issued: 1997
Value: $54

13

Henry Bearymore
*May Department
Store Company*
14" • #94156MC
Issued: 1999
Value: N/E

14

Heywood Barlinski
Bon-Ton
14"
Issued: 1999
Value: N/E

Bears

	Price Paid	Value
1.		
2.		
3.		
4.		
5.		
6.		
7.		
8.		
9.		
10.		
11.		
12.		
13.		
14.		
Totals		

Exclusive Bears

1

Holly
Lord & Taylor
8"
Issued: 1999
Value: N/E

2

Holly Bearberry
QVC
Issued: 1996
Value: $56

3

PHOTO UNAVAILABLE

Honey B. Bear
Spiegel
Issued: 1994
Value: N/E

4

Honey B. Elfberg
Parade Of Gifts
14" • #94578POG
Issued: 1998
Value: $38

5

Honey B. Growin
Parade Of Gifts
14"
Issued: 1999
Value: N/E

6

Honey B. Mine
Parade Of Gifts
14" • #94576POG
Issued: 1998
Value: $33

7

PHOTO UNAVAILABLE

Honey Bee Bear
*Faith Mountain
Company*
Issued: 1995
Value: N/E

8

Honeybunch & Uncle Gus
(sold as set with "Uncle
Gus & Gary ... The
Gift" resin piece)
QVC
13" & 6.5" & 4.75"
Issued: 1997
Value: N/E

Bears

	Price Paid	Value
1.		
2.		
3.		
4.		
5.		
6.		
7.		
8.		
9.		
10.		
11.		
12.		
13.		
14.		

Totals

9

Hubbard
QVC
Issued: 1996
Value: $60

10

Huett
QVC
Issued: 1997
Value: N/E

11

Huntley
QVC
Issued: 1997
Value: N/E

12

Ike D. Bearington
QVC
14"
Issued: 1998
Value: N/E

13

Indigo Jones
QVC
Issued: 1997
Value: $80

14

**Ingrid & Tasha
Norbruin With
Toggle F. Wuzzie
(LE-2,400)**
QVC
16" & 8" & 3"
Issued: 1999
Value: $68.50

Value Guide — Boyds Plush Animals

1
Ingrid S. Witebred
GCC
8" • #94871GCC
Issued: 1999
Value: N/E

2
Isabella
Bon-Ton
16" • #945608BT
Issued: 1999
Value: N/E

3
JC Penney Bear
JC Penney
info unavailable
Value: N/E

4
J.C. Von Fuzzner
JC Penney
14" • #773/6271/01
Issued: 1999
Value: N/E

5
J.T. Jordan
Welcome Home
Issued: 1997
Value: $50

6
Jackson
*May Department
Store Company*
Issued: 1998
Value: N/E

7
**Jacqueline K.
Bearington**
QVC
Issued: 1998
Value: $175

8
Jaime Lisa
Dillard's
Issued: 1998
Value: $68

9
Jake
Dillard's
8"
Issued: 1998
Value: N/E

10
James & Malachi
QVC
Issued: 1998
Value: $62

11
PHOTO
UNAVAILABLE
**Jameson J., Deacon T.
& Cameron G.
Bearsford**
QVC
6" & 6" & 6"
Issued: 1999
Value: $22

12
Jan B. Bearberg
Select Retailers
Issued: 1998
Value: N/E

13
Jarvis Boydsenberry
QVC
16"
Issued: 1998
Value: $75

14
Jean
Canadian
14" • #BC100905
Issued: 1997
Value: N/E

Bears	Price Paid	Value
1.		
2.		
3.		
4.		
5.		
6.		
7.		
8.		
9.		
10.		
11.		
12.		
13.		
14.		
Totals		

Exclusive Bears

1
Jeremiah
Country Living
Issued: 1997
Value: N/E

2
Jeremy
Dillard's
14" • #94712DL
Issued: 1997
Value: $45

3
Jesse
Lord & Taylor
8"
Issued: 1999
Value: N/E

4
Jillian
Dillard's
16"
Issued: 1998
Value: N/E

5
Jobie & Kibby Bearington
QVC
Issued: 1998
Value: N/E

6
Jocelyn Thistlebeary & Carson T. Bibbly
QVC
16" & 6"
Issued: 1999
Value: $42

7
Joe
Canadian
10" • #BC100508
Issued: 1997
Value: $40

8
John
Canadian
10" • #BC100505
Issued: 1997
Value: $45

Bears

	Price Paid	Value
1.		
2.		
3.		
4.		
5.		
6.		
7.		
8.		
9.		
10.		
11.		
12.		
13.		
Totals		

9
John William
QVC
Issued: 1997
Value: N/E

10
Jolee
May Department Store Company
Issued: 1998
Value: N/E

11
Joyelle
Ideation
Issued: 1998
Value: N/E

12
Julia
Dillard's
14" • #94719DL
Issued: 1997
Value: $63

13
Julian
Dillard's
info unavailable
Value: N/E

Value Guide — Boyds Plush Animals

1
Jupiter
QVC
Issued: 1996
Value: $33

2
PHOTO UNAVAILABLE
Justin
Dillard's
11" • #5106-11DL
Issued: 1997
Value: $32

3
Justina & Matthew
QVC
Issued: 1997
Value: $160

4
Karl Von Fuzzner
QVC
10"
Issued: 1998
Value: N/E

5
Kassandra Berrywinkle
QVC
12"
Issued: 1997
Value: $60

6
Kaufmann Bear
Kaufmann's
info unavailable
Value: N/E

7
Kayla Mulbeary & Krista Blubeary
QVC
6" & 6"
Issued: 1999
Value: $23

8
Kelby
Frederick Atkins
14"
Issued: 1998
Value: N/E

9
Kelsey
Dillard's
12" • #94747DL
Issued: 1999
Value: $35

10
PHOTO UNAVAILABLE
Kinsey Snoopstein (set/2)
QVC
6" & 6"
Issued: 1999
Value: $17

11
Klaus Von Fuzzner
The San Francisco Music Box Company
♪ *Let It Snow*
13" • #41-72764
Issued: 1999
Value: $50

12
PHOTO UNAVAILABLE
Knut C. Berriman
QVC
8"
Issued: 1998
Value: N/E

13
PHOTO UNAVAILABLE
Kris
Lord & Taylor
5"
Issued: 1997
Value: N/E

14
PHOTO UNAVAILABLE
Kristen
Proffitt's
6"
Issued: 1999
Value: N/E

Bears

	Price Paid	Value
1.		
2.		
3.		
4.		
5.		
6.		
7.		
8.		
9.		
10.		
11.		
12.		
13.		
14.		

Totals

Value Guide — Boyds Plush Animals

Exclusive Bears

1. Kristoff
QVC
12"
Issued: 1998
Value: N/E

2. Kyle
Select Retailers
Issued: 1998
Value: $28

3. Labelle
Ideation
8.25"
Issued: 1997
Value: N/E

4. Lara
QVC
Issued: 1997
Value: $140

5. Laura Ann
Dillard's
14"
Issued: 1998
Value: $47

6. Laura E. Bearburn (LE-5,000)
JT Webb
8"
Issued: 1997
Value: $47

7. Leo Bruinski
QVC
info unavailable
Value: N/E

8. Leon
Lord & Taylor
info unavailable
Value: N/E

9. Leonardo B. Hartbreak
QVC
12"
Issued: 1999
Value: N/E

10. Lester
Canadian
12" • #BC100705
Issued: 1997
Value: N/E

11. Letitia T. Bearington
GCC
10" • #94879GCC
Issued: 1999
Value: N/E

12. Lewis
QVC
Issued: 1998
Value: N/E

13. Lindsey
Belk
Issued: 1997
Value: N/E

14. Lindy & Nell Bradbeary
QVC
14" & 6"
Issued: 1999
Value: $68

Bears	Price Paid	Value
1.		
2.		
3.		
4.		
5.		
6.		
7.		
8.		
9.		
10.		
11.		
12.		
13.		
14.		
Totals		

196

Value Guide — Boyds Plush Animals

1
Linsey McKenzie
QVC
Issued: 1997
Value: $50

2
Little Larson
Ideation
Issued: 1997
Value: N/E

3
Liza Mae & Alex
QVC
Issued: 1998
Value: $125

4
Lizzie McBee
QVC
Issued: 1998
Value: $40

5
Logan
QVC
Issued: 1997
Value: $52

6
Lone Star
Dillard's (Texas)
#94707DL
Issued: 1996
Value: $59

7
Lucinda D. Bearsley
QVC
10"
Issued: 1998
Value: N/E

8
Lucy
Gottschalk's
12"
Issued: 1999
Value: N/E

9
Lucy Bea LeBruin
QVC
Issued: 1997
Value: N/E

10
**Ludmilla Berriman &
Ludwig Von Fuzzner
(LE-2,400)**
QVC
14" & 8"
Issued: 1998
Value: $100

11
Madeline
Elder-Beerman
8"
Issued: 1998
Value: N/E

12
Madison
Select Retailers
Issued: 1996
Value: N/E

13
Magdalena
Frederick Atkins
6"
Issued: 1998
Value: N/E

14
Mallory Witebruin
GCC
14" • #94866GCC
Issued: 1999
Value: N/E

	Price Paid	Value
1.		
2.		
3.		
4.		
5.		
6.		
7.		
8.		
9.		
10.		
11.		
12.		
13.		
14.		
Totals		

Bears

Exclusive Bears

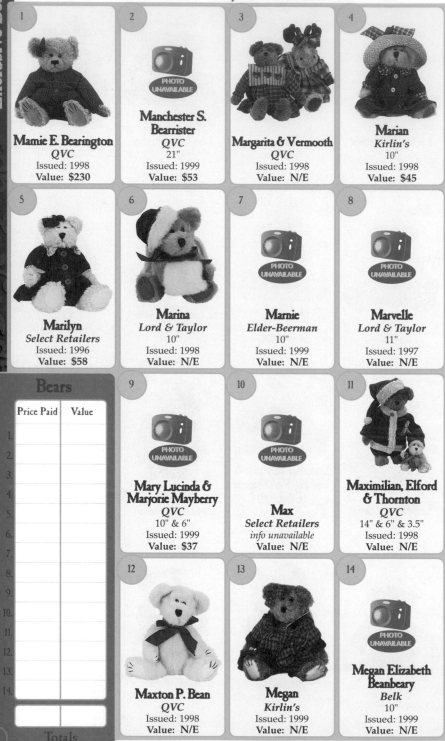

1

Mamie E. Bearington
QVC
Issued: 1998
Value: $230

2

Manchester S.
Bearrister
QVC
21"
Issued: 1999
Value: $53

3

Margarita & Vermooth
QVC
Issued: 1998
Value: N/E

4

Marian
Kirlin's
10"
Issued: 1998
Value: $45

5

Marilyn
Select Retailers
Issued: 1996
Value: $58

6

Marina
Lord & Taylor
10"
Issued: 1998
Value: N/E

7

Marnie
Elder-Beerman
10"
Issued: 1999
Value: N/E

8

Marvelle
Lord & Taylor
11"
Issued: 1997
Value: N/E

Bears

	Price Paid	Value
1.		
2.		
3.		
4.		
5.		
6.		
7.		
8.		
9.		
10.		
11.		
12.		
13.		
14.		

Totals

9

Mary Lucinda &
Marjorie Mayberry
QVC
10" & 6"
Issued: 1999
Value: $37

10

Max
Select Retailers
info unavailable
Value: N/E

11

Maximilian, Elford
& Thornton
QVC
14" & 6" & 3.5"
Issued: 1998
Value: N/E

12

Maxton P. Bean
QVC
Issued: 1998
Value: N/E

13

Megan
Kirlin's
Issued: 1999
Value: N/E

14

Megan Elizabeth
Beanbeary
Belk
10"
Issued: 1999
Value: N/E

Value Guide — Boyds Plush Animals

1
Melanie Lockley & Sam F. Wuzzie
QVC
13" & 3"
Issued: 1999
Value: $32

2
Michael
Dillard's
14" • #94717DL
Issued: 1997
Value: $40

3
Michaela
Dillard's
10" • #94718DL
Issued: 1997
Value: $40

4
Mindy Witebruin
GCC
6" • #94867GCC
Issued: 1999
Value: N/E

5
Miss Isabelle Q. Bearworthy
QVC
10"
Issued: 1998
Value: N/E

6
Miss MacIntosh & Sarabeth With Topsey (LE-3,000)
QVC
16" & 8" & 2.5"
Issued: 1999
Value: $63

7
Mohair Classic Pooh (LE-600)
Disney Gallery Stores
12"
Issued: 1999
Value: N/E

8
Mohair Santa Pooh (LE-600)
Disney Gallery Stores
12"
Issued: 1999
Value: N/E

9
Momma Bear, Allouetta & Victor (LE-1,800)
QVC
Issued: 1997
Value: $120

10
Momma Berrywinkle & Woodrow (LE-2,400)
QVC
12"
Issued: 1998
Value: $120

11
Momma McBear & Cedric
QVC
Issued: 1997
Value: $65

12
Momma McBear & Delmar
The San Francisco Music Box Company
♪ *You're Nobody 'til Somebody Loves You*
10" & 6" • #41-72585
Issued: 1998
Value: N/E

13
Momma McGoldberg & Cissy
GCC
10" • #94856GCC
Issued: 1998
Value: $43

14
Monica
Frederick Atkins
10"
Issued: 1998
Value: $32

Bears

	Price Paid	Value
1.		
2.		
3.		
4.		
5.		
6.		
7.		
8.		
9.		
10.		
11.		
12.		
13.		
14.		

Totals

Exclusive Bears

1
Mother Bearston & Bluebell
QVC
Issued: 1998
Value: $55

2
PHOTO UNAVAILABLE
Mr. Barnum
GCC
14" • #94872GCC
Issued: 1999
Value: N/E

3
Mr. BoJingles
Select Retailers
Issued: 1997
Value: N/E

4
PHOTO UNAVAILABLE
Mr. Miles & Miss Mabel Bearister
QVC
8" & 8"
Issued: 1999
Value: $30

5
Mr. Peepers
QVC
10"
Issued: 1999
Value: N/E

6
Mrs. Beariwell
GCC
10" • #94877GCC
Issued: 1999
Value: $24

7
Mrs. Bradley
Linda Anderson's Collectibles
10" • #11-0320
Issued: 1998
Value: $25

8
Mrs. Potter & Amadeus (LE-1,200)
QVC
Issued: 1997
Value: $150

Bears

	Price Paid	Value
1.		
2.		
3.		
4.		
5.		
6.		
7.		
8.		
9.		
10.		
11.		
12.		
13.		
14.		

Totals

9
Mrs. Trumbull
The San Francisco Music Box Company
♪ *Puttin' on the Ritz*
11" • #41-72769
Issued: 1999
Value: $40

10
Ms. Odetta & Neville
QVC
Issued: 1996
Value: $180

11
Nadia
Kirlin's
10"
Issued: 1998
Value: $52

12
Nadia Berriman
QVC
10"
Issued: 1998
Value: N/E

13
PHOTO UNAVAILABLE
Nancy D. Bearington
QVC
16"
Issued: 1999
Value: $121

14
PHOTO UNAVAILABLE
Nettie
QVC
Issued: 1994
Value: N/E

Value Guide — Boyds Plush Animals

1
**Niagra
(LE-3,600)**
Centre Gift Shoppe
Issued: 1999
Value: N/E

2
Nichley
Dillard's
Issued: 1998
Value: $32

3
**Nicholas, Ansel
& Fitzgerald**
QVC
Issued: 1996
Value: $162

4
**Nicholas Bearington
& Tinker F. Wuzzie**
QVC
4.5" & 2"
Issued: 1999
Value: $15.50

5
Nicholas & Nikki II
Select Retailers
info unavailable
Value: N/E

6
Nickleby S. Claus
QVC
16"
Issued: 1999
Value: N/E

7
Nicole
Dillard's
8"
Issued: 1998
Value: N/E

8
**Nicole & Amy
Berriman With
Tassle F. Wuzzie
(LE-3,000)**
QVC
16" & 8" & 3"
Issued: 1999
Value: $66

9
Nicole de la El-bee
Elder-Beerman
14"
Issued: 1997
Value: $49

10
Niklas (LE-1,800)
QVC
Issued: 1997
Value: $160

11
Noelle
Ethel M Chocolates
6"
Issued: 1998
Value: N/E

12
Olas & Omar
QVC
Issued: 1997
Value: N/E

13
Oliver
Dillard's
#94701DI.
Issued: 1996
Value: N/E

14
Oliver
GCC
#94850GCC
Issued: 1997
Value: $40

Bears		
	Price Paid	Value
1.		
2.		
3.		
4.		
5.		
6.		
7.		
8.		
9.		
10.		
11.		
12.		
13.		
14.		
Totals		

1

Olivia Q. Witebred
QVC
Issued: 1997
Value: N/E

2

Ophelia W. Witebred
QVC
Issued: 1997
Value: $60

3

PHOTO UNAVAILABLE

Oppie
Select Retailers
Value: N/E

4

Orabella Fitzbruin
QVC
Issued: 1997
Value: N/E

5

Orella Berrywinkle
QVC
Issued: 1997
Value: N/E

6

Orianna
Welcome Home
16"
Issued: 1997
Value: N/E

7

Ottilie Wilhemina
GCC
#94860GCC
Issued: 1998
Value: $40

8

PJ
Lord & Taylor
8"
Issued: 1998
Value: N/E

Bears

	Price Paid	Value
1.		
2.		
3.		
4.		
5.		
6.		
7.		
8.		
9.		
10.		
11.		
12.		
13.		
14.		

Totals

9

P.J. Bearsdale & Tink F. Wuzzie
QVC
7" & 2"
Issued: 1999
Value: $27

10

Pansy
QVC
Issued: 1995
Value: $290

11

Pee Wee
QVC
Issued: 1997
Value: N/E

12

Peyton
Frederick Atkins
14"
Issued: 1999
Value: N/E

13

Pierre
Canadian
14" • #BC100908
Issued: 1997
Value: $37

14

Prudence Bearimore
The San Francisco Music Box Company
♪ Oh, What A Beautiful Morning!
12" • #41-72765
Issued: 1999
Value: $45

Value Guide — Boyds Plush Animals

1

Puff & Poof Fuzzibutt
QVC
10" & 8"
Issued: 1999
Value: $25

2

Putnam & Kent
QVC
Issued: 1997
Value: $55

3

Quinn
Frederick Atkins
16"
Issued: 1999
Value: N/E

4

Ragna
Select Retailers
Issued: 1998
Value: $33

5

Raylee
Dillard's
14"
Issued: 1998
Value: $34

6

Reba & Roxie DuBeary
QVC
6" & 6"
Value: N/E

7

Reginald
Lord & Taylor
16"
Issued: 1996
Value: $70

8

Remington B. Bean
QVC
Issued: 1997
Value: N/E

9

Rhoda
GCC
#94854GCC
Issued: 1997
Value: N/E

10

Rocky Mountberg
Select Retailers
Issued: 1999
Value: N/E

11

Rodney
Select Retailers
Issued: 1998
Value: $28

12

Roland
Dillard's
11" • #94725DL
Issued: 1997
Value: $47

13

Ronald
Select Retailers
8"
Issued: 1997
Value: N/E

14

Rosalind
The San Francisco Music Box Company
♪ *Mr. Sandman*
14" • #41-72125
Issued: 1997
Value: N/E

Bears

	Price Paid	Value
1.		
2.		
3.		
4.		
5.		
6.		
7.		
8.		
9.		
10.		
11.		
12.		
13.		
14.		
Totals		

1
Rosalind II
The San Francisco Music Box Company
♪ *Mr. Sandman*
14" • #41-72583
Issued: 1998
Value: N/E

2
Rudolph
Select Retailers
info unavailable
Value: $30

3
Rudy Z. Mooseburg
GCC
10" • #94875GCC
Issued: 1999
Value: N/A

4
Russett
Frederick Atkins
10" • #94762FA
Issued: 1999
Value: N/E

5
Rutledge
QVC
Issued: 1998
Value: N/E

6
Sadie
Kirlin's
10"
Issued: 1999
Value: N/E

7
PHOTO UNAVAILABLE
Sadie Bearymore
May Department Store Company
8" • #94157MC
Issued: 1999
Value: N/E

8
Sakary Millenia
Select Retailers
Issued: 1999
Value: N/E

9
Samantha
Kirlin's
10"
Issued: 1997
Value: $42

10
Santa Pooh
(sold as set with "Santa Pooh" resin ornament)
Disney Catalog & Stores
9.75" & N/A • #20212MM
Issued: 1999
Value: N/E

11
Sarah Anne Bearsly & T. Foster Wuzzie
QVC
10" & 5"
Issued: 1999
Value: $33.50

12
Sarasota & Windsor
QVC
Issued: 1998
Value: N/E

13
Savannah Berrywinkle & Bentley
QVC
Issued: 1997
Value: $80

14
Scotch
Select Retailers
Issued: 1996
Value: N/E

Bears

	Price Paid	Value
1.		
2.		
3.		
4.		
5.		
6.		
7.		
8.		
9.		
10.		
11.		
12.		
13.		
14.		
Totals		

Value Guide — Boyds Plush Animals

1
Sedgewick T. Bruin
QVC
16"
Issued: 1998
Value: N/E

2
Shi Wong Panda
QVC
12"
Issued: 1999
Value: $36

3
Sidney
Dillard's
10"
Issued: 1998
Value: N/E

4
Sissy
Lord & Taylor
8"
Issued: 1998
Value: N/E

5
**The Skater
(LE-3,600)**
Canadian
12" • #BC94285PO
Issued: 1999
Value: N/E

6
Skylar & Starlynn
QVC
Issued: 1997
Value: N/E

7
Smith Witter II
*The San Francisco
Music Box Company*
♪ *You've Got A Friend*
Issued: 1997
Value: $46

8
Smokey Mountberg
Select Retailers
Issued: 1999
Value: N/E

9
**Spearmint &
Peppermint
Hollibeary**
QVC
8" & 8"
Issued: 1999
Value: $29

10
Stafford & Devon
GCC
8" • #94859GCC
Issued: 1998
Value: $56

11
**Starry
(LE-3,600)**
Canadian
8"
Issued: 1999
Value: N/E

12
Sterner
Frederick Atkins
10"
Issued: 1998
Value: $35

13
Strawbeary
Smuckers Catalog
12"
Issued: 1999
Value: N/E

14
Sunny B. Hugsworth
QVC
14"
Issued: 1999
Value: $16

Bears

	Price Paid	Value
1.		
2.		
3.		
4.		
5.		
6.		
7.		
8.		
9.		
10.		
11.		
12.		
13.		
14.		
Totals		

Value Guide — Boyds Plush Animals

1
**Sunny Buzzbee
(LE-3,600)**
J.T. Webb
10"
Issued: 1999
Value: $25

2
Susie
Lord & Taylor
8"
Issued: 1999
Value: N/E

3
Sven B. Frostman
QVC
14"
Issued: 1999
Value: $30

4
Sydney (LE-2,400)
Canadian
8" • #BC94276
Issued: 1997
Value: $50

5
T. Dean Newbearger
GCC
10" • #948656GCC
Issued: 1998
Value: N/E

6
Tammy
QVC
Issued: 1996
Value: $78

7
**Tara, Tia & Tilly F.
Wuzzie**
QVC
3" & 3.5" & 3.5"
Issued: 1999
Value: $20.50

8
PHOTO
UNAVAILABLE
Tartan Tess
Country Peddler
Issued: 1996
Value: N/E

9
Taylor
Dillard's
16" • #94705DL
Issued: 1996
Value: $78

10
PHOTO
UNAVAILABLE
Ted & Teddy
QVC
Issued: 1994
Value: N/E

11
Teddy Bauer
QVC
Issued: 1995
Value: N/E

12
Texanne
Dillard's (Texas)
14" • #94708DL
Issued: 1996
Value: $65

13
**Thea St. Griz &
Everett Elfston**
QVC
17" & 7.5"
Issued: 1998
Value: $120

14
Theodora Maria
QVC
Issued: 1998
Value: $65

Bears

	Price Paid	Value
1.		
2.		
3.		
4.		
5.		
6.		
7.		
8.		
9.		
10.		
11.		
12.		
13.		
14.		
Totals		

Value Guide — Boyds Plush Animals

1

Thor & Katrinka Berriman
QVC
12" & 7"
Issued: 1998
Value: N/E

2

Tilden, Tessa & Tori F. Wuzzie
QVC
3.5" & 3.5" & 3.5"
Issued: 1999
Value: $22

3

Tillie
Select Retailers
Issued: 1998
Value: $37

4

Tristan
Frederick Atkins
16" • #94763FA
Issued: 1999
Value: N/E

5

Tyler
Dillard's
11"
Issued: 1998
Value: $52

6

Uncle Zeb & Cousin Minnow
QVC
Issued: 1998
Value: N/E

7

Ursula Berriman
QVC
12"
Issued: 1998
Value: $57

8

Valentina, Caterina, Evalina, & Michelina
QVC
Issued: 1998
Value: $90

9

Valerie
Ideation
6"
Issued: 1999
Value: N/E

10

Venus
Elder-Beerman
Issued: 1998
Value: N/E

11

Verdeia
Frederick Atkins
16"
Issued: 1998
Value: N/E

12

Vernette
Frederick Atkins
8" • #94764FA
Issued: 1999
Value: N/E

13

Virginia Dobbsey
Coach House Gifts
12"
Issued: 1999
Value: N/E

14

Waitsfield
GCC
11" • #94853GCC
Issued: 1997
Value: $58

Bears

	Price Paid	Value
1.		
2.		
3.		
4.		
5.		
6.		
7.		
8.		
9.		
10.		
11.		
12.		
13.		
14.		
Totals		

1. Walton
Canadian
Issued: 1997
Value: N/E

2. Wesley, Willoughby & Woodward
QVC
Issued: 1998
Value: $22

3. Whihley With Winkle & Pip (LE-3,000)
QVC
12" & 6" & 3"
Issued: 1999
Value: $53

4. Will
Dillard's
6"
Issued: 1998
Value: N/E

5. Wilson (w/boat)
QVC
Issued: 1995
Value: N/E

6. Wilson (w/pie)
QVC
Issued: 1994
Value: N/E

7. Winifred
Valentine's Day
Issued: 1997
Value: $43

8. Winnie II
The San Francisco Music Box Company
♪ Love Is Blue
14"
Issued: 1999
Value: $35

9. Winstead & Pensacola
QVC
15" & 6"
Issued: 1998
Value: N/E

10. Yolanda Panda
QVC
Issued: 1998
Value: N/E

11. Younker Bear
Younkers
info unavailable
Value: N/E

12. Yu'Kon B. Bear (LE-10,000)
Canadian
10" • #BC94278
Issued: 1998
Value: $40

13. Yvonne & Yvette
QVC
Issued: 1998
Value: N/E

14. Zwick
Dillard's
#94748DL
Issued: 1999
Value: N/E

Bears

	Price Paid	Value
1.		
2.		
3.		
4.		
5.		
6.		
7.		
8.		
9.		
10.		
11.		
12.		
13.		
14.		
Totals		

EXCLUSIVE CATS

A new litter of exclusive kittens is born every year from a wide variety of outlets including Dillard's, Elder-Beerman, Gift Creations Concepts (GCC), The San Francisco Music Box Company and QVC.

1

Allie Fuzzbucket & Mugsy Tirebiter
QVC
9" & 9"
Issued: 1998
Value: N/E

2

Aspen P. Ninelives
GCC
12" • #94870GCC
Issued: 1999
Value: N/E

3

Caleigh
Dillard's
11"
Issued: 1998
Value: N/E

4

Casper Cat O'Lantern
Select Retailers
11"
Issued: 1999
Value: N/E

5

Cher S. Fussberg
Select Retailers
Issued: 1998
Value: N/E

6

Claudia & Rowena Pussytoes
QVC
Issued: 1997
Value: $50

7

Cleo P. Pussytoes
QVC
Issued: 1997
Value: $62

8

Cleo P. Pussytoes
The San Francisco Music Box Company
♪ *What's New Pussycat?*
16" • #41-72140
Issued: 1998
Value: N/E

9

Crackers & Roquefort
QVC
Issued: 1998
Value: $42

10

Fuzzy Jake Cattington
QVC
10"
Issued: 1999
Value: N/E

11

Grosvenor Catberg
QVC
Issued: 1997
Value: $80

12

Heranamous
The San Francisco Music Box Company
♪ *Ebony And Ivory*
17" • #41-72639
Issued: 1998
Value: N/E

Cats

	Price Paid	Value
1.		
2.		
3.		
4.		
5.		
6.		
7.		
8.		
9.		
10.		
11.		
12.		
13.		
14.		
Totals		

Value Guide — Boyds Plush Animals

1

Holly
Elder-Beerman
8"
Issued: 1999
Value: N/E

2

Ivana Purrkins
QVC
11"
Value: $40

3

Jenna
Dillard's
11"
Issued: 1999
Value: N/E

4

Katie Kat
Lord & Taylor
16"
Issued: 1998
Value: $50

5

Leslie G. Catberg
Select Retailers
Issued: 1998
Value: N/E

6

**Lindsey II &
Tucker F. Wuzzie**
QVC
Issued: 1998
Value: N/E

7

**Lyndon B. & Mondale
W. Cattington**
QVC
Issued: 1998
Value: N/E

8

**Margaux P.
Pussyfoot**
QVC
14"
Issued: 1999
Value: $32

9

PHOTO
UNAVAILABLE

**Miss Annie
Fuzzybuns**
QVC
14"
Issued: 1999
Value: $20

10

Mrs. Petrie
QVC
13"
Value: N/E

11

**Muffles T.
Toastytoes**
QVC
11.5"
Issued: 1999
Value: $25

12

**Nana Purrington
& Gouda**
Select Retailers
Issued: 1999
Value: N/E

13

Pepper
Dillard's
11" • #94746DL
Issued: 1999
Value: $20

14

Pussy Broomski
Select Retailers
5.5"
Issued: 1999
Value: N/E

Cats		
	Price Paid	Value
1.		
2.		
3.		
4.		
5.		
6.		
7.		
8.		
9.		
10.		
11.		
12.		
13.		
14.		
Totals		

Value Guide — Boyds Plush Animals

1

Salem Thumpkin
Select Retailers
16"
Issued: 1999
Value: N/E

2

Terence, Thad &
Thristan
QVC
info unavailable
Value: N/E

3

Thomasina Purrkins
QVC
info unavailable
Value: N/E

4

Whitefurd Felinsky
QVC
12"
Value: N/E

5

Zoe R. Grimilkin
QVC
11"
Issued: 1997
Value: $47

EXCLUSIVE COWS

Ms. "Myrtle MacMoo" joined "Adelaide & Aggie" as the only heifers to be offered as exclusives. All three of the cows were available through the home shopping network QVC.

6

Adelaide & Aggie
QVC
Issued: 1998
Value: $50

7

Myrtle MacMoo
QVC
11"
Issued: 1999
Value: $19

EXCLUSIVE DOGS

It's a dog-eat-dog world out there, as collectors will discover when they try to find these cuddly canines, the last of which was available in 1998. To dog-loving collectors' dismay, no new puppies were released since.

8

Ambrose P.
Hydrant III
QVC
Issued: 1997
Value: N/E

9

Ambrose Q. Hydrant
Lord & Taylor
Issued: 1998
Value: N/E

10

Bath & Body
Works Dog
Bath & Body Works
Issued: 1996
Value: $45

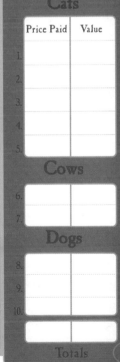

Cats	
Price Paid	Value
1.	
2.	
3.	
4.	
5.	

Cows	
6.	
7.	

Dogs	
8.	
9.	
10.	

Totals

Exclusive Dogs/Donkeys/Frogs/Gorillas

1	2	3	4

Buzz	**Caesar Q. &**	**Corky**	**Salty**
Lord & Taylor	**Cosmo G. Hydrant**	*QVC*	*Casual Living*
10"	*QVC*	Issued: 1998	Issued: 1995
Issued: 1997	10" & 10"	Value: N/E	Value: $50
Value: N/E	Issued: 1998		
	Value: N/E		

EXCLUSIVE DONKEYS

Everyone's favorite doleful donkey, Eeyore, took on a new role for the 1999 holiday season as Boyds and Disney teamed up to present a collection of plush characters and resin ornaments.

5

Elf Eeyore (sold as set with "Elf Eeyore" resin ornament)
Disney Catalog &Stores
8" • #20214MM
Issued: 1999
Value: N/E

Dogs

	Price Paid	Value
1.		
2.		
3.		
4.		

Donkeys

5.		

Frogs

6.		

Gorillas

7.		

Totals

EXCLUSIVE FROGS

"Nikali Q. Ribbit" continues to be the leaping lord of the exclusive pond as the first frog to hop into the collection.

6

Nikali Q. Ribbit
QVC
Issued: 1997
Value: N/E

EXCLUSIVE GORILLAS

Collectors went "ape" over these three burly brothers, who were available through QVC in 1998. The set makes a perfect family addition to "Joe Magilla" and "Mike Magilla," who are available in the regular line.

7

Jake, Jay & Jette Magilla
QVC
Issued: 1998
Value: N/E

EXCLUSIVE HARES

The collection of exclusive hares has multiplied like rabbits over the past few years, with a (w)hopping 44 pieces introduced since 1995.

1

Allison Babbit
The San Francisco Music Box Company
♪ *I Only Have Eyes For You*
14" • #41-72141
Issued: 1998
Value: N/E

2

Alpine
Select Retailers
info unavailable
Value: N/E

3

Anissa
Select Retailers
Issued: 1998
Value: $40

4

Ashley
The San Francisco Music Box Company
♪ *Love Me Tender*
14" • #41-66847
Issued: 1997
Value: N/E

5

Bath & Body Works Snowbunny
Bath & Body Works
Issued: 1997
Value: N/E

6

Belle
Harry & David
8"
Issued: 1998
Value: N/E

7

Brittany
Dillard's
8" • #94711DL
Issued: 1997
Value: $33

8

PHOTO UNAVAILABLE

Caitlin
Dillard's
8"
Issued: 1997
Value: N/E

9

Chantanay
Select Retailers
info unavailable
Value: N/E

10

Demi
QVC
Issued: 1996
Value: $35

11

Dutch
Select Retailers
Issued: 1998
Value: N/E

12

Ellie
Select Retailers
Issued: 1998
Value: N/E

Hares	Price Paid	Value
1.		
2.		
3.		
4.		
5.		
6.		
7.		
8.		
9.		
10.		
11.		
12.		
Totals		

Exclusvie Hares

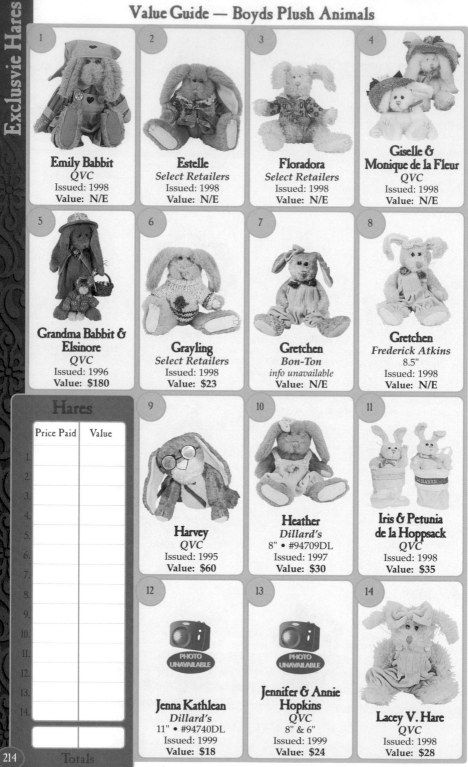

1

Emily Babbit
QVC
Issued: 1998
Value: N/E

2

Estelle
Select Retailers
Issued: 1998
Value: N/E

3

Floradora
Select Retailers
Issued: 1998
Value: N/E

4

**Giselle &
Monique de la Fleur**
QVC
Issued: 1998
Value: N/E

5

**Grandma Babbit &
Elsinore**
QVC
Issued: 1996
Value: $180

6

Grayling
Select Retailers
Issued: 1998
Value: $23

7

Gretchen
Bon-Ton
info unavailable
Value: N/E

8

Gretchen
Frederick Atkins
8.5"
Issued: 1998
Value: N/E

Hares

	Price Paid	Value
1.		
2.		
3.		
4.		
5.		
6.		
7.		
8.		
9.		
10.		
11.		
12.		
13.		
14.		
Totals		

9

Harvey
QVC
Issued: 1995
Value: $60

10

Heather
Dillard's
8" • #94709DL
Issued: 1997
Value: $30

11

**Iris & Petunia
de la Hoppsack**
QVC
Issued: 1998
Value: $35

12

PHOTO
UNAVAILABLE

Jenna Kathlean
Dillard's
11" • #94740DL
Issued: 1999
Value: $18

13

PHOTO
UNAVAILABLE

**Jennifer & Annie
Hopkins**
QVC
8" & 6"
Issued: 1999
Value: $24

14

Lacey V. Hare
QVC
Issued: 1998
Value: $28

Value Guide — Boyds Plush Animals

1

Lady Harington
QVC
Issued: 1997
Value: $42

2

Lady Harriwell
QVC
Issued: 1998
Value: $23

3

Lady Pembrooke
The San Francisco
Music Box Company
♪ *Music Box Dancer*
12" • #41-72647
Issued: 1998
Value: N/E

4

**Lavinia V.
Hariweather**
The San Francisco
Music Box Company
♪ *You Are My Sunshine*
10" • #41-72644
Issued: 1998
Value: N/E

5

Lindsey
Dillard's
8" • #94710DL
Issued: 1997
Value: $30

6

Lindy
Elder-Beerman
13"
Issued: 1999
Value: N/E

7

**Mandy, Melissa &
Michael**
QVC
Issued: 1998
Value: $28

8

Meredith
Frederick Atkins
10"
Issued: 1999
Value: N/E

9

**Ms. Magnolia,
Lauren & Elizabeth**
QVC
Issued: 1997
Value: $110

10

**Nanna O'Harea &
Audrey**
QVC
11" & 6"
Issued: 1998
Value: N/E

11

Natalie
Dillard's
14" • #94716DL
Issued: 1997
Value: N/E

12

Parker
Select Retailers
Issued: 1998
Value: $25

13

Pauline
Kirlin's
10"
Issued: 1997
Value: $45

14

Penelope
Select Retailers
10"
Issued: 1998
Value: N/E

Hares

	Price Paid	Value
1.		
2.		
3.		
4.		
5.		
6.		
7.		
8.		
9.		
10.		
11.		
12.		
13.		
14.		
Totals		

Exclusive Hares/Lambs/Lions

1

Reno
Select Retailers
info unavailable
Value: N/E

2

Stamford
QVC
Issued: 1997
Value: $45

3

Stanford
QVC
info unavailable
Value: N/E

4

Zelda Fitzhare
The San Francisco Music Box Company
♪ *Feelin' Groovy*
17" • #41-72643
Issued: 1998
Value: N/E

EXCLUSIVE LAMBS

The lamb collection has doubled in size recently as the two "gentle giants" Ivy M. Fuzzyfleece" and "Lucy Belle Lambston" made their QVC debut.

5

Abbey Ewe
The San Francisco Music Box Company
♪ *Mairzy Doats*
14" • #41-72648
Issued: 1998
Value: N/E

6

Brianne
Select Retailers
Issued: 1997
Value: $27

Hares

Price Paid	Value

Lambs

7

Ivy M. Fuzzyfleece
QVC
10"
Issued: 1999
Value: $19

8

Lucy Belle Lambston
QVC
14"
Issued: 1999
Value: N/E

EXCLUSIVE LIONS

Lion and lamb teamed up and were jamming in 1999, as "Marley Dredlion & Maybelle B. Bahoodle" joined the collection to become the coolest king and queen of the jungle.

9

Braden
Select Retailers
Issued: 1997
Value: $25

Lions

Totals

1

**Marley Dredlion &
Maybelle B. Bahoodle**
QVC
9" & 9"
Issued: 1999
Value: $12

2

Zack
QVC
Issued: 1997
Value: $34

EXCLUSIVE MICE

The phrase "quiet as a mouse" does not apply to these four pieces, which all scampered into the collection with a bang.

3

PHOTO UNAVAILABLE

**Colby &
Port S. Mouski**
QVC
6" & 6"
Value: N/E

4

Dick, Harry & Tom
QVC
Issued: 1997
Value: $36

5

Gouda & Edam
QVC
Issued: 1998
Value: $50

6

Havarti Chrismouse
GCC
#94864GCC
Issued: 1998
Value: $35

EXCLUSIVE MOOSE

Four more friends from the north recently wandered into the collection, bringing the total to well over 10 pieces. Dillard's, Gift Creations Concepts and QVC had more moose to offer.

7

Eddie Bauer
Eddie Bauer
Issued: 1994
Value: $90

8

Emily Ann
Lord & Taylor
17"
Issued: 1997
Value: $68

9

Izzy
Dillard's
#94745DL
Issued: 1999
Value: N/E

10

Magnus P. Mossfield
QVC
17"
Value: $75

Lions	Price Paid	Value
1.		
2.		

Mice		
3.		
4.		
5.		
6.		

Moose		
7.		
8.		
9.		
10.		

Totals

217

Value Guide — Boyds Plush Animals

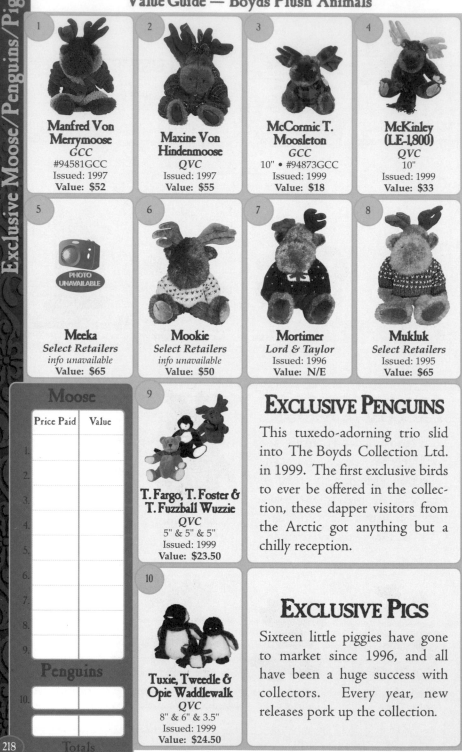

1 Manfred Von Merrymoose
GCC
#94581GCC
Issued: 1997
Value: $52

2 Maxine Von Hindenmoose
QVC
Issued: 1997
Value: $55

3 McCormic T. Moosleton
GCC
10" • #94873GCC
Issued: 1999
Value: $18

4 McKinley (LE-1,800)
QVC
10"
Issued: 1999
Value: $33

5 Meeka
Select Retailers
info unavailable
Value: $65

6 Mookie
Select Retailers
info unavailable
Value: $50

7 Mortimer
Lord & Taylor
Issued: 1996
Value: N/E

8 Mukluk
Select Retailers
Issued: 1995
Value: $65

9 T. Fargo, T. Foster & T. Fuzzball Wuzzie
QVC
5" & 5" & 5"
Issued: 1999
Value: $23.50

10 Tuxie, Tweedle & Opie Waddlewalk
QVC
8" & 6" & 3.5"
Issued: 1999
Value: $24.50

Moose

	Price Paid	Value
1.		
2.		
3.		
4.		
5.		
6.		
7.		
8.		
9.		

Penguins

10.		

Totals

EXCLUSIVE PENGUINS

This tuxedo-adorning trio slid into The Boyds Collection Ltd. in 1999. The first exclusive birds to ever be offered in the collection, these dapper visitors from the Arctic got anything but a chilly reception.

EXCLUSIVE PIGS

Sixteen little piggies have gone to market since 1996, and all have been a huge success with collectors. Every year, new releases pork up the collection.

Value Guide — Boyds Plush Animals

1

Baby Rosebud
Harry & David
Issued: 1996
Value: N/E

2

Big Pig, Little Pig
Canadian
12" & 9" • #BC94279
Issued: 1998
Value: $53

3

Big Pig, Little Pig
Select Retailers
10" & 8"
Issued: 1998
Value: N/E

4

Erin
Dillard's
8"
Issued: 1998
Value: N/E

5

G. Wilbur McSwine
QVC
8"
Issued: 1997
Value: $38

6

Hamilton
Cracker Barrel
11"
Issued: 1999
Value: N/E

7

Kaitlin & Kendall McSwine
QVC
8" & 5"
Issued: 1998
Value: N/E

8

Katie
Select Retailers
info unavailable
Value: N/E

9

Katie O'Pigg
Dillard's
Issued: 1997
Value: $27

10

Lena O'Pigg
Dillard's
12" • #94706DL
Issued: 1997
Value: $36

11

Merentha
Dillard's
11" • #94727DL
Issued: 1997
Value: $50

12

Olympia
QVC
Issued: 1997
Value: N/E

13

Primrose
QVC
11"
Issued: 1999
Value: $17

14

Rosebud
Harry & David
8"
Issued: 1998
Value: N/E

Pigs

	Price Paid	Value
1.		
2.		
3.		
4.		
5.		
6.		
7.		
8.		
9.		
10.		
11.		
12.		
13.		
14.		

Totals

219

1

Rosie O'Pigg
The San Francisco
Music Box Company
♪ *Second Hand Rose*
11" • #41-72641
Issued: 1998
Value: N/E

2

Santa's Helper Piglet
(sold as set with
"Santa's Helper Piglet"
resin ornament)
Disney Catalog &
Stores
6" • #20215MM
Issued: 1999
Value: N/E

EXCLUSIVE TIGERS

Disney's "Tigger" bounced into the line in 1999, becoming the first tiger to be made available through The Boyds Collection Ltd. Decked out in holiday costumes, he is sure to put a little spring into your collection.

3

Elf Tigger
(sold as set with
"Elf Tigger" resin orna-
ment)
Disney Catalog &
Stores
11" • #20213MM
Issued: 1999
Value: N/E

EXCLUSIVE ORNAMENTS

From musical bears to a set of flying lambs, you can find nearly anything you need to decorate your home all year round with over 40 pieces in this category.

4

Angelina
The San Francisco
Music Box Company
♪ *Love Me Tender*
6" • #41-72768
Issued: 1999
Value: $10

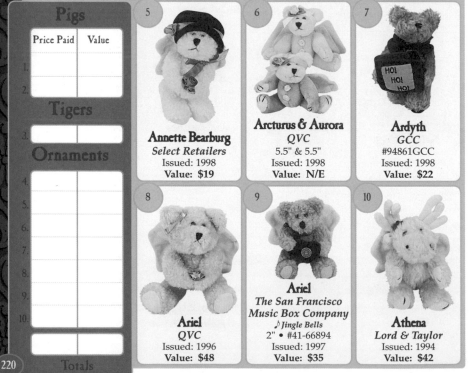

Pigs

	Price Paid	Value
1.		
2.		

Tigers

3.		

Ornaments

4.		
5.		
6.		
7.		
8.		
9.		
10.		

Totals

5

Annette Bearburg
Select Retailers
Issued: 1998
Value: $19

6

Arcturus & Aurora
QVC
5.5" & 5.5"
Issued: 1998
Value: N/E

7

Ardyth
GCC
#94861GCC
Issued: 1998
Value: $22

8

Ariel
QVC
Issued: 1996
Value: $48

9

Ariel
The San Francisco
Music Box Company
♪ *Jingle Bells*
2" • #41-66894
Issued: 1997
Value: $35

10

Athena
Lord & Taylor
Issued: 1994
Value: $42

Value Guide — Boyds Plush Animals

1

Baby Bailey (set/2)
QVC
6" & 6"
Issued: 1999
Value: $18

2

**Barret, Belinda &
Berg Blizzard**
QVC
4.5" & 4.5" & 4.5"
Issued: 1999
Value: N/E

3

Comet
Lord & Taylor
Issued: 1996
Value: N/E

4

Dolly & Jed
QVC
Issued: 1997
Value: N/E

5

Eeyore
Disney Catalog
Issued: 1998
Value: $35

6

Evergreen Elfston
GCC
#94876GCC
Issued: 1999
Value: N/E

7

**Fenton & Forest
Silverton**
QVC
Issued: 1998
Value: N/E

8

Galaxy
The San Francisco
Music Box Company
♪Twinkle, Twinkle,
Little Star
7" • #41-72767
Issued: 1999
Value: $15

9

Juliette
The San Francisco
Music Box Company
♪ Love Me Tender
4" • #41-72646
Issued: 1998
Value: N/E

10

Lapis
QVC
Issued: 1996
Value: $35

11

Matilda
Lord & Taylor
Issued: 1994
Value: N/E

12

Max
Lord & Taylor
8"
Issued: 1999
Value: N/E

13

PHOTO
UNAVAILABLE

**Mimsie, Myrtle &
Melba Bahsworth**
QVC
5" & 5" & 5"
Issued: 1999
Value: $17.50

14

Morley (set/3)
QVC
Issued: 1998
Value: N/E

Ornaments

	Price Paid	Value
1.		
2.		
3.		
4.		
5.		
6.		
7.		
8.		
9.		
10.		
11.		
12.		
13.		
14.		
Totals		

Exclusive Ornaments

1

Morty
Elder-Beerman
5"
Issued: 1999
Value: N/E

2

Mrs. Bear In-The-Moon
Lord & Taylor
Issued: 1996
Value: N/E

3

Piglet
Disney Catalog
Issued: 1998
Value: $35

4

Pooh 1999
Disney Catalog
Issued: 1999
Value: N/E

5

Pooh 2000
Disney Catalog
Issued: 1999
Value: N/E

6

Pooh, Tigger, Eeyore & Piglet
Disney Catalog
8.5" & 8.5" & 8.5" &
8.5" • #19725MM
Issued: 1999
Value: N/E

7

Priscilla
Lord & Taylor
10"
Issued: 1997
Value: N/E

8

Sheila
Lord & Taylor
5"
Issued: 1999
Value: N/E

9

Snowbeary (set/3)
QVC
Issued: 1998
Value: N/E

10

Tessa
Lord & Taylor
8"
Issued: 1999
Value: N/E

11

Tigger
Disney Catalog
Issued: 1998
Value: $38

12

Timmy
Lord & Taylor
5"
Issued: 1999
Value: N/E

13

Winnie The Pooh
Disney Catalog
Issued: 1998
Value: $35

Ornaments

	Price Paid	Value
1.		
2.		
3.		
4.		
5.		
6.		
7.		
8.		
9.		
10.		
11.		
12.		
13.		
Totals		

EXCLUSIVE PUPPETS

Even though he was the very first exclusive puppet to appear on stage, "Maxwell Mittbruin" suffered no stage fright during his debut on QVC in 1999.

Maxwell Mittbruin
QVC
16"
Issued: 1999
Value: $35

EXCLUSIVE TREE TOPPERS

"Auriela Angelfrost" flew into the collection in 1999. She and her sister "Arielle," who is available in the regular line, make great "guardian angels" all year round.

Auriela Angelfrost
QVC
10"
Issued: 1999
Value: N/E

Puppets		
	Price Paid	Value
1.		

Tree Toppers		
2.		

| Totals | | |

Future Releases

Use this page to record future Boyds Plush Animals releases.

Boyds Plush Animals	Item #	Status	Price Paid	Market Value

Page Total:	Price Paid	Value

Future Releases

Use this page to record future Boyds Plush Animals releases.

Boyds Plush Animals	Item #	Status	Price Paid	Market Value

Page Total:	Price Paid	Value

Total Value Of My Collection

Record the value of your collection here!

Boyds Plush Animals			Boyds Plush Animals		
Page Number	Price Paid	Market Value	Page Number	Price Paid	Market Value
Page 39			Page 71		
Page 40			Page 72		
Page 41			Page 73		
Page 42			Page 74		
Page 43			Page 75		
Page 44			Page 76		
Page 45			Page 77		
Page 46			Page 78		
Page 47			Page 79		
Page 48			Page 80		
Page 49			Page 81		
Page 50			Page 82		
Page 51			Page 83		
Page 52			Page 84		
Page 53			Page 85		
Page 54			Page 86		
Page 55			Page 87		
Page 56			Page 88		
Page 57			Page 89		
Page 58			Page 90		
Page 59			Page 91		
Page 60			Page 92		
Page 61			Page 93		
Page 62			Page 94		
Page 63			Page 95		
Page 64			Page 96		
Page 65			Page 97		
Page 66			Page 98		
Page 67			Page 99		
Page 68			Page 100		
Page 69			Page 101		
Page 70			Page 102		
Subtotal:			Subtotal:		

Page Total:	Price Paid	Value

Record the value of your collection here!

Boyds Plush Animals

Page Number	Price Paid	Market Value
Page 103		
Page 104		
Page 105		
Page 106		
Page 107		
Page 108		
Page 109		
Page 110		
Page 111		
Page 112		
Page 113		
Page 114		
Page 115		
Page 116		
Page 117		
Page 118		
Page 119		
Page 120		
Page 121		
Page 122		
Page 123		
Page 124		
Page 125		
Page 126		
Page 127		
Page 128		
Page 129		
Page 130		
Page 131		
Page 132		
Page 133		
Page 134		
Subtotal:		

Boyds Plush Animals

Page Number	Price Paid	Market Value
Page 135		
Page 136		
Page 137		
Page 138		
Page 139		
Page 140		
Page 141		
Page 142		
Page 143		
Page 144		
Page 145		
Page 146		
Page 147		
Page 148		
Page 149		
Page 150		
Page 151		
Page 152		
Page 153		
Page 154		
Page 152		
Page 153		
Page 154		
Page 155		
Page 156		
Page 157		
Page 158		
Page 159		
Page 160		
Page 161		
Page 162		
Page 163		
Subtotal:		

	Price Paid	Value
Page Total:		

Boyds Plush Animals

Page Number	Price Paid	Market Value
Page 164		
Page 165		
Page 166		
Page 167		
Page 168		
Page 169		
Page 170		
Page 171		
Page 172		
Page 173		
Page 174		
Page 175		
Page 176		
Page 177		
Page 178		
Page 179		
Page 180		
Page 181		
Page 182		
Page 183		
Page 184		
Page 185		
Page 186		
Page 187		
Page 188		
Page 189		
Page 190		
Page 191		
Page 192		
Page 193		
Page 194		
Subtotal:		

Boyds Plush Animals

Page Number	Price Paid	Market Value
Page 195		
Page 196		
Page 197		
Page 198		
Page 199		
Page 200		
Page 201		
Page 202		
Page 203		
Page 204		
Page 205		
Page 206		
Page 207		
Page 208		
Page 209		
Page 210		
Page 211		
Page 212		
Page 213		
Page 214		
Page 215		
Page 216		
Page 217		
Page 218		
Page 219		
Page 220		
Page 221		
Page 222		
Page 223		
Page 224		
Page 225		
TOTAL:		

Page Total:	Price Paid	Value

GRAND TOTAL:	Price Paid	Value

Burke P. Bear Sees The World

One special bear in particular is touching lives in a very deep, profound way. Please meet "Burke P. Bear."

"Burke P. Bear" is named after Burke Derr, a young man who lost his fight with cystic fibrosis (CF) on June 17, 1997. Inspired  by the story of the courageous teen and avid Boyds collector (Burke had well over 100 Boyds bears in his collection), Head Bean Gary Lowenthal named a bear after this fan.

When Pennsylvania retailer Lucinda Marks learned of "Burke P. Bear's" story, she suggested that retailers donate $1 to Pennsylvania Cystic Fibrosis, Inc. (PACFI) for every "Burke P. Bear" sold. The idea caught on and more than 134 retailers across the United States and Canada have joined in the effort. "Burke" has become the catalyst for PACFI's "Million Dollar Bear" campaign to aid in CF research. Its goal is to raise $1 million by the end of the year 2000, the year Burke would have graduated from college.

The Burke P. Bear North American Tour to spread awareness about CF and the "Million Dollar Bear" campaign began on October 9, 1998. Since then, "Burke" has met with notable individuals ranging from the governor of Oklahoma to musician John Tesh. The city of Auburn, Massachusetts proclaimed May 8, 1999 to be "Burke P. Bear Day." He was also honored when designated "Pennsylvania's Ambassador for Love, Peace, Having Fun and Curing Cystic Fibrosis."

To date, "Burke" has helped to raise over $60,000 and his travels now span the globe. For more information, please contact PACFI at 1-800-900-2790, bobderr@sunlink.net or PACFI, P.O. Box 29, Mifflinburg, PA 17844.

Secondary Market Overview

While the shelves of your local Boyds retailer is your best source for making plush acquisitions, you may not find every piece you are looking for. Although The Boyds Collection Ltd. announces retirements in advance, pieces can slip through the fingers of even the most diligent collectors. That is where the secondary market comes into play. It is here that collectors are given a second chance to obtain those elusive retired and limited plush critters once they climb off of those shelves.

The Internet has emerged as the primary source for finding those coveted secondary market items. Collectors are no longer limited by geography or distance in finding that special piece. Nor do they even have to leave their homes to do so.

Retailers from all over the country can be found selling their wares on the Internet. With a few mouse clicks, you can shop among stores worldwide in search of the lowest price or best deal. On-line auctions are ideal for collectors who miss the thrill of scouring flea markets and newspaper classifieds and still crave excitement in their hunts.

In Internet shopping, it is very important, and not very difficult to protect yourself. While buying collectibles sight unseen is unwise, it is sometimes unavoidable over the Internet. Make sure to examine any available pictures of the item you are buying on-line and don't be afraid to ask questions. Find out if there is a return policy if you are unhappy with the condition of your purchase. Buying through reputable dealers goes a long way to ensuring peace of mind. Talk with other collectors to get a feel for which Internet retailers provide the best service. If the auction site provides feedback ratings, take advantage of this opportunity to see what comments other buyers had regarding a particular seller.

The Internet can also put you in touch with like-minded collectors from all around the world. Search for bulletin boards and chat rooms that are devoted to Boyds plush animals. Here you might find collectors who can offer information, advice and maybe even that piece you have been searching for.

There are also other more personal means to finding your pieces. Swap & sells are one of the most popular. These events usually bring out collectors from all over the state, region or even country. Usually there are rows of tables stocked full of merchandise. Flea markets also the offer this type of atmosphere. There are also exchange services and the classifieds section of the newspaper offers another route, usually on a local level.

Most retailers do not take part in the secondary market; however, they can act as a liaison between collectors. Some retailers provide lists of collectors looking to buy, sell or trade pieces, as well as information pertaining to swap & sells around the area.

What factors affect secondary market values? Condition plays a large part. Who wants a plush animal that looks like something the cat dragged in? Make sure all original packaging is intact. The *Mohair Bears* come in special gift boxes that should appear as brand new as the bear inside. Availability is also a key factor. Pieces usually see their largest increases in value after they retire. Limited editions also see rising values on the secondary market. Once there are not enough of these pieces to go around to all who want them, the demand for those pieces increases.

Remember that market values are always fluctuating. The only constant is the love you feel for a particular plush animal. If you buy for the love of the piece, you will never be disappointed!

Variations

J ust as no two people are exactly the same, neither are two Boyds plush animals. When differences arise between two animals whether from either human error or an intended alteration of the original design or pattern, the result is what the collectible industry calls a variation.

Variations can range from changes in wardrobe to changes in eye and fur color, name and stock number. In addition, there are many other minor variations that may occur naturally during production.

A WARDROBE FOR EVERY OCCASION

It turns out that some Boyds plush animals are just as fashion conscious as humans. "Helmut" the moose had originally been seen braving the elements in a green hooded sweater. Soon, the green sweater was gone, replaced by a red one. Moose aren't the only critters that can't always decide on a wardrobe. The spring 1994 "Edmund" bear has occasionally been spotted in blue overalls instead of his usual black ones, making this already valuable bear even more so. The bear and hare pair of "Alastair & Camilla" first sported a sweater and dress, respectively, but now they wear matching sweaters.

SEEING THE WORLD THROUGH DIFFERENT EYES

Boyds plush cats experience variations in the blink of an eye. "Dewey R. Cat," "Dewey Q. Grimilkin" and "Ophilia Q. Grimilkin" are just some of the many cats who have changed their eye color.

A DYE JOB?

When people get older they tend to find a few more gray hairs (or hares in the case of rabbits). Boyds plush animals occasionally undergo a similar hair-raising change. The fur of "Corinna" the bear has ranged from dark brown to light brown. The bears "Callaghan" and "Leon" have also been found with varying shades of fur.

A LITTLE LIFT, A SMALL TUCK, A BIT OF COLOR

Facial patterns have been altered for those Boyds creatures seeking a new look. The bear "Avery B. Bean" is more tight-lipped than his open mouthed predecessor, giving him a more stately appearance. Cows such as "Bessie Moostein" and "Elmo Beefcake" lost their baby faces of pink noses and chubby cheeks and grew into a more streamlined appearance. Early "Sherlock" bears-dressed-as-hares had pink paws, while later ones pattered about with gray paws.

A TECHNICAL CHANGE

Changes aren't always cosmetic. Item numbers, sizes and even names have been known to change. These name changes range from slight ("Alec" the bear is also known as "Alex") to drastic ("Diana" the hare is also known as "Elizabeth"). "Fitzroy" the bear has seen not only his wardrobe change, but his item number, also!

BEAUTY IS IN THE EYES OF THE BEHOLDER

With so many variations out there, it is important to remember that not every one experiences a dramatic rise in value. And it is impossible to know which ones will. But a plush variation just might be the perfect conversation piece to round out your Boyds collection.

Insuring Your Collection

When insuring your collection, there are three major points to consider:

1. **KNOW YOUR COVERAGE:** Collectibles are typically included in homeowner's or renter's insurance policies. Ask your agent if your policy covers fire, theft, natural disasters and damage or breakage from routine handling. Also, ask if your policy covers claims at "current replacement value" – the amount it would cost to replace items if they were damaged, lost or stolen. This is extremely important since the secondary market value of some pieces may well exceed their original retail price.

2. **DOCUMENT YOUR COLLECTION:** In the event of a loss, you will need a record of the contents and value of your collection. Ask your insurance agent what information is acceptable. Keep receipts and an inventory of your collection in a different location, such as a safe deposit box. Include the purchase date, price paid, size, issue year, edition limit/number, special markings and secondary market value for each piece. Photographs and video footage with close-up views of each piece, including tags, boxes and signatures, are good back-ups.

3. **WEIGH THE RISK:** To determine the coverage you need, calculate how much it would cost to replace your collection and compare it to the total amount your current policy would pay. To insure your collection for a specific dollar amount, ask your agent about adding a Personal Articles Floater or a Fine Arts Floater or "rider" to your policy, or insuring your collection under a separate policy. As with all insurance, you must weigh the risk of loss against the cost of additional coverage.

Production, Packaging And Pricing

Where do Boyds plush animals come from? It's not the mere story of the birds and the bees. It's an involved process from the drawing board to the finished product which results in the creation of these lovable critters.

Ideas initially spring from the fertile imagination of Boyds artist Gary Lowenthal. These ideas take shape in the form of sketches drawn by Gary himself. It often takes multiple tries before he can get the design to look just like what he had in mind.

The piece literally begins to take shape when the designs are received by a seamstress. Patterns are cut by hand, but because of the complexity of some of the Boyds plush designs, a machine is sometimes used for this task.

Pieces are then hand-stitched together, with room left to add stuffing. The stuffing helps give the plush animals their own individual feel and shape. Once stuffed, the animals are stitched up and are ready for their finishing touches.

The mouth, nose and paws are the final pieces to be added. These hand-made additions contribute to the uniqueness of each piece. The animals are now completed and ready to begin their journey to store shelves!

Most of the animals come packed in bags, although *The Mohair Bears* arrive in their own special gift boxes, an honor befitting their "uppah clahss" status. Most animals have a hang tag that provides basic information about the character and his or her series, as well as space for recording the cuddly critter's name.

There are plush animals available for every budget, with prices ranging from $6 to $50. Most fall in the $15 to $25 range, making them the perfect gift which will tax the heart but not the wallet.

Accessories

Are your animals looking a bit bored? Boyds makes a plethora of accessories to spice up their (and your) lives. From playing dress-up to coordinating boat races down at the lake, your animals are guaranteed to keep busy 24 hours a day with their new playthings! Here are a couple of items to get them started.

FASHIONABLY LOUD AND PROUD

Boyds animals are very fashion-conscious. Whether they come dressed in an elaborate matching ensemble or a simple bow around the neck, your animals are sure to want to add more to their wardrobe (greedy little critters, aren't they?). Boyds has created sweaters, hats and glasses that are just the right size and fit for these unique-sized animals, and they are fashionable enough to ensure that yours is the best looking critter on the block.

A BEAR'S WORK IS NEVER DONE

GARDENING – Have some bears or hares who love to play in the dirt? Put them to work with some of Boyds' handy gardening tools, such as "Nanette's Garden Wheelbarrow" and watch them go! "Caroline's Strawberry Baskets" are perfect for gathering up fresh flowers and re-potting them indoors in "Emily's Flower Pots" for everyone to enjoy! Just make sure to keep them watered with "Bailey's Watering Cans!"

CONCESSION STANDS – Keep your critters busy all day by letting them run their own business! Boyds makes several concession stands at which your bear can sell honey, watermelon or even the items that your plush friends grew in their garden!

ALL WORK AND NO PLAY ...

Fortunately, this isn't the case for Boyds bears and friends. These critters can play all day long if they want to! And you should have lots of toys and activities around to keep them occupied!

WATCHING THE BIG GAME – It's the biggest football game of the year and no one wants to miss it, including your plush! Help them get settled on any one of their custom-sized loveseats or armchairs, such as "Indy's Blue Denim Couch" and root along with them for their favorite team (the Chicago Bears, perhaps!).

CAMPING – Teddy bears need vacations too! Let your animals visit their friends and relatives in "the great outdoors" by sending

them on their own camping trip! The "Bearibriar Campfire Set" is perfect for frying up those fish that were caught while sailing down the river in one of the three colored "Wooden Rowboats" that are available through Boyds.

TOY BOX TREASURES – For bear cubs, stock up on the latest and greatest toys made by Boyds! There is something for everyone in the Boyds toy box, from "planes, trains and automobiles" to soap box racers, tic-tac-toe sets and winter sleds, and they are all sure to be appreciated by your younger plush pals!

FOR HIM, HER AND HOME

Not to be outdone, Boyds moms and dads can now stock up on Boyds paraphernalia as well. "Bearware" is available for every room in the home, as well as the closet!

KITCHEN – Those smiling bears and hares are sure to warm up your kitchen! Since 1997, Boyds has produced Bearware Potteryworks, a line of ceramic cookie jars, mugs and salt and pepper shakers that are designed in the images of your favorite Boyds pieces. In addition, each cookie jar is further individualized with a special quote inside! The salt and pepper shakers make a great conversation piece (as well as collectible!), and are sure to liven up your kitchen or dining room. So why not let your favorite Boyds critters celebrate your holidays and family dinners with you?

HOME – Scatter votives, picture frames and musicals through other parts of your home to give it that true "Boydsian" feel. *Le Bearmoge™ Collection* is a line of porcelain boxes created by Boyds. Each box features a different character perched on top of a box that has a special surprise inside. These delicate containers make great jewelry boxes, sewing kits or even decorations! Likewise, *The Beatrice Collection™* (named after Gary's mother) features similar Bearstone-themed porcelain boxes that make great gifts and accessories.

FASHION – And don't limit your love of Boyds to the home! Pins are a popular (and subtle) way of expressing your "love of Boyds" while hats (with or without ears) and sweatshirts are also available for Boyds-aholics who want to parade their Boyds pride around town.

LICENSED PRODUCTS

Boyds can only do so much at one time, and with such an overwhelming (and growing) demand for more products, the company is working with licensees to help take the pressure off and meet the collectors' demands.

In 1997, Sunrise, a leading manufacturer of greeting cards, became Boyds' first official licensee and produced a line of bear- and hare-themed greeting cards. The cards were an immediate success, and soon the company began to expand its line of Boyds-themed products. Now Sunrise note cards, stationery, blank journals, party invitations, gift bags, tissue wrap and scrapbook kits are all available through national retail stores that carry Boyds products.

Manual Woodworkers and Weavers became Boyds' second licensee when they developed a line of soft chenille afghans, throws, pillows, wall hangings and tapestry calendars that feature the lovable Boyds critters and are just as cuddly as the animals themselves!

Uptown Rubber Stamps joined forces with The Boyds Collection to produce a series of rubber stamp kits. The kits are ideal for personalizing invitations, envelopes, lunch bags and more. But watch out, because the habit can be addictive! Some collectors have been known to get carried away and even stamp family members!

For years, High Wind Productions has designed T-shirts and sweatshirts for Boyds employees to wear to trade shows and similar events. They have now made their products available to the public. In addition to the T-shirts and sweatshirts, tote bags, embroidered polo shirts and denim shirts have been recently added to the collection.

Concept Direct also has a wide variety of Boyds-themed address labels for your enjoyment and convenience. Both large- and small-sized labels can be purchased through the company.

Boyds has an accessory for every reason and season, a piece to keep every collector (and animal) satisfied. To find out what pieces are available to complement your collection, contact your local Boyds retailer, and check *The Boyds Bear Retail Inquirer* for updates and information on the latest accessories.

The Warm And Fuzzy World Of Wuzzies

Your Wuzzies can now join in the fun with pint-sized accessories made just for them! "Wuzzie at Workbench," "Wuzzie Picnic Lunch Stop," "Wuzzie Lazy Day Fishing Pier" and "Elmer's Mini Locomotive Express" will keep your Wuzzies hard at play!

– Key –

All Boyds plush animals are listed below in alphabetical order. The first number refers to the piece's location within the Value Guide section and the second to the box in which it is pictured on that page.

ACKNOWLEDGEMENTS

CheckerBee Publishing would like to extend a very special thanks to Suzie Hocker. We would also like to thank Linda Brand, Julie Christensen, Harry and Millie Croft, Melisa Dutton, Mellissa Gabbard, Darlene Johanson, Linda and David Reinhart, Linda Wise and the many collectors and retailers who contributed their valuable time to assist us with this book. Also many thanks to the great people at The Boyds Collection Ltd.